w/D

THEODORE HOOK
AND HIS NOVELS.

LONDON : HUMPHREY MILFORD.

OXFORD UNIVERSITY PRESS.

THEODORE HOOK.

*Reproduced from Eddis's portrait in the National Portrait
Gallery; by permission of Emery Walker, Ltd.*

THEODORE HOOK
AND HIS NOVELS.

BY

MYRON F. BRIGHTFIELD,

ASSISTANT PROFESSOR OF ENGLISH IN
THE UNIVERSITY OF CALIFORNIA.

CAMBRIDGE:

HARVARD UNIVERSITY PRESS.

1928.

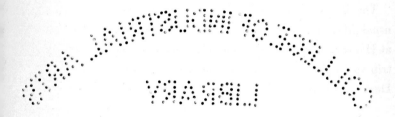

PRINTED AT

THE HARVARD UNIVERSITY PRESS,

CAMBRIDGE, MASSACHUSETTS, U.S.A.

PREFACE.

IN its original form this work was presented as a dissertation for the degree of Doctor of Philosophy at Harvard University. It has since been enlarged and rewritten. At Harvard the work had the encouragement of Dr. Gustavus Howard Maynadier, and the careful reading and criticism of Professor Bliss Perry. They, however, are in no way responsible for the errors it may contain.

The British Museum Library granted me the usual privileges. The staff of the Widener Library at Harvard has been very kind and obliging. My trip to England was made possible by a Charles Dexter Scholarship.

MYRON F. BRIGHTFIELD.

BERKELEY, CALIFORNIA,
July, 1928.

CONTENTS.

INTRODUCTION 3

I. PARENTAGE AND BOYHOOD. 16

II. THE WRITER OF PLAYS 29

III. THE *Gamin de Londres* AND THE IMPROVI-
SATORE (1805–1813) 59

IV. THE MAURITIUS INTERLUDE 95

V. PAMPHLETEER, EDITOR, JOURNALIST, AND
NOVELIST (1819–1841) 112

VI. SOCIAL LIFE (1819–1841) 166

VII. HOOK'S NOVELS:

I. PUBLICATION 224

II. PLOTS 234

III. CHARACTERS 250

IV. BACKGROUND 270

VIII. HOOK'S IMPORTANCE AS A NOVELIST . . 293

APPENDIX: SYNOPSES OF HOOK'S NOVELS . . . 339

BIBLIOGRAPHY OF THE WRITINGS OF THEODORE
HOOK 363

INDEX 373

THEODORE HOOK
AND HIS NOVELS.

INTRODUCTION.

JUST off the busy London thoroughfare, Fulham Road, and not a hundred yards from the north end of Putney bridge, is the quiet churchyard of the Fulham parish church of All Saints. In the eastern corner of this small plot, near the graves of several bishops of London, is a plain grave whose old but well-preserved headstone bears the following inscription:

THEODORE EDWARD HOOK
DIED 24TH AUGUST 1841
IN THE 53RD YEAR OF HIS AGE.

He died in a little cottage (whose site is now included in Bishop's Park) fronting on the Thames, not a stone's throw from his grave. Although he was universally known in London society at the time of his death, his body was accompanied from the cottage to the churchyard only by his nephew, the distinguished Rev. Walter Farquhar Hook, and by a half-dozen sincere friends and neighbors. Among the mourners there were none who might represent the aristocratic and literary circles among which the dead man had moved with great applause for almost two-score years.

Popular rumor had it that Theodore Hook at his death was in debt to the enormous sum of

thirty thousand pounds. The privileged creditor
was the government (a Tory government — and
Hook from childhood had been an ardent Tory),
which accordingly took possession of all his effects,
and they were sold by Mr. Edmund Robins at his
auction rooms in Covent Garden, on Friday, November 19, 1841, beginning at half-past twelve
o'clock precisely. The sale lasted four days and
brought £2500. This sum was turned over to the
Lords of the Treasury as part payment for the
Mauritius defalcation for which Hook had been
held liable — the shadow of which had hung over
the entire latter half of his life.

Theodore Hook left another very unfortunate
complication behind him. Twenty years before
his death he had been living in complete obscurity
in Somers Town, constantly expecting immediate
arrest and imprisonment. There he had met a
young woman who, although certainly of a not
elevated social station, had been, by common
report, of respectable conduct previously. With
this woman Hook lived from that time till his
death, but he did not marry her. She bore him
five children — four girls. All were left utterly
destitute by Hook's death. A subscription was
taken for their relief. The king of Hanover (Duke
of Cumberland), at whose London residence
Hook had often dined, gave £500. William John
Broderip, a magistrate in the Thames Police

Court and the staunchest friend Hook ever had, gave to the limit of his means. But practically all of Hook's aristocratic acquaintances refused to give anything, on the score of morality — for in this instance morality and economy happily supported each other. Hence the amount realized by the subscription was not large. The boy was given a small clerkship in India. The four girls and their mother sink from sight soon after.

Theodore Hook's place as editor of Colburn's "New Monthly Magazine" was quickly and satisfactorily filled. "On August 24, 1841, Theodore Hook died," writes Walter Jerrold, the biographer of Thomas Hood, "and within a week an emissary from the publisher, Colburn, visited Hood to offer him the succession to the editorship of the 'New Monthly Magazine.'" The prince of punsters was the logical successor, for he had been for two years the magazine's most important contributor.

At the time of his death, Hook still received a salary as editor of the Sunday newspaper, the "John Bull." But the salary was insignificant and the duties nominal. His interest in this paper, which, under his direction, had achieved so brilliant a *succès de scandale* in 1821, had long since waned, and the paper itself had sunk to colorless obscurity and a circulation of only four or five thousand copies.

The publishers, Henry Colburn and Richard

Bentley, had reason to regret Theodore Hook's death. He had first become associated with them in 1824, when they were in partnership. In 1832 Bentley bought out Colburn, who agreed not to engage in the publishing business in London. He made trial elsewhere, but he soon came back to the city, paid the forfeit prescribed, and set up a rival publishing house. Hook remained on good terms with both of these men (who now hated each other bitterly), although most of his dealings were with Colburn. A new novel by Theodore Hook spelled a certain and considerable profit to its publisher, for of such a work at least four thousand copies could be sold in the "three decker" form, at the usual and exorbitant price of one pound ten shillings. A few years later the novel could be republished in one volume in Colburn's "Modern Standard Novelists" or in Bentley's "Standard Novels," and it would find a greater sale at the reduced price at which such works were marketed. The loss of a novel writer of proved popularity was a financial blow distinctly felt by his publishers.

A good outline of the life and literary achievements of Theodore Hook appeared in "Bentley's Miscellany" for September, 1841. This account was partly reproduced and considerably augmented by the "Gentleman's Magazine" of October, 1841. The October numbers of the "New

Monthly" and of "Fraser's Magazine" also contained short estimates. Among the weekly periodicals, the "Athenæum" noted Hook's death and viewed his accomplishments on September 4, 1841. William Jerdan, editor of the weekly "Literary Gazette," had been Hook's personal friend for many years, and it is with a friend's grief that he writes in his magazine of August 28:

It is too early a time to speak of this singularly gifted individual except in the spontaneous and general terms of that sorrow which flows from the thought that we shall never listen to his voice again; never hear those sparkling sallies which used to set the table in a roar; never dwell with unmingled admiration on those extemporaneous effusions, in which he never had an equal, and which were the delight and wonder of all who knew him; never witness that unabating spirit and unflagging mirth which made him the soul and centre of the convivial circle; never hearken him on to new efforts and additional triumphs, after he had achieved more than would have been fame to twenty acknowledged wits; never look upon that bright, dark flashing eye, illuminating with mind and the glance of the forthcoming lightning; never feel the force of that manly sense, acute observation, and accumulated intelligence, which rendered him as instructive when gravity prevailed, as he was unapproachable when festivity ruled the hour. Alas, dear Hook! there is now a void indeed where you filled an enviable place, a gloom where you so gloriously shone.

In 1842 Colburn brought out Hook's last full novel, "Fathers and Sons," most of which had appeared in instalments in the "New Monthly."

The first volume of the novel contained an exceedingly brief but very accurate memoir of the author.

In the "Quarterly Review" for May, 1843, appeared a lengthy article containing a sketch of Hook's life and a critical estimate of his writings. The facts it presents are not always accurate, and they are frequently set down in the compressed form demanded of the periodical article. Yet this account is the best survey of the life and works of Theodore Hook that has ever appeared. It came out anonymously, but there is no doubt as to the identity of the author. He was John Gibson Lockhart, a close acquaintance of Hook's for twenty years. "I have been neither well nor in good spirits," he writes to John Murray, the owner of the "Quarterly," on March 28, 1843, "but I have worked hard for a while on Hook's papers." [1] The papers consisted chiefly of a diary or journal kept irregularly over many years. It has since disappeared, but if it is lost, the loss is not a great one. It consisted, to judge from Lockhart's liberal extracts, of a few wistful but conventional regrets about the rapid flight of time and human life, together with a record of the social events to which its author was invited and the distinguished per-

---

[1] Samuel Smiles, *A Publisher and His Friends* (1891), ii, 505 f.

sonages whom he encountered on such occasions. The remaining "papers" can have been great neither in number nor in importance. The diary, then, and the memoirs of Hook which appeared in periodicals immediately after his death, and further anecdotes and information arising from his personal acquaintance with Hook and from talks with other friends — these formed the materials with which Lockhart worked. The result of his labor was the best "Quarterly" article, probably, that Walter Scott's son-in-law ever wrote, and the most popular as well, for it passed through at least three editions when printed separately in Murray's "Reading for the Rail." [1]

In 1847 — induced probably by the success of Lockhart's essay — the publisher, Bentley, decided to put out a collection of verse and prose pieces contributed by Hook to the newspaper "John Bull." He thereupon engaged Richard Harris Dalton Barham, the son of Richard Harris Barham, who wrote the "Ingoldsby Legends," to arrange the collection and to write a brief life of Hook to serve as an introduction. The man Bentley employed was well qualified. He was later to

---

[1] Andrew Lang, *The Life and Letters of John Gibson Lockhart* (1897), ii, 265 f.: "Among Lockhart's *Quarterly* articles, the most permanently valuable are his brief contributions to biography. Of these the essay on Theodore Hook (1843, no. 143) is the best known, having been published separately in Murray's *Railway Reading*, and is, perhaps, the best."

be the biographer of his own father, "Ingoldsby" Barham. The latter was one of Hook's half-dozen most intimate friends. To "Ingoldsby," Hook had related many of the amusing incidents of his life; these the younger Barham was able to recover and record. In addition, he had read Lockhart's essay, and he collected reminiscences from many of his subject's early friends. With such materials, this life sketch, crowded with anecdote, grew under the younger Barham's hand to the respectable size of two hundred pages duodecimo. The entire volume appeared in 1848 as "The Life and Remains of Theodore Edward Hook."

After 1850 the name of Theodore Hook is still frequently met with. Many of his novels were reprinted both in England and in America. All of them were put out in a cheap and uniform edition by Routledge in the early eighteen-seventies. In 1872 Bentley collected in one small volume Hook's well-known "Ramsbottom Letters," originally contributed to "John Bull." A year later J. C. Hotten brought out a rival edition of the same work. In 1889 Chatto and Windus published a volume entitled "The Choice Humorous Works of Theodore Hook." This work was a collection of Hook's verse and shorter prose pieces to which was prefixed a Life. The verse and prose, however, had practically all been printed in Barham's volume of 1848, and the life sketch was shamelessly plagiarized from Barham and from Lock-hart.[1]

The appearance of this volume, added to the fact that the centenary of Hook's birth occurred in 1888, caused a small flurry of periodical articles, chiefly in the less-known magazines, in the years immediately before and after 1890. These articles, almost without exception, consist of a retelling of humorous anecdotes concerning the man, collected from Barham and Lockhart. For twenty or thirty years previous to 1890, Hook's name had been appearing not infrequently in memoirs written by, and biographies written of, the men of his day.

In our own century almost the very name of Theodore Hook has been forgotten. If his memory is now to be revived among men, his entire story must be told anew: his deeds must be relived and his literary productions must be reconsidered. For his life, Lockhart and Barham must still be the principal reliance of the present-day writer, yet the material they present will endure assortment and correction, and it can be augmented by a not inconsiderable amount of additional information which has appeared since 1850. As for Hook's literary labors, the perspective of a century makes possible a much truer estimate than could be at-

---

[1] This plagiarism is noted by Richard Garnett in his article on Theodore Hook in the *Dictionary of National Biography*.

tempted even by a Lockhart in the decade immediately following his death.

The only remaining consideration is, then, is
the attempt worth the effort? It gives every appearance of being so. It is no ordinary man who
can, in one lifetime, be a playwright, a courtier, an
editor, a government official, a writer of verse, a
novelist, a clubman, and a celebrated wit. It is no
ordinary man, moreover, who can know, in their
most intimate and convivial moments, the royalty,
the aristocracy, and the literary class of his day —
and, among the last named, such men as Sheridan,
Colman the younger, Leigh Hunt, Campbell,
Coleridge, Byron, and Disraeli. Such a life is the
many-sided reflection of an age.

When one turns to Hook's literary achievement,
the prospect seems fully as promising. He
flourished during the years 1825 to 1840, a period
which is not often entered by the critic of English
literature, but one whose marked significance is
ably asserted by Mr. Hugh Walker, in his work
on the literature of the Victorian era, in these
terms:

The years 1825 to 1840 show a comparatively meagre
list of memorable works. In the writings of the younger
generation we have only a partial counterpoise to the
loss caused by the failing powers and thinning ranks
among their elders. We can see in it numerous begin-
nings and rich promise, but the actual performance is
poor beside that of the preceding fifteen years, which in-

cludes all that matters of Byron, the best of Scott's prose, and Miss Austen's, and all of Shelley and Keats, together with much of Coleridge and Wordsworth. But the true significance of the years after 1825 will be missed unless we bear in mind that they were the seed-time of all the rich literature of the early and intermediate Victorian era. By the greatness of that literature we must estimate the importance of the years in which it was germinating.

Again, it is as a writer of novels that the name of Theodore Hook assumes its greatest literary importance. In the English novel this period of fifteen years saw a marked change of dynasty. In 1825, the Waverley Novels had given to historical romance and to Sir Walter Scott the reigning influence. In 1840 the monarch was Charles Dickens, firmly established as a realist portraying the life of contemporary England. The history of this change inevitably involves the name of Theodore Hook. His importance has not been denied by the few who have considered it. Lockhart writes in 1843:

His defects are great; but Theodore Hook is, we apprehend, the only male novelist of this time, except Mr. Dickens, who has drawn portraits of contemporary English society destined for permanent existence. A selection from his too numerous volumes will go down with Miss Edgeworth and Miss Austen. His best works are not to be compared with theirs, either for skilful compactness of fable or general excellence of finish. His pace was too fast for that. But he is never to be confounded for a moment either with their clumsier and weaker followers, or with the still more tedious imitators of their only modern superior.[1]

Lockhart's prediction has not been fulfilled. Hook's right to a place among English novelists has been almost entirely overlooked. The result has been, writes Professor George Saintsbury, in 1924, in his "English Novel," that his achievement has never received proper acknowledgment:

> Yet for all this, Hook has a claim on the critical historian of literature, and especially of the novel, which has been far too little acknowledged. And this claim does not even consist in the undoubted fact that his influence both on Dickens and on Thackeray was direct and very great. It lies in the larger and more important, though connected, fact that at a given moment his were the hands in which the torch of the novel-procession was deposited.

A judgment which implies that Theodore Hook received the "torch of the novel-procession" from Walter Scott about 1825, that he passed it to Charles Dickens in 1840, and that he, during the years between, carried that torch in his own hands, may seem extravagant. Its soundness can be proved or its extravagance demonstrated only by a comprehensive study of Hook's novels. With the exception of a few pages by Professor Saintsbury in his "Essays in English Literature, 1780–

---

[1] The "only modern superior" is Dickens. Lockhart wrote before the full powers of Thackeray had become manifest.

1860," of a longer but not illuminating chapter by Wilhelm Dibelius in his "Englische Romankunst," and finally, of scattering remarks in popular histories of the English novel, there has been no endeavor to fix the position of Theodore Hook as a novelist.

CHAPTER I.

PARENTAGE AND BOYHOOD.

In 1763 John Wesley abandoned the Norwich Tabernacle as a hopeless undertaking. In 1775 it came into the hands of that interesting woman, Selina, Countess of Huntingdon. During the intervening twelve years it was presided over by the Reverend John Hook, a Church of England clergyman, of a family whose residence in Norfolk began at least as early as the reign of Elizabeth. John Hook's only child, James, was born on June 3, 1746. The infant lost no time in displaying the precocity characteristic of the family, for he could perform on the pianoforte at the age of four, and he appeared in public at six. His father, however, intended him for a trade, until the sudden development of the affliction vulgarly called club-foot made it certain that the boy would never walk without canes. John Hook thereupon allowed his son to follow his bent, and sent him to study with Garland, the cathedral organist.

When he was about twenty-one years old, James Hook came to London, and he is first heard of as the composer of a group of songs sung at Ranelagh and at the New Theatre at Richmond, and published as his first work. He found employment, too, from 1769 to 1773, as organist at Marylebone Gardens. In 1774 he became the "organist and composer" at Vauxhall Gardens; he held this position until 1820, thus spanning the interval between the evening when Fanny Burney's Evelina was insulted there when she inadvertently strayed on one of the darker paths, and the night when Pierce Egan's Tom and Jerry had rather dull amusement knocking down a dandy and dancing with a few Cyprians "till daylight had long given them the hint it was time to think of home."

In the eighteenth century, particularly on the gala nights, Vauxhall was one of the famous sights of the metropolis, and all classes rubbed shoulders there. In the nineteenth, it came gradually to be a resort where the shopkeeper and his family spent their Sunday "mornings" from two to six o'clock, and where, after dark, the light-fingered gentry mingled with a set of rough apprentices and doubtful women, skilfully starting up brawls in various parts of the gardens by which they were enabled the more expeditiously to ply their profession. James Hook's duties at this resort included the playing of an organ concerto every evening during the season, which began early in June. He also assisted the well-known Barthelemon in conducting the orchestra, which had among its members, Fisher, the best oboe player of his day. Moreover, he contracted to compose a certain number of songs to be sung by Mrs. Weichsell, the leading soloist and the mother of the famous Mrs. Billington, and by various other singers from Drury Lane and Covent Garden who were glad enough, one imagines, to be employed in the dead season of the theatrical year.

But Mr. Hook (to give him the invariable title by which he is known on Vauxhall programmes and on the title-pages of his published works) had time for other profitable pursuits. He gave piano lessons, and his receipts from only two schools, — one in Chelsea and one at Stepney, — where he was the regular instructor, were no less than £600 a year. In her "Recollections of a Literary Life," Mary Russell Mitford confesses candidly that, when she was a girl at Mrs. St. Quintin's school in London, from 1798 to 1802, her father insisted that she continue her piano lessons, although instructor after instructor had discovered that she had "neither ear, nor taste, nor application." She adds:

The regular master employed in the school was Mr. Hook (father of Theodore), then a popular composer of Vauxhall songs, and an instructor of average ability. A large, smooth-faced man he was, good-natured and civil spoken; but failing, as in my case everybody else had failed, to produce the slightest improvement, my father, not much struck by his appearance or manner, decided, as usual, that the fault lay with the teacher.

Mr. Hook's book of instruction, the "Guida di Musica," was widely known, and through it many a fashionable young woman was introduced to a polite knowledge of the pianoforte. He was also for many years organist at St. John's Church, Horsleydown.

The stage furnished another outlet for the indefatigable energies of James Hook. As a song writer for the theatre he ranks with men like Charles Dibdin, William Shield, Stephen Storace, and Thomas Linley, the father-in-law of Richard Brinsley Sheridan. The market for songs was good. Every play written between 1780 and 1820 contained at least a song by the comedian and a plaintive air or two by the heroine; while the "opera," or more properly the "ballad opera," which was perhaps the chief dramatic product of the period, required an overture, several dances, and three or four songs to an act. For a ballad opera which held the boards for ten or a dozen nights (and only one in twenty ran longer) the composer could expect about £75. And Mr. Hook composed with astounding rapidity; for he wrote the music for over thirty plays and ballad operas which appeared at the three theatres royal between 1770 and 1810. He knew too that the librettist regularly fared better than the composer, inasmuch as the former, in addition to receiving his share of the receipts of the play, could frequently sell his copyright to a publisher for a sum which was often respectable. Therefore, Mr. Hook endeavored to raise up a librettist from his own family; for among the thirty plays were one written by his wife in 1784, two by James Hook, his elder son, in 1795 and 1797, and nine written between 1805 and 1809 by his younger son, Theodore Edward Hook.

This indomitable composer, in fact, wrote one hundred and forty complete works, more than two thousand songs, at least one oratorio, and many concertos and sonatas. This mass has met the fate of all the huge piles of music put out in those days — a few of the songs or glees still survive. For example, the once famous Dr. Arne is now known almost entirely for his "Lass with the Delicate Air." Similarly, of the enormous mass of music produced by Mr. Hook, there survives possibly the song, "The Lass of Richmond Hill," — sung originally by Incledon in the "Gentle Shepherd," in 1795, and popularly accepted as a reference to Mrs. Fitzherbert, the morganatic wife of the Prince of Wales, later George IV, — and certainly the song "'T was Within a Mile of Edinborough Town." He made a good living from his musical activities; his yearly income must have averaged two thousand pounds.

Mr. Hook's talent was genuine. The renowned Dr. Burney is said to have spoken highly of him. The musician W. T. Parke, whose "Musical

Memoirs" contains practically all of the extant biographical information about Mr. Hook, is always open in his admiration of his talent both as a composer and as a virtuoso. Parke adds, however, an outright, if softened, accusation of plagiarism — considering Hook's offences "to have been the effect of haste, not design." Now certainly one who composed so voluminously may well have been a plagiarist, or, at least, was almost certain to have the offence charged against him. Yet it is possible that Parke is merely repeating a baseless slander set forth by an anonymous pamphlet, printed at Bath in 1780, called the "A.B.C. Dario Musico" — a Grub Street tract which singles out certain contemporary musicians for excessive vilification, while it heaps effusive plaudits upon certain others. Mr. Hook, as may be seen from the following extract, fares evilly indeed:

H——K. — Bred up to trade at Norwich. He early disclosed a love for music, and has on all occasions shown himself familiar with the works of the best composers. If a deluge should obliterate all traces of music, and the elaborate works of this gentleman only escape, they would serve as an Ark to convey to posterity a satisfactory idea of the music of all the composers of this age. Indeed, Mr. H——k's merit to collect has been unceasing. On the opening of the Artist's Room in the Strand, an Ode was performed, by Mr. H——k. When the performance was over, some of the cognoscenti, discussing its merits, appealed to Giardini (who had conducted) for his decision; he asserted with peculiar gravity that it was the best music he had heard.

"Why," says one, "it is not all his own." "True," replied the keen Signor, "that is the reason it is so good."

To the modern ear, Mr. Hook's songs — which regularly celebrate the joys of rural life, the ardent advances of Strephon, the shy reticence of Delia, and the pangs of disprized Arcadian love — seem rather to plagiarize from each other, for they all sound nearly alike.

In 1770, or a year later, James Hook married Miss Madden, who was, writes the musician Parke, "the daughter of an officer in the British service." It seems most probable that her family was Irish. Did she belong to the famous Madden family, of Irish extraction, which numbered among its members Major General Sir George Allan Madden, a hero of the Peninsular Campaign, and William John Madden, a captain of the Royal Marines and father of Sir Frederic Madden, the famous antiquary? Was she one of the seven sisters of these two brothers? That fact does not transpire. She was highly talented, and her education had been elegant and aristocratic. The young composer must have thought himself extremely fortunate to win her. "She was," Parke continues, "a genteel and accomplished lady and greatly excelled as an artist in miniature painting." She is known to the stage as the author, in 1784, of "The Double Disguise," an inoffensive little two-act farce on the conventional mistaken-

identity pattern — for which her husband provided the music. In her later days she became
vehemently religious, and Henry Angelo, the son
of the popular Eton fencing-master, speaks of her
then, in his "Reminiscences," as "an affable,
pleasant lady, inclined to be lusty."

The first child of this marriage was James Hook,
junior, who was born in June, 1772. At Westminster School, which he entered on January 16,
1786, he became engaged in a contest of epigrams
with George Canning, then at Eton, through the
medium of the school papers, the Westminster
"Microcosm" and the Eton "Trifler." Later
James Hook went to Oxford, matriculating there
as a student at St. Mary Hall on June 8, 1792, at
the age of nineteen. In due course he received his
A.B. and A.M. degrees — the latter in 1799. In
1795, and again two years later, he attempted to
assist his father by writing the librettos of two
ballad operas. The first of these, "Jack of New-
bury," was acted on May 6, 1795, at Drury Lane;
the second, "Diamond Cut Diamond, or Venetian
Revels," came out at the same theatre on May 23,
1797. The second play was a complete failure.
The first, through strenuous efforts, was kept
alive for some half-dozen nights. John Adolphus,
biographer of the famous comedian John Bannister, writes of it:

In an unlucky hour, it occurred to Mr. Hook, eldest son of Mr. James Hook, the composer, that he would write an opera. He chose for his subject "Jack of New-bury." Bannister played in it; and Signora Storace, Mrs. Crouch, and Mrs. Bland lent their aid; there was also a masque introduced in honour of the Prince of Wales's marriage: but all would not do; poor Jack was kept in a state of precarious existence for a few nights, and then disappeared for ever.

Neither of these pieces was ever published.

In 1796 young James Hook took holy orders. In 1797 he accomplished the most successful achievement of his life: he contracted a most fortunate marriage with Anne, the second daughter of Sir Walter Farquhar, the physician and confidential friend of the Prince of Wales. After his marriage, James's advance was rapid. He became private chaplain for a time to the Prince and to the King, and "is known to have been honoured," writes the "Gentleman's Magazine," in 1828, with George III's "particular personal regard." Accordingly, piece after piece of preferment fell his way, and he became Dean of Worcester in 1825. He was one of those entirely secular ministers of religion very common in the days before the Oxford Movement — preaching the cause of the Established Church on the grounds of constitutional law, expressing (with manly good sense and in favor of the king and the Tory party) decided opinions on all political questions,

drinking deeply and convivially, combatting
Methodism and all apostles of gloom, taking his
cirrhosis of the liver manfully, and dying on February 5, 1828, at the not advanced age of fifty-
five, to be buried in Worcester Cathedral after
services by the bishop. His oldest child, born in
London, March 13, 1798, was the well-known
Walter Farquhar Hook, Vicar of Leeds and later
Dean of Chichester, whose principal literary accomplishment was the immense "Lives of the
Archishops of Canterbury."

In temperament and attainments James Hook,
junior, was much like his younger brother, Theodore. Not only was his boyish temper spirited if
not fractious, and not only did he write for the
stage, but he published two novels, "Pen Owen"
in 1822, and "Percy Mallory" in 1824, and contributed several articles to Theodore's newspaper,
"John Bull." W. R. W. Stephens, the son's biographer, adds:

James inherited the talents of his father and mother,
and added to them very considerable powers of his own.
It was truly remarked by one of his friends that had he
devoted his whole attention to painting, music, or
literature, he would have achieved a high reputation in
either of the three professions. . . . Some of his juvenile
sketches were shown to Sir Joshua Reynolds, who was
so much struck by the genius of the young artist that he
strongly recommended the boy's parents to have him
trained for the profession of painter. . . . In music he had
the same aptitude as his brother Theodore for playing

impromptu on the piano, and was superior to him in execution and general knowledge of the art; but although a ready versifier, he did not improvise verses to his own accompaniments, the accomplishment for which Theodore earned such a remarkable reputation.

But there was to be one material point of difference between the brothers. James, at the earnest solicitation of his mother, took holy orders. His life was honorable, respectable, and a trifle dull. Theodore, under no importunity or restraint, strayed on the uncharted Bohemian side paths. His career was mutable, violent, and very interesting. The man who must point his moral may point one here in either direction.

Theodore Edward Hook, the second son of James Hook the composer, was born in Charlotte Street, Bedford Square, London, on September 22, 1788. He was sixteen years younger than his brother.

Lockhart's "Quarterly" essay and Barham's Life relate many incidents of Theodore's boyhood. They agree that the phenomenon exhibited by that boyhood is one of an exuberant spirit unrestrained by any determined, and especially by any enduring, discipline. From a school in the neighborhood of Vauxhall kept by Mr. Allan, Theodore was sent to a "seminary for young gentlemen" in Soho Square, where, a decade before, J. M. W. Turner, the future landscape

painter, had been a student.[1] Matters culminated
here in March, 1802, on the day of the celebration
for the Peace of Amiens. Our school had declared
a holiday, Theodore had announced; but when his
brother, by chance in London at the time, in-
quired at the school, he discovered not only that
the day was *not* a holiday, but that nothing had
been seen of Theodore for three weeks. The truant
youth was thereupon sent to the boarding school
of Dr. Curtis at Linton in Cambridgeshire, which
for some reason — perhaps because the art of the
cane was only imperfectly understood — the boy
seems genuinely to have liked. But the school was
removed to Sunbury, and Theodore probably decided that of schools near London he preferred
Harrow.

To Harrow, therefore, he went, entering in the
Easter–Midsummer term of 1804 at the comparatively late age of fifteen. At the school at this
time were (Sir) Robert Peel and Byron. Only a
year before his death, as Barham records, Hook,
during a convivial evening with Ingoldsby,

mentioned several anecdotes of his early life; among
others, he said that on the day on which he was first
sent down to Harrow school, Lord Byron, who was there
at the time, took him into the square, showed him a
window at which Mrs. Drury [wife of the celebrated

---

[1] This Soho Square school was then well known. It has disappeared, but it is mentioned by Mr. E. Beresford Chancellor,
in his *History of the Squares of London* (1907), pp. 125 f.

Latin master] was undressing, gave him a stone, and bid him "knock her eye out with it." Hook threw the stone and broke the window. Next morning there was a great "row" about it, and Byron, coming up to him, said, "Well, my fine fellow, you've done it! She had but one eye [the truth], and it's gone!" Hook's funk was indescribable.[1]

One may call this piece of juvenile contumacy characteristic either of the uncurbed Theodore or of the headstrong young lord, were it clear whether the latter's instigation limited itself merely to suggestion, or whether he was subjecting the new arrival to some process of hazing.

Theodore did not stay long at Harrow. Early in 1805 he came home to Charlotte Street, called there by the illness of his mother. She died, after a long period of decline, on October 18 of the same year. What little pressure of restraint and precept had been exerted on the headstrong boy was now entirely removed.

---

[1] This incident is quoted from R. H. D. Barham's *Life and Letters of the Rev. Richard Harris Barham* (1870), ii, 109 f. Thus Barham, in addition to writing a biography of Hook, was also the biographer of his own father. To avoid possible confusion herein, I may say that by "Barham" I always mean R. H. D. Barham and his biography of Hook; by "Ingoldsby," I mean Richard Harris Barham, author of the "Ingoldsby Legends" and the father of Hook's biographer.

CHAPTER II.

THE WRITER OF PLAYS.

IT is not to be supposed that the old composer, now approaching his sixtieth year, could spare much time from his multifarious pursuits to exercise a proper parental control over the sixteen-year-old Theodore. Indeed, granted the leisure, the temperament was lacking. "A large, smooth-faced man he was," Mary Russell Mitford has already been quoted as saying, "good-natured and civil spoken." And young Angelo knew him as a witty old gentleman whose spectacles "did not disguise his good-humoured countenance; he always had something to say to make others smile." James Hook must have thought his younger son a prodigiously clever lad. Thus from the position of son and schoolboy Theodore at once advanced to become his father's associate and collaborator. And, to put a final touch to the situation, the composer, on November 6, 1806, married Miss Harriet Horncastle James, who could not have been many years older than Theodore himself.[1] It is not sur-

---

[1] Granting that Miss Middleton is correct, in her article on James Hook, senior, in the *Dictionary of National Biography*, in giving April 5, 1873, as the date of the death of the second wife. The British Museum *Catalogue of Printed Books* is in error when it ascribes to Mrs. Harriet Horncastle Hook the authorship of the play "The Double Disguise." This play, it has been noted, was the work of the first wife, born Miss Madden.

prising that, in the words of Lockhart, "Theodore found not — what in spite of a thousand proverbs many men have found under such circumstances — a second mother."

Left to his own devices, the youth naturally drifted to the theatres, where his father's reputation readily procured him admission both before and behind the curtain. The air of the green room became Theodore's native element. It was there, writes an actor, that "every evening, between the play and the afterpiece, noblemen, authors, and artists used to assemble on the footing of the most social intimacy. Everyone came provided with his anecdote or *bon mot*. In no other place have I ever seen so perfect an equality between talent, wealth, and rank." And thus, running to get a fan for some famous and beautiful actress of magnificent bust and neat silken ankles, chatting with a man of title intent upon pleasant diversion or with some dashing young blade of fashion, listening to the clever reminiscences of renowned actors and managers, in the genially affable atmosphere of people of easy manners and sharp wits, lavish with money provided the effect was striking, with the whole scene framed in the brilliant illusory background of bright lights, sparkling tinsel, grease-paint, and rouge — thus it was that Theodore's character was formed at his most impressionable age.

At Drury Lane he could see Richard Brinsley Sheridan, the manager and chief proprietor. From him and from Thomas Harris, manager of Covent Garden, he would hear of the peculiar adaptability of the two large theatres for elaborate stage tableaux, and of the new type of drama from France, the *melo-drame*, which abounded in such spectacles. At the Haymarket, George Colman the younger might lend the bright young man a few French plays and vaudevilles, after exhorting him to take good care of them, for they were no longer easy to procure now that "Boney" was roaming the Continent again. Here, too, Theodore might hear some envying three-pound-a-week actor tell of the thousand pounds this George Colman made at one swoop from his play "John Bull," of 1803. Finally, at the "Hay," Hook made the acquaintance of Charles Mathews, of comedians *facile princeps*, and was witness to his uncanny ability at impersonation. "But I have no chance of showing these tricks in public," Mathews would probably say, "for the comedy parts in standard drama are straight parts. What I need are farcical afterpieces which are written purposely for me — or even good farcical situations which I can fill out as I please."

Naturally Theodore Hook decided to write a few plays himself — or, it should be said rather, to continue his boyish efforts in that direction; for in a family in which father, mother, and elder brother had all been concerned in stage productions, it was impossible to avoid the contagion. Announcement of his intention at home met with whole-hearted encouragement and promise of coöperation from his father. The little back drawing-room was allotted to Theodore, and he set to work. A friend from the theatre, Sam Beazley, architect and dramatist (whose railway stations, however, proved more durable than his farces), describes the room: "Tables, chairs, mantelpiece, piano, were all covered with a litter of letters, MS. music, French plays, notes, tickets, rhyming dictionaries — not a seat to be had."

The result proved that this young man in his teens could write plays as well as could any dramatist of his day. In explanation of this phenomenon a few observations are necessary. The entire first half of the nineteenth century saw the English drama in a most lamentable state. "The period exhibits," writes Mr. Harold Child in the "Cambridge History of English Literature," "a confusing jumble of trivial aims and poor accomplishments; from which may be extricated two principal characteristics — the degeneration of comedy into farce, and the growth of what is known as melodrama." Of this half-century, the decade 1805 to 1815 is certainly the poorest of the poor. In 1805 Sheridan still lived, a prosperous gentleman, it is true, for the burning of Drury Lane, which ruined him, did not occur till 1809. But his duties as member of Parliament, his responsibilities as manager of a theatre, and his fear, evident in his later life, to compete with the author of the "School for Scandal," kept him from writing; *that* career had ended even before he brought out his last play "Pizarro," in the Kotzebue vein, in 1799. At the Haymarket, George Colman the younger practically ceased writing (not to mention a few translations and adaptations) after the success of "John Bull" in 1803. To name other writers for the stage at the time is to unearth such misty creatures as Dibdin, Morton (whose "Speed the Plough" of 1800 was successful enough to fix one of its characters, Mrs. Grundy, in literature), O'Keefe, and Frederick Reynolds.

Theodore Hook essayed each of the three kinds of drama then being written — the ballad opera, the melodrama, and the farce.

He wrote two ballad operas. These ballad operas (the term is a present-day coinage, for they were then called "operas," or "comic operas") were plays containing, like Gay's "Beggar's Opera," much music — but music merely incidental, not blended with the plot to form, as in present-day grand opera, one unified production. The first of Theodore's attempts was also his first play. It was the two-act "The Soldier's Return;

or, What Can Beauty Do?" produced at Drury Lane on March 23, 1805, the music being by his father. It was, writes James Smith (co-author of the "Rejected Addresses"), at the school of Dr. Curtis in Cambridgeshire "during the hours allotted for recreation, that he planned and wrote entirely his first piece, called 'The Soldier's Return,' which, after laying by for two years, was produced at Drury-Lane Theatre in the season of 1804–5." As the work of a boy of thirteen, the play certainly merits astonishment. But otherwise it is a lifeless affair, which has for its central piece of business the return of a soldier reported dead, and his reunion with his beloved just as she is about to marry, for the sake of protection, his own father, whose new title, as it has changed his name, has completely mystified the son. The source of this plot, it is to be feared, would quickly be revealed by a short subterranean exploration among the buried farces of the day. The comic part, played by John Bannister, is described by the comedian's biographer, Adolphus:

In "The Soldier's Return" Bannister played Rocket, a man of fashion — a coxcomb of the coarsest mould, a pedant of the humblest description; he had two humours, that of dressing so that no one suspected him to be a gentleman, and of introducing the names of men of celebrity, such as Dryden, Newton, and Shakespeare, for the purpose of displaying his memory, by reciting the dates of their birth and death, and their principal productions, in the manner of a compendium of certain articles in an abridged biographical dictionary.

In other words, the hand of the precocious school-boy is everywhere apparent. The chief marvels of the business are that patient audiences heard without protest on eleven successive evenings the announcement of the repetition of this lifeless play on the succeeding evening; that it was published; and that Genest, in his monumental "History of the English Stage," could call it "a moderate comic Op." As his share of the proceeds the sixteen-year-old boy received a check for £50 — a fact which certainly did not dampen his ardor.

The second of Hook's ballad operas came out four years later, in 1809, at the Lyceum Theatre, whither the Drury Lane company had moved after the destruction of their theatre. This was "Safe and Sound, an opera in three acts, the music by Mr. Hook." This musical play is merely his own farce "Catch Him Who Can," with a change of scene from Spain to Prussia.

Theodore Hook played a considerable part in introducing melodrama into England. The originator of the melodrama — the specific type of drama known by that name — was the Frenchman, Guilbert de Pixerécourt, although the thing itself is connected also with the name of Kotzebue, and with a native English impulse evident in such a play as Monk Lewis's "Wood Demon." To the Frenchman, melodrama meant a play with a happy ending, much music, and one or more startling stage spectacles. Into Hook's hands came Pixerécourt's "Tékéli" of 1803. He made a free translation of it; his father composed or selected music for it; and it was produced, in three acts, at Drury Lane on November 24, 1806, as "Tekeli; or, The Siege of Montgatz." Elliston played the title rôle, and Charles Mathews the comic part of Bras-de-fer. There is spectacular action in each of the three acts — a fight in the forest, the concealment of Count Tekeli in a cask and his escape in a sack of grain, and a final combat between Austrians and Hungarians, in addition to an elaborate tableau when the courageous countess pulls aside a curtain and discloses to the astonished Austrian envoy her faithful followers ready to hurl the besiegers from the walls. "Tekeli" was a tremendous success. It ran over fifty nights at Drury Lane, and three years later a shorter version was revived at the Haymarket.

Of course Hook immediately translated another Pixerécourt melodrama. Out of his "La Forteresse du Danube," popular at Paris in 1805, he fashioned "The Fortress," which was first given at the Haymarket on July 16, 1807, and had a very moderate run of twelve nights. The play — which recounts the heroic efforts made by the beautiful daughter of Count Everard of Suabia to enable her father to escape from a prison, in which he has been placed through the malevolence of political enemies, despite the vigilance of her lover, Oliver, who is in charge of the fortress and is naturally torn between love and duty — is inferior to "Tekeli." It is, as Genest writes, "better calculated for representation than perusal," for the main effect of the piece depends upon the stage trick by which the escape is effected.

The next logical step was for Hook to write a melodrama of his own. He called it the "Siege of St. Quintin; or, Spanish Heroism," and attuned it to catch the enthusiasm generated by the Peninsular campaign. It was a comparative failure ("a poor piece," writes Genest), for it ran only nine times at Drury Lane after November 10, 1808; and it probably owed even this short run to the fact that the management had spent too much money on costumes and scenic effects to abandon the piece immediately. The play was never printed, but an extensive summary of the plot was given by the "Monthly Mirror," a dramatic periodical,[1] in November, 1808. The summary reveals that Hook modelled the play very closely after the two plays of Pixerécourt he had translated, using in particular the *motif* of the escape effected by means of a stage trick. The most in-

---

[1] Very few copies of this magazine are extant. Its owner was Tom Hill, the editor was Dubois, and James Smith wrote for it. All these men are mentioned in a succeeding chapter as friends of Theodore's youth.

teresting fact in connection with the piece is that
it was extensively revised by the manager of
Drury Lane, Richard Brinsley Sheridan. The
"Monthly Mirror," which had, for some reason,
an animus against Sheridan, speaks as follows:
"Mr. Johnstone is introduced as an Irishman,
without any rhyme or reason — without rhyme,
because he has no song to sing, and without reason, because his character of an Irishman is
wretchedly drawn, or is rather no character at all.
For this personage Mr. Hook is indebted to Mr.
R. B. Sheridan, the dramatist defunct." Of another scene it writes: "This scene, we say, is also
written by the author of the 'School for Scandal,'
and is the worst in the piece. As some other little
touches have been given to it by Mr. Sheridan, we
are tempted to ascribe to him a share in the opening of the third act" — another particularly bad
place, in the opinion of the reviewer.

In 1809, in his "English Bards and Scotch Re-
viewers," young Byron turned an affrighted eye
to the British drama:

> Now to the Drama turn — Oh! motley sight!
> What precious scenes the wondering eyes invite:
> Puns, and a Prince within a barrel pent.

He appends a footnote to the last line: "In the
melo-drama of 'Tekeli,' that heroic prince is clapt
into a barrel on the stage; a new asylum for dis-

tressed heroes." In Byron's first draft of his poem, this final line read:

> Princes in barrels, Counts in arbours pent;

and his footnote was: "In the melodrama of 'Tekeli,' that heroic prince is clapt into a barrel on the stage, and Count Everard in the fortress hides himself in a green-house built expressly for the occasion. 'T is a pity that Theodore Hook, who is really a man of talent, should confine his genius to such paltry productions as 'The Fortress,' 'Music Mad,' etc. etc." Again, in his final draft of the poem, the young lord continues:

Gods! o'er those boards shall Folly rear her head,
Where GARRICK trod, and SIDDONS lives to tread?
On those shall farce display buffoonery's mask,
And HOOK conceal his heroes in a cask?

It was a play like "Tekeli," therefore, that Byron thought emblematic of the complete stagnation of the drama.[1]

And Byron is right, of course. The melodrama committed the drama to the stage spectacle and the acrobatic feat — to the leap for life, the thrilling rescue from real flames, the storming of the fortress walls, the clever ruse, the quick change of disguise. Thus the emphasis is no longer on dialogue but on stage carpentry; and the play, effec-

---

[1] The quotations are taken from *The Works of Lord Byron*, edited by Ernest Hartley Coleridge (1898), i, 341 and 344.

tive as it may be in presentation, cannot be read as literature. Again, this sort of thing attracts a different audience, or it at least changes the taste of the existing one. As a result "legitimate" drama becomes less and less popular, and managers can no longer profitably put it on. Finally, Covent Garden will naturally strive to outdo Drury Lane, and will set its carpenters to work to construct more effective scenery. Drury Lane will counter by placing a pool of real water on the stage. Covent Garden will retaliate with a tournament on horseback. Thus the way is made clear for Van Amburgh and his performing lions; we are then in the music hall and no longer in the theatre.

The situation is a bad thing for the genuine dramatist; it means his downfall. This is clearly recognized by George Cumberland, editor of a series of plays by contemporary dramatists called the "British Theatre," in an article in the "Monthly Mirror" for April, 1807.

Since [he writes] the stages of Drury-Lane and Covent-Garden have been so enlarged in their dimensions as to be henceforward theatres for spectators rather than playhouses for hearers, it is hardly to be wondered at if their managers and directors encourage those representations to which their structure is best adapted. The splendor of the scenes, the ingenuity of the machinist, and the rich display of dresses, aided by the captivating charms of music, now in a great degree supersede the labours of the poet. There can be nothing very gratifying in watching the movements of an actor's lips, when we cannot hear the words that proceed from them; but when the animating march strikes up, and the stage lays open its recesses to the depth of a hundred feet for the procession to advance, even the most distant spectator can enjoy his shilling's-worth of show. What then is the poet's chance?

To return to Byron's protest. He is right in holding that melodrama has much blame to bear for ruining legitimate drama. But with what peculiar unfitness the protest comes from a romanticist! The poems that Byron was to write — on just such provender did the melodrama feed. The audience that applauded melodramas idolized Monk Lewis and Mrs. Radcliffe, and took Byron and Walter Scott into its embrace. Just a short time later, Daniel Terry achieved triumph after triumph by turning Waverley Novels into melodramas. Place the romantic movement behind the footlights and you will have what the early nineteenth century called a melodrama.

With his writing of farces Theodore Hook began modestly enough. He read a newspaper account of a French vaudeville (the pieces themselves were almost impossible to procure because of the blockade), the "Babillard" of Charles Maurice, and borrowed the idea, which was that of having one character do all the talking. The resultant play was the one-act afterpiece, "The Invisible Girl." It was written expressly for Bannister, and was first given on his benefit night at Drury Lane,

April 28, 1806. "He played," says Adolphus, "Captain Allclack, a gentleman infected with such an overpowering *cacoëthes loquendi*, that talk to whom he will, he repels all their attempts to partake in the discourse, anticipates their thoughts, answers himself in their supposed words, and expresses resentment if he only surmises that they intend to utter a syllable." Bannister succeeded with it — no slight feat, for, as Genest writes, "the actor who attempts this part with any prospect of succeeding in it must have a versatility of talent, and a happy memory — if he should pause for a moment for the Prompter, the part would be spoilt."

Hook's next farce, "Catch Him Who Can," was the first of his Haymarket farces, being acted there on June 12, 1806. It was an attempt to write something which would bring out the unique ability of Charles Mathews to change instantly from the impersonation of one character to that of an entirely different character by the aid of only a few slight changes in make-up. Mathews, therefore, was cast for seven changes of disguise; and they were so effectively made, writes Mrs. Mathews in her "Memoirs" of her husband, that they almost defeated their purpose — the audience consistently failed for a long time to recognize the comedian after each change. The display of this remarkable gift is the chief business of the piece, although the cast included also the comedian Liston, and Mrs. Mathews as the heroine. The plot is nondescript. It concerns the duel of two spirited young men, the flight of each, thinking the other has been killed, the seeking of revenge by the father of one, the falling in love of the one with the sister of the other — and the final happy revelation that neither of the duellists has been injured. "The foundation of the plot, and nothing more," Genest avers, "seems to have been borrowed from Madame [de] Genlis." Again, then, Hook's source was probably a newspaper account of the plot of a French comedy. He thought that plot good enough to use again in his opera "Safe and Sound."

Hook's next effort, the one-act farcical sketch, "Music Mad," was also written for Mathews. It was first acted on his benefit night at the Haymarket, August 27, 1807, and for six evenings thereafter. The main idea of the play was again a borrowed one; it was taken from a fairly well-known Italian piece, "Il Fanatico per la Musica," the success of which had been established by the celebrated actor, Naldi. As in the "Invisible Girl," there is a single farcical situation. Sir Christopher Crochet (Mathews), an old man so passionately fond of music that he dresses his servant (Liston) in a waistcoat scored all over with musical notes, calls his relatives about him and leaves his money to, as he thinks, the most unfortunate of them — the young sailor, Hawser, who, unlike the other prospective heirs, makes no pretense of knowing anything about music. The piece is extremely slight. The author admits that it is but a sketch, and declares that he allowed it to be printed only "that the town, seeing how weak it is in itself, may know what is due" to Mathews and to Liston.

It was as the author of the two-act farce, "Killing No Murder," that Hook was best known, perhaps, to the theatregoers of his day. This play opened on July 1, 1809, at the Haymarket. It ran for thirty-five performances, — a longer run than any other play at a London theatre that year, — and it was revived at Drury Lane in 1823. "Killing No Murder" was written expressly for Mathews, and he succeeded so well with it that it became one of the stock pieces that he played at provincial theatres during his tours over the country. His part was that of Buskin, an actor. He was, in fact, the creator, not only of the rôle, but also of the character; for, writes Mrs. Mathews: "The truth is that the first act of 'Buskin' was a sketch, which Mr. Mathews filled up *ad libitum*, and from this it became much the fashion amongst authors to trust to his working up their 'raw material,' and thus he seldom got a ready-made part given to him in a new piece."

The comedian, Liston, was given the rôle of Apollo Belvi, a Methodist dancing master. Now by one of those humorous accidents, very common before the passage of the Reform Bill, Mr. John Larpent, besides holding four or five other remunerative sinecures, accepted £400 a year as the "Reader of Plays," in addition to two guineas for each and every play to which he granted a license. Mr. Larpent was a staunch Methodist, although one marvels at the remarkably elastic conscience which could reconcile Methodism and play-licensing. "Killing No Murder" contained one extremely caustic, not to say indecent, scene, in which Apollo Belvi describes the process of, and the reasons for, his conversion to Methodism. Accordingly, Larpent refused to issue the license and thereby made the piece famous. For Hook, after securing the license by suppressing the scene, caused the actors to substitute the words "what I must not mention" for the words "Methodist minister," introduced the entire controversy into the play in carefully guarded language, and made all the circumstances known to the public by printing the suppressed scene with the play and writing a long explanatory introduction in which he posed as a martyr to the freedom of the drama. The dramatic critics and the playgoers, who, together with the clergymen of the Established Church, hated Methodists *ex officio*, naturally supported Theodore wholeheartedly. Genest, too, stands squarely behind Hook: "and if every person who may be aggrieved by the Licenser, would, like Hook, bring the circumstances of the case before the public, it might possibly bring that petty tyrant to reason." Larpent had probably made himself obnoxious on previous occasions.

This incident, together with the acting of Mathews and Liston, would have been sufficient, probably, to have assured the play's popularity. But the play itself, a farce of comic incident with a double plot, has certain merits. The high-life intrigue involves Bradford's successful elopement with Nancy, in spite of the watchfulness of her amorous aunt and of her uncle. The second and principal plot is that of Buskin, an actor, who loves Fanny, sister of Tap, the inn-keeper. Fanny loves Buskin, but she has been promised to Apollo Belvi, a dancing master. Buskin persuades Apollo that Fanny is being married to him because she has lost her reputation, and he advises Apollo to declare himself his own cousin and announce his own death, in order to release himself from his engagement to wed. Apollo, therefore, kills himself off without murder, and Buskin marries Fanny, winning the favor of Tap by employing his theatrical talents to extricate the inn-keeper from a difficult situation. It is true that the high-life plot is commonplace, and that the two plots hang but loosely together. Mathews found no difficulty in separating them and giving the Buskin-Apollo plot by itself as a complete one-act farce, to which he gave the title, "A Day at an Inn." Nevertheless, "Killing No Murder" is good average farce — as good, surely, as anything of its kind written between 1805 and 1815.

This respectable level Hook maintained in his two-act "Trial by Jury," acted eighteen times at the Haymarket after May 25, 1811, with Liston and Elliston in the leading parts. The comic action of this play, a bewildering maze of mistaken identity, — which reaches its height when Sanford, the hero, disguised as a gardener in the house of his beloved, is bribed by his rival to act as if he were Sanford, — has some newness about it.

Encouraged by the favorable reception of "Trial by Jury," Hook made another experiment with the theme of mistaken identity in his "Darkness Visible," produced on September 23, 1811, at the Haymarket, with Munden and Elliston. It had some success, but it is decidedly below the level of his two previous farces.

In the preface to "Darkness Visible," Theodore Hook pays his respects to the farce-writer's profession in a boyish pronunciamento which, though certainly not unattended by the pride that apes humility, is candid enough.

Serious criticisms upon broad farces [he writes] seem to me like architectural discussions upon the construction of mouse-traps, and a man might be censured for making a mouse-trap, because it happened not to be a county gaol, with as much reason as a writer is condemned for making his farces light and laughable, because they are not comedies. To the writer of comedy — talents, genius, imagination, knowledge of the world, and ten thousand other qualities are essential; but a farce is allowed to be a collection of possible improbabilities, outré characters, and forced incidents, so put together, as to raise a laugh, and please for the moment. These materials, in the hands of favourite performers, are enough to answer the purpose for which they were intended, and from the actors, generally speaking, the piece receives its popularity. No man ever expected to become famous for writing farces.

Considered for themselves, the plays of Theodore Hook have no interest to-day for the student of literature. They are the work of a bright boy with an excellent memory and very little power of invention. The central ideas of most of them are borrowed. Many of their jokes, characters, and situations are second-hand also. "It is unsafe," declares Lockhart, "to depend on the originality of anything in these early pieces of Hook's." And the "Monthly Mirror" of November, 1809, points out a passage in "Killing No Murder" pillaged almost entire from Samuel Foote's "Commissary." Moreover, the plays abound in mediocre puns, and the characters bandy epithets dear to the vulgar. A joke which has fared well in one play will certainly appear in a following play. Since claptrap succeeds well in war-time, the gallant English sailor is pulled forward whenever possible. Certain situations are worked hard: the idea of an escape effected by means of a trick or ruse is employed in no less than five of the plays. Above all, the extreme haste with which all of them were composed shows with what a careless eye their author viewed them. The "Monthly Mirror" (normally very favorably disposed toward Hook) feels bound to protest, in September, 1809, in a review of the ballad opera "Safe and Sound," as follows:

To speak or sing *extempore* is laudable — but to write and represent *extempore* is neither respectful to the public nor creditable to oneself. We are far from decrying old age. We admire old friends and venerate old wine: but as to old puns and old music, represented as new, we desire none of their company. Woe be to the man who suffers a drama to escape him without due revision.

Hook's dramatic career has a certain interest in that it shows the progress of an apprenticeship. It is not surprising that a youth in his teens, with no knowledge of the world, begins in the tradition of unreal and artificial farce, with trifles involving a single ridiculous character, as in "Music Mad" and "The Invisible Girl," or capitalizing one single accomplishment of a comedian, as in "Catch Him Who Can." But in a few years this youth reaches the level of "Killing No Murder" and "Trial by Jury." In these the humor no longer proceeds exclusively from puns and ridiculous epithets, but largely from situation and plot complication, and there comes to be a certain amount of freshness about the material and the way it is handled. By 1811, in short, Hook had served almost the whole of his apprenticeship; he was learning to write good farce. It is easy to see whose career he was attempting to emulate. "As I take it," he writes in 1811, in dedicating his "Darkness Visible" to George Colman the younger, "you and I are the two most distinguished dramatic writers of the age — you as the best, and I as the worst." For the Haymarket manager, Theodore had an awed respect; "for *his* powers," writes Barham, quoting another, "he had a respect bordering on fear, and with him he rarely ever ventured to enter the lists." An ambition which fixed George Colman's accomplishment as its summit was surely modest. There can be little doubt that, had Hook continued to write plays, he would soon have equalled "John Bull"; in fact, it seems certain that he would have gone beyond it into a higher type of drama — into comedy. For the farces of Samuel Foote, by which Theodore was much influenced, may occasionally be dignified by the title of "comedies of manners." Foote, particularly when he is scourging hypocrites, frequently through his characters throws a true light on the realities of the life of his day. That Theodore as he learned those realities would have reflected them in his plays seems unquestionably proved by the content of the novels he wrote twenty years later.

Theodore Hook's youthful stage efforts owe the greatest interest they possess to the fact that they are an epitome of the state of the London stage at the time. The degraded condition of the drama in the early part of the nineteenth century is, it has been noted, a commonplace of literary criticism. But to see further into the complex chain of events and circumstances which made that degradation inevitable, no point of vantage can be more favorable than that offered by Hook's dramatic career.

During the first fifteen years of the century, the enormous growth of the population of London meant a doubling or trebling of the ranks of playgoers. In spite of the war, — perhaps, indeed, because of it, — a large group of people who had never visited the theatre before were now present at each performance.

The natural response to an increased volume of theatregoers should have been more theatres. But the ancient licensing system, a pure anachronism, still endured. The only houses to which the royal license was granted were the two large theatres, Drury Lane and Covent Garden, and, since the days of Foote, the Little Theatre in the Haymarket, which was too small to admit of productions on the scale of those in the two traditional houses. Other theatres were restricted to musical productions, Christmas pantomimes, variety, vaudevilles, and trained animal acts. They could not produce standard, legitimate drama. That there *were* other theatres is shown by a glance at any newspaper of the period. Also, they could and did evade the licensing act by adding a few songs to a play by Shakespeare, for instance, or by playing a few musical numbers between acts — and calling the performance a musical production. But they had no prestige among actors or playgoers; the matter of their solvency and continued existence was very often continually in question; and, as they could produce no new play, the dramatist considered them not at all.

Another method of providing for increased audiences was to increase the seating capacity of the two larger houses. This was done to Covent Garden after the fire of 1808, to Drury Lane after the fire of 1809. The result was, as has already been noted, further to degrade literary drama. When the theatre becomes so large that the spoken word can be only imperfectly heard, then the eye, not the ear, must be the object of appeal. The new type of play, the melodrama, was at hand to meet the requirement. And melodramas, although they may be very effectively presented, cannot be perused as literature.

The Haymarket Theatre had, in Mathews and Liston, the two greatest comedians of the day. They excelled in that simple, rude, obvious type of humor, now called "slapstick comedy," which requires farce as its proper medium. As a matter of course they played the regular comic parts in legitimate drama. But what attracted the multitudes, what the new audiences demanded more and more of, were the afterpieces, written especially for these comedians, to enable them to display their peculiar talents — their sleight-of-hand tricks, their facial contortions, their impersonations. Here, then, lay open the simplest and easiest field for the play writer — to put together something which might enable famous comedians to exhibit their wares.

Under such circumstances the cause of literary or legitimate drama was hopeless. When old established actors and actresses like Mrs. Siddons and the Kembles wished for a play, they turned naturally to Shakespeare. Or, there were plenty of other old tested favorites — "Venice Preserved," "The Orphan," "The Fair Penitent," "Jane Shore," the comedies of Farquhar, Cibber, Goldsmith, and Sheridan. But even these traditional favorites were financial successes no longer. The tastes of the new audience had apparently broken with the traditions of the past. And it logically followed that new plays in the old tradition were not wanted; manager after manager discovered that audiences would not gather to see them. The result of such a condition of affairs was that the stage ceases to be of any importance to the progress of English literature. On the indistinct side-path of the drama are to be met only such little-known writers as J. R. Planché, Dion Boucicault, and H. J. Byron. In the main stream of literature there are, indeed, great men of letters who are writers of dramas. But these productions are of necessity closet dramas; their authors are not familiar with the practical considerations demanded by the stage — with the limitations of an acted play. Nor have they the desire to learn, for they can receive more money from their published poems, essays, and novels than they could from the theatre. And this situation is apparent during the entire period from Wordsworth and Coleridge's "Borderers," from Byron's "Cain," to the dramas of Tennyson and Browning. Indeed, the only exceptions are a few plays by Sir Edward Bulwer-Lytton.

These were the conditions that produced for the stage a writer like Theodore Hook. He translated two melodramas; he composed a third. The failure of the third caused him to abandon the type, for the alterations and revisions demanded by Sheridan, as well as the delays and difficulties attending the production of a full three-act melodrama, probably convinced him that the chance of reward was not worth the effort. He wrote only two ballad operas, for this type of production was almost entirely superseded by the melodrama, which also had much music. He gave most of his efforts to the writing of farces. These provided the most money for the least effort. They were short; they could be quickly composed. The antics of Mathews could make successful even a most indifferent farce. To the credit of young Theodore, then, it must be said that he knew what the theatre and the conditions of his day demanded. As an execrable phrase has it, he "gave the public what it wanted."

But if Hook had so excellently gauged his times and his public, why did he give up writing plays after 1811? The answer is that his splendid government appointment, received early in 1812, entirely removed the necessity of earning a living by writing. But in 1819, when he again faced the world of literature, he tried the stage once more and found that he could make no money by it. Why could he not? It might be imagined, since the number of farce writers was not great, that the field would hold excellent pecuniary possibilities; and, moreover, since large audiences were still restricted to attendance at only two large theatres, that the managers of those two would be wealthy and successful and would feel well disposed to reward the dramatist liberally. The true situation was the exact opposite of this. The history of managers of the licensed theatres is a record of one bankruptcy after another.

For, to begin with, the managers of Drury Lane and Covent Garden were obliged to pay too high a rental to the owners of the theatre. In the next place, the melodramas they produced were expensive, because they necessitated the expenditure of much money for costumes, for stage carpentry, and for the hiring of "extras" to swell the numbers that filled the stage when the march music started up. Nor could the manager raise the price of admission to his theatre. The prolonged and serious character of the Old Price riots at Covent Garden in 1809 showed the strength of the popular resistance to increased prices. Again, the danger of a disastrous fire was not the least of the manager's liabilities. But his severest burden came from a source which would be little suspected by one not familiar with the theatre of the day. And here it is best to allow one of those managers to put his own case. Alfred Bunn, lessee at one time both of Drury Lane and of Covent Garden, wrote his memoirs in 1840, to explain his bankruptcy.[1]

---

[1] *The Stage: Both Before and Behind the Curtain.*

Looking back at his unfortunately terminated managerial days, Bunn, after cursing the temperamental impudence of actors, writes:

But the *ne plus ultra* of the pretensions of performers has within the last few years been arrived at, by the alteration they have thought it proper to make in the scale of their emoluments. This added to other causes and probably taking the lead of them all, will sooner or later entirely close the doors of the two large theatres.

Good actors now cost twenty or thirty pounds a week as compared with a former ten or fifteen pounds. A few have demanded fifty pounds a night.

The result, however, of their presumption has not been visited on managers alone, but on another class of persons, to whom they are equally, if not more indebted, for having been in a situation to exercise such presumption. I allude to dramatic authors, very few of whom the stage can now boast of. Within the last fifty years, and until within the last twenty, these gentlemen were enabled to obtain a comfortable living, and by virtue thereof, contributed to the amusement of the public, the benefit of the performers and managers, and the general advancement of the drama.

Colman received a thousand pounds for "John Bull," and Morton a similar amount for "Town and Country"; but now the dramatist receives scarcely any financial return.

To this shameful disparity may be attributed in a great degree the falling off in our dramatic literature; for as our original dramatists can, for the most part, obtain a much greater remuneration by composition for periodical publications, than they can upon the scene of their *quondam* glory, so the managers, from the impossibility of paying actor and author on the same scale, are compelled to apply to translators and adapters, and support their own upon the resources of a foreign stage.

CHAPTER III.

THE *GAMIN DE LONDRES* AND THE IMPROVISATORE (1805–1813).

IT is not to be imagined that, while Theodore Hook was writing for the stage, he was a pale slave of the lamp and of the little back parlor in Charlotte Street. He was thoroughly at home at Vauxhall Gardens, where his father's name carried weight. At the theatres he was pointed out and welcomed as the precocious boy who had produced a successful play at sixteen. He became the pet of the green room; he was indulged on every hand. He became intimate with comedians whose best farces were their lives, and who did not cease their antics when they left the footlights and rubbed off the grease-paint. But, indeed, Theodore's natural temperament needed little incitement. Horatio Smith, who collaborated with his brother James, to produce the immensely popular "Rejected Addresses" of 1812, has left a picture of Hook at this time. His vivacity, writes Horace [1] in pompous vein, was "a manifest exuberance from the conjunction of rampant animal spirits, a

---

[1] In his *Graybeard's Gossip About His Literary Acquaintances,* quoted in Arthur H. Beavan's *James and Horace Smith* (1899), p. 222.

superabundance of corporeal vitality, a vivid sense of the ludicrous, a consciousness of his own unparalleled readiness, and a self-possession, not to say an effrontery, that nothing could daunt. Indulging his natural frolicsomeness rather to amuse himself than others, he was not fastidious about the quality of his audience, whom he would startle by some outrageous horseplay or practical joke, if he found them too stupid for puns, jests, and songs. Thus you were always sure of him; he required no preparation, no excitement, he was never out of sorts, never out of spirits, never unprepared for a sally, however hazardous."

Pierce Egan's "Life in London" discloses the presence in that city of groups of fast young blades, mostly of good family, who, after witnessing a cock fight or a prize fight, or creating brawls in the low dives of the Haymarket, sallied forth overturning watch-boxes containing sleeping watchmen, — for the safety of the metropolis was still dependent on these helpless old men, — tearing signposts off hinges, and bearing Highlanders from the fronts of tobacconists' shops. They are undoubtedly direct descendants of the Whipping Toms, Muns, Hectors, Nickers, and Mohocks of a former day, although their violence is now set at a lower pitch than that of the "sons of Belial, flown with insolence and wine," who swaggered forth in the days of Sedley and Rochester to commit assault upon the unfortunate person abroad after dark.

It is against such a background that one whole side of the early life of Theodore Hook belongs. He was continually ready for every sort of horse-play, not always of the most innocent nature. He possessed the necessary qualities of a successful practical joker — he had a most imperturbable effrontery, back of which played an imagination that enabled him quickly to follow up any initial stroke; and he had a genuinely keen eye for the ludicrous. He was a young scamp bent on mis-chief.

But here it is well to pause. If his conduct was incorrigible, boisterous, and hilarious, there is no evidence that it was immoral, licentious, or de-praved. This is apparent even when a bitter enemy makes charges against his conduct. In 1825, after the appearance of his first series of "Sayings and Doings," there came out a miser-able Grub Street pamphlet of fifty pages,[1] the author of which, in attacking Hook, asserts that he has personal knowledge of various knavish tricks executed by the boy Theodore.

It was at school [writes the anonymous assailant] I first fell within the sphere of his excellencies. How often have I seen him run, at the downfall of any mar-

---

[1] *Sayings and Doings Considered. With On Dits, Family Memoirs, etc. etc. etc.* London, printed for T. & J. Allman, 1825.

ket-woman's basket, and, while receiving the thanks of the sufferer for the assiduity with which he stopped the rolling of her oranges or apples, has he, by dropping them among the eggs or other brittle ware, contrived to make his salvage destroy twice its value; while the sorrow depicted so artfully on his countenance has saved him, when discovered, from the chastisement which he deserved! How many a blind or decrepit old man has he caused to fall, by sliding on the path, and rendering that part slippery which was about to receive the tottering foot of the helpless creature, who imagined all the while the dear little boy was running to tend his guidance.

Also writes the pamphleteer:

His art of mimicry began at a very early period: in the parish church, when the banns of marriage have been proclaimed, and the young espoused has been glistening with rapture at the announcement of her name, he has mimicked an aged voice and forbade the match; the revulsion of the feelings of the poor girl has satisfied his spirit and consoled him for the short-livedness of the joke.

The miserable nature and purpose of this pamphlet is evident from its tenor. But it is significant that Theodore stands charged in it only with thoroughly naughty schoolboy tricks.

As a matter of fact, the young Theodore's pranks were by no means so reprehensible and malicious as the anonymous writer would make them. His forte was practical jokes, openly executed to astonish and delight his audience. It is true that popular leniency toward such jokes no

longer exists; and much of what Hook's contemporaries would have called high-spirited fun,
we should call deliberate mischief or pointless
buffoonery. But things were different then.
Every-one was attempting practical jokes; the
perpetrator of to-day's might be the victim of to-
morrow's. "To club wit and club society of that
period," writes the actor and dramatist, Frederick
Reynolds, in 1827, "may be appropriately applied
the thought of Montecuculi, as only three single
points were necessary to effect the supposed existence of the former and the real happiness of the
latter, viz: — first, practical jokes; second, practical jokes; and third, practical jokes." [1] Again,
nearly all of these jokes were committed before
Theodore was twenty-one years old, and may
therefore be regarded with the leniency with
which college-boy pranks are yet viewed. He himself later repented of many of them, for there was
a change of attitude toward them between his
earlier and his later years. Finally, the point of
each joke lies in the way it is told later at a dinner
party. In the presence of an audience which has
just eaten and drunk its fill and is favorably disposed toward being amused, even a somewhat
pointless joke can be made amusing in the telling,
if a touch or two is added to accord with poetic

---

[1] *The Life and Times of Frederick Reynolds, Written by Himself* (1827), ii, 166.

justice, and if the narrator possesses the art of dilating upon each trivial incident to form an irresistibly comic whole. Hook was a man above all others who had mastered this accomplishment. These jokes, writes Lockhart,

are nothing without the commentary of that bright eye — the deep gurgling glee of his voice — the electrical felicity of his pantomime — for in truth he was as great an actor as could have been produced by rolling up Liston and Terry and Mathews into one. So told, no mirth in this world ever surpassed the fascination of these early mountebankeries.

Over the relation of one of them Lockhart had seen "austere judges, venerable prelates, grand lords, and superfine ladies all alike overwhelmed and convulsed." [1]

Theodore's first exploit was the acquisition of a "museum."

He commenced [writes Barham], as a very young man, of course, with the establishment of a museum, which boasted the most complete collection of knockers, the finest specimens of sign-painting, the most magnifi-

---

[1] Three years earlier, the author of a sketch of Hook in *Fraser's Magazine* (November, 1841, xxiv, 518–524) had written: "Mr. Hook's early love of fun was uncontrollable; his perceptions of the ridiculous, keen and unerring; and his desire to amuse himself and others with his observations and experiments upon folly and credulity was irresistible. His descriptions, then and since, of circumstances, men, and things, were curiously graphic and entertaining; and the most trivial particulars in detail were made important and laughable by his peculiar style of narration."

cent bunches of grapes, the longest barbers' poles, and the largest cocked hats that the metropolis could produce.

It probably boasted also, as did a similar collection described by G. A. Sala in his memoirs,[1] of

all the brass plates bearing announcements relative to academies for young ladies, medical practitioners, agents to the Moon Fire Insurance Office, and professors of the pianoforte; all the knockers, ranging from the fierce lion's head in iron to the diminutive sphinx in brass; all the bell-pull handles and signboards; all the Original Little Dust Pans; the huge red effigies of human hands which had hung over glovers' shops; the arms brandishing hammers which had been the signs of goldbeaters.

After Theodore began to frequent the green room, the theatre naturally became the scene of many of his jokes. Ingoldsby Barham's diary records one which occurred behind the scenes at Drury Lane in April, 1807.[2]

He was there one evening, during the heat of the Westminster election, at the representation of "The Wood Demon," and observing the prompter with the

---

[1] *Things I Have Seen and People I Have Known* (1894), ii, 81 f. Hook's collection so impressed Ingoldsby Barham that he introduced a description of it into his novel, "My Cousin Nicholas."

[2] In Barham's life of his father. It is in Ingoldsby's record of a day with Hook on the river on August 21, 1839. The theatre is recorded as the Haymarket, but this is an error, since Sheridan was manager of Drury Lane, and since Monk Lewis's play was presented only at Drury Lane and during the month of April, 1807.

large speaking trumpet in his hand, used to produce his
supernatural voices incidental to the piece, he watched
him for some time, and saw him go through the business
more than once. As the effect was to be repeated, he
requested of the man to be allowed to make the noise for
him; the prompter incautiously trusted him with the
instrument, when, just at the moment when the
"Fiend" rose from the trap, and the usual roar was to
accompany his appearance, "Sheridan for ever!" was
bawled out in the deepest tones that could be produced
— not more to the astonishment of the audience than to
the confusion of the involuntary partisan himself, from
whom they seemed to proceed.

"Never shall we forget," writes the author of
the memoir of Hook prefixed to Colburn's edition
of "Fathers and Sons" in 1842,

the effect produced upon Dowton and the other actors
on the stage during one of the serious scenes of a senti-
mental comedy of the day, by Hook's possessing himself
of the livery coat of one of the under-performers, and
with a tragedy strut marching on to the stage to present
a letter to Dowton, who, taken by surprise at the sight
of the new performer, could not utter a word, while the
rest of the actors were convulsed with laughter.

And the same account continues:

But one of the most amusing of his pranks consisted
in secretly accompanying Liston, when singing a particularly quaint song in the "Finger Post," with a penny
trumpet, from which, at the end of every line, he elicited
such odd sounds, that at the conclusion the audience
rapturously encored the performance. This he repeated
in conjunction with the singer: the latter all the while
completely mystified as to the character and where-
abouts of his unknown coadjutor.

Hook's intimate companion at this time was the comedian, Charles Mathews.[1] With the mornings and evenings of each devoted to the theatre, there were still the afternoons to employ in long country excursions, during which endless opportunities were presented to "startle the natives" with some wild prank. Thus at Croydon Fair a good-sized commotion was created when Hook suddenly broke away from Mathews and appealed loudly to the sympathies of the crowd, asserting that he was a maltreated younger brother whose brother was trying to get him into an asylum in order to deprive him of his property. Mathews, as the wicked brother, declared Hook a harmless lunatic. Both found supporters and sympathizers, and the crowd was worked to a fighting pitch. At Woolwich, Mathews for two days successfully masqueraded as the Spanish ambassador, expressing a preference for outlandish foods and talking a gibberish which the crowds who gathered to see him imagined to be Spanish. On another famous afternoon the two are on the Thames. They land

---

[1] Mrs. Mathews, *Memoirs of Charles Mathews* (1839, 2nd edition), ii, 78: "His intimate acquaintance at this time with a kindred spirit kept alive the desire to astonish others, for his own amusement, longer than it might otherwise have lasted, and gave, perhaps, a new impetus to his fanciful will. The youthful Theodore Hook had a head to devise, and nerve to execute, and lent himself, heart and mind, to every occasion of mirth; and where injury was to be punished or folly reproved, these 'two were a multitude' in furthering the end."

on a beautiful lawn, despite a sign forbidding all landing. The owner sends out his servant to warn them off. The intruders pay no attention to him or to the owner himself, but go through the motions of surveying. They are employees, they finally explain, of the Thames Improvement Commission, and they are measuring the ground for a new canal which will cut through the lawn and just miss the tip of the conservatory adjoining the owner's residence. At once the portly old gentleman becomes very gracious. He introduces his wife and daughters; he presses an invitation to dinner. The best food and the choicest wines are served. A hint is passed that perhaps matters can be arranged. In her very popular "Memoirs" of her husband, Mrs. Mathews gives many more of these adventures.[1] "There was no end," she writes, "to these instances of frolicking, and Mr. Hook could never resist a temptation to display some of his inexhaustible stock of humour for the entertainment of his companions."

Sometimes the actor Daniel Terry, or the before-mentioned Sam Beazley, was Hook's abettor

---

[1] The three instances given are from the first hundred pages of her second volume. Lockhart and Barham copy them from this source. Barham says, concerning the Woolwich adventure, that he has heard "a different and somewhat less triumphant termination to the adventure." He also doubts many particulars of the surveying incident; but Mrs. Mathews's version agrees with Hook's own account of the joke given in his novel *Gilbert Gurney*.

in these escapades. Horace Smith describes a typical one.

One Sunday afternoon a party of us were strolling through the village just as the inhabitants were returning from church, when Hook, having suddenly turned down his shirt collar, pushed back his curly hair, and assumed a puritanical look, jumped into an empty cart by the roadside, and began to hold forth in the whining tones of a field preacher. Gathering ourselves in front to listen to him, we formed the nucleus of a congregation, which presently included a score or two of open-mouthed labourers and country crones. So enthusiastic and devout were the sham preacher's manner and matter, that he commanded the deep attention of his audience, until, with a startling change of voice and look, he poured forth a volley of loud and abusive vulgarities, jumped from the cart, and ran across the fields, pursued by a couple of incensed rustics, who soon, however, abandoned a chase which they found to be hopeless.

The pages of Barham, Lockhart, and Mrs. Mathews are filled with descriptions of high jinks of this sort — of jokes ranging all the way from the innocent one of plastering round black wafers on a white horse in order to attract attention in the next village, to the thoroughly reprehensible one of getting a free ride home in a cab by riding in it to a physician's house, springing out, urging the physician to make haste to attend a critical case, leaving him to drive alone to a fictitious address — and to pay the cabman.

In the London "Times" of Tuesday, October 31, 1809, there is the following curious item:

The neighborhood of Bedford-street, Covent-Garden, was the scene of much confusion yesterday. Some wag had taken the trouble of going to different trades-people, and ordered various articles of furniture, and of other descriptions, to be sent to the house of Mr. Grif-fith, an apothecary in that street. At an early hour in the morning, carpets, boxes of candles, articles of house-hold furniture, &c. were sent. The family being out of town, and no person but the maid servant at home, she of course refused to receive them; the consequence was, that the porters were obliged to take up their loads and walk home again, amidst the jeers of an immense con-course of people, assembled to witness this curious hoax. Fresh arrivals in the course of the day induced the crowd still to remain; among these arrivals was a patent mangle, an enormous large rocking horse, three wagon load of coals, &c. At length, to complete the joke, at the dining hour arrived eight post-chaises, from different parts of the country, with some of the most intimate friends of Mr. Griffith, all anxious, having received cards of invitation for that purpose, to taste his poultry and game, but the populace made game of them, and dis-appointment being the order of the day, the horses' heads were turned and the guests departed amidst the loud cheers of the spectators. The arrivals of goods continued till a late hour in the evening.

Theodore, confessing to Ingoldsby many years later, declared himself to be the sole originator of this hoax, and added (to indicate that the touch of genius had been present) that among the articles delivered at the house "were the dresses of a Punch and nine blue devils, and the body of a man from Lambeth bonehouse, who had the day before been found drowned in the Thames." This particular form of hoax was probably an original discovery of Theodore's. Its success was so happy that he followed this first attempt a year later with the famous Berners Street hoax, which caused a very gratifying sensation at the time and is still mentioned in an occasional London guidebook. His confederates in this immense project were Henry H —, a Brazenose College man who later entered holy orders, and a well-known actress. The victim was a Mrs. Tottenham at 54 Berners Street. Why this unfortunate woman was selected, does not appear. The street itself formed a *cul-de-sac*, thus enormously increasing the confusion. Several thousand letters were dispatched; the conspirators engaged a room on the opposite side of the street, and awaited the event. Of what followed, a faint idea may be gathered from an article in the "Morning Post" of November 28, 1810.[1]

MOST EXTRAORDINARY SCENE
BERNERS–STREET IN AN UPROAR

The greatest *hoax* that has ever been heard of in this metropolis was yesterday practised in Berners-street, Oxford-street. The house of Mrs. Tottenham, a lady of

---

[1] Lockhart gives the date of the hoax as 1809 and Barham follows him. I am the first to discover the true date by a search in the newspapers.

fortune, at no. 54, was beset by about a dozen trades-people at one time, with their various commodities, and from the confusion altogether such crowds had collected as to render the street impassable. Waggons laden with coal from the Paddington wharfs, upholsterer's goods in cart loads, organs, piano-fortes, linen, jewellery, and every other description of furniture, sufficient to have stocked the whole street, was lodged as near as possible to the door of no. 54, with anxious trades-people and a laughing mob. The Lord Mayor of London also arrived in his carriage and two livery servants, but his Lordship's stay was short, and he was driven to the Marlborough-street Police Office.

At the office his Lordship informed the Sitting Magistrate that he had received a note purporting to have come from Mrs. Tottenham, which stated that she had been summoned to appear before him, but that she was confined to her room by sickness, and requested his Lordship's favour to call on her. Berners-street at this time was in the greatest confusion from the multiplicity of trades-people who were returning with their goods and spectators laughing at them. The officers belonging to the Marlborough-street Office were immediately ordered out to keep order, but it was impossible for a short time. The first scene witnessed by the officers were six stout men bearing an organ, surrounded by coal merchants with permits, barbers with wigs, mantua-makers with band-boxes, opticians with their various articles of trade, and such was the pressure of trades-people who had been duped, that at four o'clock all was consternation and confusion.

Every officer that could be mustered was enlisted to disperse the people, and they were placed at the corners of Berners-street to prevent trades-people from advancing towards the house with goods. The street was not cleared at a late hour as servants of every denomination wanting places began to assemble at five o'clock. It turned out that letters had been written to the different trades-people, which stated recommendations from persons of quality.

A reward has been offered for the apprehension of the author of the criminal hoax.

This hoax exceeded by far that in Bedford-street a few months since; for besides a coffin, which was brought to Mrs. Tottenham's house, made to measure, agreeable to letter, five feet six, sixteen, there were accoucheurs, tooth-drawers, miniature-painters, artists of every description, auctioneers, undertakers, grocers, mercers, post-chaises, mourning-coaches, poultry, rabbits, pigeons, &c. In fact, the whole street was literally filled with the motley group.

The conspirators must have spent weeks so wording each letter that it would prove acceptable bait to the functionary to whom it was addressed — for not only the Lord Mayor, but practically every officer of government, from royalty downwards, received letters. Theodore had, writes Lockhart, describing his repentance in later years for some of the liberties he took,

no objection to bodying forth the arrival of the Lord Mayor . . . but he would rather have buried in oblivion that no less liberty was taken with the Governor of the Bank, the Chairman of the East India Company, a Lord Chief Justice, a Cabinet Minister — above all with the Archbishop of Canterbury and His Royal Highness the Commander-in-Chief.[1] They all obeyed the summons — every pious and patrotic feeling had been most movingly appealed to.

---

[1] That is, the Duke of York. Barham, however, says that the royal livery seen on the occasion was not that of the commander of the military forces, but that of the Duke of Gloucester, another of the sons of George III.

Theodore's escape from detection was miraculous; indeed, had there been any serious and concerted effort at an inquiry, his identity must have become known. Had he been discovered it would not have gone easy with him.

> Not merely in this case [observes Barham] were the comforts of a single family suspended, or a few movables demolished, but a quarter of the town was disturbed — a whole street was thrown into a state of uproar, which lasted from morning till night — hundreds of individuals, servants, artisans, tradesmen, great and small, from all parts of London, professional men of every class, not to speak of princes, potentates, and nobles of high degree, swelled the catalogue of the victims.

It is difficult to imagine how any practical joke, short of one inaugurating a civil war, could have exceeded in effect the Berners Street hoax. It quite fittingly represents, therefore, Theodore's last serious public exertion. There were a few more, of course. In 1813, the Regent gave a fête at Carlton House. Hook thereupon "invited" the *soi-disant* actor, "Romeo" Coates. Romeo went, was informed that the invitation was spurious, and returned home discomfited. To the Regent's credit it must be added that, on hearing of the incident, he sent a personal invitation the next day, and himself showed the actor through Carlton House. To bring out the humorous point of the joke and to excuse Hook in some measure, the long story of Romeo's character and career must be told — a ridiculous little fop with a sublime satisfaction with himself and not the slightest talent for acting, who rode in a bright green chariot shaped like a sea-shell, and who further immortalized the immortal Will by inscribing in the church at Stratford-on-Avon the lines:

> His name in ambient air still floats,
> And is adored by Robert Coates.[1]

But in general, after 1810, Hook devoted himself to another and far better kind of humor.

In 1808, in the midst of his career as a writer for the stage, he wrote, under the pseudonym of "Alfred Allendale," a novel called "The Man of Sorrow," of which scarcely any copies were sold.

Toward the end of 1809, Theodore's brother, the Reverend James, made a vigorous protest against the life he was leading. The consequence was that, in the early months of 1810, Theodore and James went up to Oxford and made inquiries about entering. Theodore was almost debarred at the outset by a characteristic piece of levity; for, when he was asked by Vice-Chancellor John Parsons, Master of Balliol, whether he was ready to subscribe to the Thirty-nine Articles, he replied, "Oh, certainly sir, forty if you wish." He was told that he might enter after spending a few months in a course of

---

[1] The entire incident is recorded in John R. and Hunter H. Robinson's *Life of Robert Coates* (1891).

prescribed reading. Accordingly, Theodore matriculated in the University on July 2, 1810, at the age of twenty-one, as a resident of St. Mary Hall (called the "Skimmery"), his brother's college.

Barham records two or three rough pieces of horseplay set in motion by Theodore at Oxford during his residence of only two terms. But life there must have seemed dull to a youth accustomed to the excitement of the theatre, and he came there at almost too late an age to change his habits and break with his former Bohemian existence. He therefore soon abandoned his project, perhaps never very seriously entertained, of studying for the law, and returned to London. At Oxford he first met Richard Harris Barham, author of the "Ingoldsby Legends," and father of the biographer of both.

Early in 1809, Hook became interested in private theatricals, and found opportunity both of acting and writing at the "Grange Theatre" of Mr. John Rolls in the Kent Road. Rolls, who himself acted, engaged Mr. and Mrs. Mathews and several other professionals, in order to give the productions a more finished character. "The evening's amusement," writes Mrs. Mathews, "was a *mélange* of every kind of lively conceit that wit could devise and talent execute — pieces written for the occasion, with local hits, &c." On January 30, 1809, Hook appeared as Sir Callaghan

O'Brallaghan in "Love à la Mode," and experienced, much to the amusement of Mathews's
gifted wife, a considerable amount of stage fright.
On the same night he played Horatio in "Ham-
let," and appeared in a very thin travesty of that
play, written by himself, called "Ass-ass-ination;
or, The Oracle." This sketch is crammed with all
the strained puns which Theodore affected in his
early years, and it has been preserved, with all its
imperfections on its head, by being printed years
after Hook's death in "Bentley's Miscellany." [1]
One year later, on January 30, 1810, the same actors appeared in a play of Hook's called "The Will
and the Widow; or, Puns in Plenty" — which is
probably sufficiently described by its second title.
At the third and last Rolls entertainment — on
January 30, 1811 — another play by Theodore
saw the light. This was "Black and White; or,
Don't be Savage," which was, when the author, in
1819, was in great need of money, remodelled as
"Pigeons and Crows," and brought out at the
Haymarket.

---

[1] Vol. xxii (1847): "Ass-ass-ination. An historical tragedy
in Two Acts. Edited by Theodore Edward Hook, Esq. Discovered in an old building near Stratford-upon-Avon, Sept. 9,
1798, and said to have been written by Mr. William Shakespeare. Performed at the Grange in the Kent Road, the seat of
John Rolls, Esq. on Jan. 30th, 1809 or 1810." It was performed both in 1809 and in 1810.

Along with all the mad and frequently reprehensible pranks of Theodore's youth, the great
redeeming aspect of those days had been rapidly
developing. That remarkable ability at extempore versifying which he possessed — and in which
possession he stands absolutely alone in English
literary biography — now demands consideration.

The old composer, Theodore's father, had a
considerable reputation as a wit and punster. The
musician Parke records many of his jokes, and at
least one good one — the following:

> Whilst walking with Hook one day in the Strand, we
> were impeded in crossing the road from Norfolk Street
> to the opposite side of the way by a hackney chariot,
> whose number was the unit one. The carriage being
> extremely clean and neat, and in good preservation,
> particularly claimed my notice, and induced me to ob-
> serve to Hook as it passed, that it appeared to be almost
> as good as new; adding, "It has been well taken care
> of." "There is nothing extraordinary in that," said
> Hook, "for everybody takes care of number one."

From infancy, Theodore was a true child of his
father. Beazley writes of the boy as he was in
1805:

> Already he possessed all the powers of entertainment
> which have since made him so celebrated as a table-
> companion, and in the confined circle of the family he
> would exhibit them with the same zeal and effect as
> when in the most brilliant society, with the eyes of the
> gifted and great upon him. His wit was never depen-
> dent upon excitement, but flowed spontaneously on
> every occasion, early or late.

Mrs. Mathews describes Theodore's first considerable public exercise of the gift which made him famous.

The election for Westminster had recently taken place [May, 1807], and Mr. Sheridan was chosen one of its representatives, on which occasion the actors of Drury-lane celebrated their proprietor's triumph by giving him a dinner at the Piazza Coffee-house. To this dinner Mr. Hook was invited. In the course of the day many persons sung, and Mr Hook being in turn solicited, displayed, to the delight and surprise of all present, his wondrous talent in extemporaneous singing. The company was numerous, and generally strangers to Mr. Hook; but without a moment's premeditation, he composed a verse upon every person in the room, full of the most pointed wit, and with the truest rhymes, unhesitatingly, gathering into his subject as he rapidly proceeded, in addition to what had passed during the dinner, every trivial incident of the moment. Every action was turned to account; every circumstance, the look, the gesture, or any other accidental effects, served as occasion for more wit; and even the singer's ignorance of the names and condition of many of the party, seemed to give greater facility to his brilliant hits than even acquaintance with them might have furnished. Mr. Sheridan was astonished at his extraordinary faculty, and declared that he could not have imagined such power possible, had he not witnessed it. No description, he said, could have convinced him of so peculiar an instance of genius, and he protested that he should not have believed it to be an unstudied effort, had he not seen proof that no anticipation could have been formed of what might arise to furnish matter and opportunities for the exercise of this rare talent.

The fruition of this gift for improvisation belongs to a later period in Theodore's life. But even in these early days, men of intellect and ability professed themselves amazed at Hook's powers.

Horace Smith has left record of one evening.

The century must have been young when I first met him at the house of the late Nat Middleton the banker, then living in Charles Street, St. James's Square. A large dinner party was assembled, and before the ladies had withdrawn, the improvisatore was requested to favor the company with a song; his compliance was immediate and unembarrassed, as if it were an affair of no difficulty; and the verses, turned chiefly upon the names of the guests, only once varied by an allusion to some occurrence of the moment, were so pointed and sparkling, that I hesitated not to express my total disbelief in the possibility of their being extemporaneous, an opinion which some "good-natured friend" repeated to the singer. "Oh, the unbelieving dog!" exclaimed the vocalist. "Tell him if I am called upon again, he himself shall dictate the subject and the tune, which of course involves the metre; but it must be some common popular air." All this took place, and the second song proving still more brilliant than the first, I made a very humble palinode for my mistrust, and expressed the astonishment and delight with which his truly wonderful performance had electrified me. Not without difficulty, however, had I been enabled to believe my own ears, and several days elapsed before I had completely recovered from my bewilderment, for, as an occasional rhymester, I could well appreciate the difficulty of the achievement.

A short time later Horace took refuge at Theodore's house during a thunderstorm. The young improviser thereupon composed an extemporaneous defiance of the storm — Horace being in some trepidation at such an impious scorn of thunder and lightning — and followed this performance with an entire improvised operetta — the sort of ballad opera the old composer Hook was in the habit of supplying music for — consisting of "the morning song of Patty the dairymaid . . . the meeting and the duet with her rustic lover . . . the advent of the squire, his jovial hunting song, his dishonorable proposals to Patty, and their indignant rejection . . . his ignominious retreat, and the marriage of the happy pair." [1]

In 1812 Thomas Campbell wrote in a letter:

Yesterday an improvisatore — a wonderful creature of the name of Hook — sang some extempore songs, not to my admiration, but to my astonishment. I prescribed a subject — "pepper and salt" — and he seasoned the impromptu with both — very truly Attic salt. He is certainly the first improvisatore this country ever possessed — he is but twenty.[2]

In 1808 or 1809, Leigh Hunt heard Theodore one day at Sydenham when Campbell was also there. Hook's "extempore verses," writes Hunt,[3]

---

[1] Both of these incidents are related by Horace in his *Graybeard's Gossip About His Literary Acquaintances*, quoted in Beavan, *op. cit.*

[2] *Life and Letters of Thomas Campbell*, edited by William Beattie, M.D. (1849), ii, 219. Hook was twenty-three in 1812.

[3] *Autobiography of Leigh Hunt* (1903), i, 240 ff. It is to be noted that Hunt's general attitude toward Hook was by no means favorable. He was politically at the opposite pole. He

were really surprising. It is easy enough to extemporize in Italian — one only wonders how, in a language in which everything conspires to render verse-making easy, and it is difficult to avoid rhyming, this talent should be so much cried up — but in English it is another matter. . . . In Hook the faculty was very unequivocal. He could not have been pre-informed about all the visitors on the present occasion, still less of the subject of conversation when he came in, and he talked his full share till called upon; yet he ran his jokes and his verses upon us all in the easiest manner, saying something characteristic of everybody, or avoiding it with a pun; and he introduced so agreeably a piece of village scandal upon which the party had been rallying Campbell that the poet, though not unjealous of his dignity, was, perhaps, the most pleased of us all. Theodore afterwards sat down to the pianoforte, and, enlarging upon this subject, made an extempore parody of a modern opera, introducing sailors and their claptraps, rustics, etc., and making Campbell and his supposed flame the hero and heroine. . . . Campbell certainly took the theme of the parody as a compliment; for having drunk a little more wine than usual that evening, and happening to wear a wig on account of having lost his hair by a fever, he suddenly took off the wig and dashed it at the head of the performer, exclaiming, "You dog! I'll throw my laurels at you."

The combination of Theodore's ability in improvisation with the imperturbability of nature

---

spent two years in jail for libelling the Regent; Hook was the Regent's ardent supporter at all times. Hook also made sport of Hunt in his newspaper, "John Bull," and the following squib printed therein must have rankled:

> "O! Crimini, Crimini!
> What a nimini pimini
> Story of Rimini!"

which carried him through his various practical jokes proved the source of many pleasant adventures. There were certainly many escapades like the one recounted by Barham. Hook and Terry, walking down the street in the evening before the play, observe that there is to be a dinner party at a certain house. Hook wagers that he will be in the house in the midst of the guests at ten o'clock, and asks Terry to call for him there at that time. Theodore thereupon enters the house with the guests and is not noticed in the excitement. At the dinner table his sallies make him the centre of all attention. The host, after racking his memory and consulting his wife, finally asks Theodore his name. The latter, after relating with his usual sang-froid the story of an invitation to the house of a relative known to him only by correspondence, affects suddenly to become conscious of the mistake he has made, and asks leave to depart immediately. The host will not permit it. So Theodore seats himself at the piano and fully repays his host for what he has eaten and drunk by giving the party one of his unrivalled extempore performances. When Terry arrives at ten o'clock, he sees Hook still at the piano, but singing now his final quatrain:

> I am very much pleased with your fare,
>   Your cellar's as prime as your cook; —
> My friend's Mr. Terry, the player,
>   And I'm Mr. Theodore Hook.

About 1808, Hook became acquainted with Thomas Hill, a little old man, by trade a drysalter, by nature one of the most inquisitive beings in England. He was also — with his "Pooh, pooh! I happen to *know*" — one of the best-informed gossips in the city.[1] Although Hill had no literary tastes himself, he collected a good library and aspired to be a sort of literary patron on the strength of his ownership of the "Monthly Mirror," a theatrical paper (which has several times been quoted in these pages in connection with Hook's dramatic career) of a very moderate circulation. He consequently became, writes Cyrus Redding, "a character long known wherever a quorum of literary men chanced to meet." He gave each Sunday at his villa at Sydenham, eight miles out, "plain dinners and good wine, in exchange for which his guests used to play upon his idea of being a literary patron, to his infinite gratification." The exchange was a fair one, therefore. Hill had no difficulty in gathering about him ambitious young theatrical and journalistic men who were glad of a chance to eat a good dinner and amuse themselves and him by talking about literature. To do them justice, they probably had a real liking for their kindly host.

---

[1] The best accounts of him are in Cyrus Redding's *Fifty Years' Recollections*, in Barham, and in Leigh Hunt's *Autobiography*.

The poet, Campbell, lived close by and was often present at these parties. From the theatre were Hook, Mathews, and sometimes George Colman. Edward Dubois, lawyer by necessity, litterateur by temperament, was the editor of Hill's "Monthly Mirror." Leigh Hunt, theatrical critic of his brother John's paper, the "News," was often of the group. The brothers, James and Horace Smith, had not yet written the "Rejected Addresses," but they had for some time been dabbling in literature, and James was assisting Dubois with the "Mirror." Finally, among the guests of prominence, there was Thomas Barnes, schoolfellow of Leigh Hunt at Pembroke, who was now doing literary odd jobs, but who was soon to settle into his proper vocation as the highly successful editor of the London "Times."

The guests usually walked to Sydenham in groups, and the peaceful Sunday morning calm of many a country neighborhood was blasted by the boisterous jokes which Theodore Hook and his companions perpetrated along the way. At the host's house, Leigh Hunt writes: "The wine flowed merrily and long; the discourse kept pace with it; and the next morning, in returning to town, we felt ourselves very thirsty. A pump by the roadside with a plash round it was a bewitching sight." In his novel "Gilbert Gurney," Hook was later to recount at great length the happenings at one of these convivial Sydenham Sundays.

But there was another world to conquer for a young man with a natural gift as unique as Theodore's. Aristocratic society was small and admission to it was difficult. But a successful passport was wit. The well-turned epigram, the sparkling *jeu d'esprit*, the pointed *vers de société* — these were prized even more than dress or personal appearance by the beaux of the Regency.[1] And Theodore, in addition, was a personable youth. He was at this time, writes a eulogistic critic in "Fraser's Magazine" of November, 1841, "a tall, slim, fashionable-looking youth with a fine figure; black clustering curls hanging about his animated face, every line of which was full of intelligence and genius." Leigh Hunt, who did not like Hook, writes of him: "He was then a youth, tall, dark, and of good person, with small eyes, and features more round than weak; a face that had character and humour, but no refinement." An etching of Theodore at the age of twenty, done by Bennett of Bath, and appearing in the "Monthly Mirror"

---

[1] The literature on the social life of the Regency is very large. The contemporary accounts which best repay perusal are, I have found, the journal of Thomas Raikes, Lady Charlotte Bury's *Diary Illustrative of the Times of George the Fourth*, Robert Huish's *Memoirs of George the Fourth*, and the amazing *Memoirs of Harriette Wilson*. As to present-day accounts of the time — Mr. Lewis Melville's *The Beaux of the Regency* (1908) is good and contains a bibliography. Charles Whibley's *Pageantry of Life* contains an introduction which gives an excellent short view of the entire age.

of September, 1807, shows certainly that if "refinement" is indicated by the thin pale face of the scholar or the slender nose of the "blue," then Theodore was not refined. It is an open face there depicted — a face which discloses completely the nature of its possessor. It is marked above all by eagerness and animation. It shows a disposition fun-loving and careless, but well-meaning and hearty. The features are not coarse or weak; the nature is not malicious, although it may be unmethodical, sanguine, and impatient of restraint.

We believe [says Lockhart] he owed his first *entrée* to the impression made on Sheridan by his improvisation at the Piazza Tavern. He soon afterwards became familiar with Sheridan's amiable and richly-gifted son Thomas, and through him with various young men of his own standing who moved in the atmosphere of fashion.

Richard Brinsley Sheridan was indeed a useful patron, and Hook was much in his company. Mrs. Mathews speaks of Mrs. Richard Wilson's parties in Lincoln's Inn Fields, where frequent guests were Lords Eldon and Erskine, Sir Samuel Romilly, and others. There came also

dear old Captain Morris with his songs and his singing, and charming society; Sheridan and others of his noted contemporaries; the youthful Theodore Hook and Horace Twiss (just rising from their teens), stood prominently forward, full of the buoyancy, wit, and talent which have established their respective positions in the high and intellectual society in which they both live.

And on the same night with Sheridan, Lord Petersham and others, Hook was elected a member of the "Eccentrics." This club had first been a tavern club called the "Brilliants."

It had existed chiefly [writes Mr. T. H. S. Escott in his "Club Makers and Club Members"], to judge from Gilray's caricatures, for bestial drunkenness, tempered by extravagantly high play. Afterwards reorganized or revived as the Eccentrics, it grew greatly in numbers and distinction, including at different times Fox, Sheridan, Petersham, Melbourne and Brougham, as well as, before its close, Theodore Hook, who took from it many characters and scenes for his novels.

But it is the Marchioness of Hertford with whom Theodore's real introduction to society is associated. At her dinners and *soirées*, Hook, because of his powers of entertainment, soon became a frequent and welcome visitor. She had been the celebrated Maria Fagniani, the well-beloved "Mie Mie" of George Selwyn (the great wit of a former age), and she was a remarkable woman. It was she who, in 1811 and for several years following, swayed the opinions of the Regent (and it is worthy of remark, in connection with the Regent, to say that she swayed them without transgressing the bounds of decorum), for it was mainly because of the influence of the Hertfords that he left Fox and the Whigs and became definitely Tory. The Regent's visits to Manchester Square were frequent, and it was here that Theodore was first presented to him.

We have heard him [says Lockhart] describe his presentation to the Prince: — his awe at first was something quite terrible — but good-humoured condescension and plenty of champagne by and by restored him to himself, and the young man so delighted his Royal Highness, that as he was leaving the room he laid his hand on his shoulder and said, "Mr. Hook, I must see and hear you again." After a few more similar evenings at Lady Hertford's, and, we believe, a dinner or two elsewhere, the Regent made inquiry about his position, and, finding that he was without profession or fixed income of any sort, signified that "something must be done for Hook."

There is very little record of Hook's doings from 1811 to 1813. That he was known to the famous beaux of the Regency — men like Brummell, Alvanley, Petersham, the diarist Raikes, Rufus Lloyd, Richard Fitz-Gibbon, "Kangaroo" Cooke, and others — is practically certain. Without question he knew the survivors of this group twenty years later. It is probable that he was a guest at Devonshire House, for Sheridan was frequently there, and it was the resort of almost all the wits and beaux of the time. He struck up an intimacy with the Reverend Edward Cannon, whose blunt speech and affected selfishness repelled those who did not know him well, and led finally to his falling into the disfavor of the Regent because of the enmity of that prince's morganatic wife, Mrs. Fitzherbert.

The "Reminiscences and Recollections of Captain Gronow," in describing the useless and super-

annuated Generals of the Guard, records the following incident, which occurred in 1811 or 1812:

> One of them, General Thornton, was afflicted with
> the idea that of all persons in the world he was the only
> one who understood the art of waltzing. In fact, it was
> quite a mania with him, and he might be seen at nearly
> every party of note, making himself exceedingly ridicu-
> lous by teaching young ladies to waltz. . . . Theodore
> Hook gave him the *soubriquet* of the "waltzing Gen-
> eral"; this occasioned a violent altercation between
> them at a ball in Portman Square, where, it is said, the
> General received a more personal affront from Hook;
> which, however, he did not resent according to the then
> received notions of honour, by calling him out. The in-
> quiry into this affair by a committee of the other officers
> of the Guards . . . found that General Thornton had
> been guilty of cowardice in not demanding immediate
> satisfaction of Hook, and he was therefore desired to
> quit the regiment forthwith.

The story seems to set forth Hook's act as an un-
provoked assault upon a helpless old officer, and it
may possibly have been that. But there is no evidence to show that Hook knew the old man to be
too helpless and meek-spirited to resent the affront
in the usual manner. And it is hard at this day to
recall the excitement caused by the introduction
of this new dance. Hook's opposition to it was
sincere enough. To the end of his life he lost no
opportunity to curse the intimate contact of partners in the waltz, and to condemn, moreover, another innovation, the ballet dance, because of the
shocking exposure of the lower extremities which

took place whenever the dancer's skirts became elevated by a rapid pirouette. It is amusing, however, to find the superannuated officer highly approving of the waltz, and the dashing young Theodore condemning this German innovation as immoral!

Another incident of these years concerns Hook's schoolfellow at Harrow, Lord Byron. The latter, by the way, must have heard some of Theodore's extemporaneous performances, for Thomas Medwin, recording Byron's conversations at Pisa, in 1821 and 1822, makes him say: "Why should we not be able to improvise in hexameters as well as the Italians? Theodore Hook is an improvisatore." Young Henry Angelo was at Newmarket watching a race when he met Byron driving a barouche. Angelo climbed in upon invitation, and was delighted to find that "my old acquaintance Theodore Hook was in the barouche." Angelo and Hook drove to Cambridge with Byron, had dinner with him and several college students, took places on the London mail-coach, drank a parting draught of the famous Cambridge beer handed up to them by Byron, and drove off into the evening shadows with his lordship huzzaing and twisting his hat to them until they were out of sight.

The Prince Regent's intention to "do something for Hook" had been sincere. While Theodore was in the midst of his pleasant and expensive social career, therefore, he received the information, early in 1812, that he had been appointed accountant general and treasurer of the island of Mauritius, or Isle de France, which had been taken in 1810 but was not yet formally ceded by France.[1] This office returned to its possessor over two thousand pounds a year.

There is nothing mysterious or unparalleled in this appointment. A good musician won his way to the Regent's heart almost as quickly as did a beautiful woman. He was an instrumentalist of a sort himself; he belonged to the "Nobleman's and Gentleman's Catch and Glee Club," and he occasionally tried his hand at composing a verse for a glee. "It is not generally known," writes Huish in his "Memoirs of George the Fourth," "that a certain ambassador at one of the northern courts owes his elevation principally to the skill which he displayed at Carlton House on the violincello, the favorite instrument of his Royal Highness." Moreover, thinks the memoir writer, it is "a curious coincidence that two of the most confidential servants of his Royal Highness owed their

---

[1] Lockhart says that the appointment was made "late in 1812"; but Mrs. Mathews quotes a letter to her husband from George Colman, dated April 4, 1812, in which the dramatist writes: "Hook certainly goes to the Isle of France, at which I grieve; but with a good appointment, at which I rejoice; but shall lose a most pleasant, clever, and good fellow." Notice of the appointment is not in the *Annual Register*, nor can I find it in the *Gazette*.

elevation to their skill in music." Again, the poet
and songster, Tom Moore, got a government appointment in the West Indies, and Tom Sheridan,
son of the dramatist, was made colonial treasurer
at the Cape of Good Hope. Since the Regent,
then, was delighted and astonished at Hook's extemporaneous performances, his appointment of
the youth to a responsible government position
was quite in accord with his custom and character.
He probably expressed his intention to help Theodore to his physician and confidential friend, Sir
Walter Farquhar, the father-in-law of James
Hook, Theodore's brother. Sir Walter would then
remind the Prince that his brother, Robert Townshend Farquhar, had, in 1811, been appointed
governor general of the newly conquered island of
Mauritius. Thus the Regent's appointment took
the direction it did.

That Theodore Hook would accept this splendid
appointment goes without saying, if only from the
fact that he was heavily in debt. His plays and
copyrights had surely returned him more than two
thousand pounds; he was living at home, where he
had no board to pay or furniture to buy. Yet he
was considerably over two thousand in debt — a
thing almost incredible to one not accustomed to
the scale of expenditure in the social life of the
Regency. He was beginning to be harried by duns.
Hook "was one of my earliest and most intimate

companions," wrote Beazley years later, "and I smuggled him off to Mauritius in spite of debtor and dun. What buoyant spirits were his in those days!" On September 24, 1812, Theodore wrote to his friend, John Elliot, requesting a loan of £300, saying:

I am on the point of sailing for the Cape in the Semiramis with Admiral Tyler, on my way to the Mauritius. The opportunity is given me of realizing a fortune, every facility afforded me in embracing it and every advantage likely to result from it, but I am checked at the moment of starting by some debts which I feel myself bound in honor to pay before I leave the country, the amount of which is between three and four hundred pounds — I cannot leave the kingdom happily without discharging them, and my own connections have done so much in preparing me for the voyage, fitting me out and procuring me the passage, &c., &c. that I cannot apply to them for more assistance to defray debts already incurred.[1]

The application was successful; the most persistent creditors were appeased; and Theodore soon began his voyage to the far-off African island.

---

[1] Quoted from G. F. Waugh's "Unpublished Letters of Theodore Hook," in the *Gentleman's Magazine* of April, 1896.

CHAPTER IV.

THE MAURITIUS INTERLUDE.

AFTER a voyage of four months and six days, Theodore Hook arrived at Mauritius on October 8, 1813, and was installed in office the next day. He remained on the island until April 18, 1818. For a young man just entering his twenty-sixth year, the future, in 1813, could not have been more roseate. His official position was enviable. He was third or fourth in rank in the island; he was a civil official, appointed by the Crown and responsible only to the governor. This governor, the supreme autocrat of the island, was also a civil official, and was the uncle of the wife of Theodore's brother. "The governor," wrote Hook after he arrived, "is everything that is excellent, and I, as I should be, everything that is grateful." He appointed Hook to his personal staff, thus enabling the young man to live at his official residence, and probably a good deal at his expense. He procured for him, in addition to his offices of treasurer and accountant general, the posts of inspector general and superintendent of the public press, and commissioner and comptroller of stamps. The total

salary from all these sources was the magnificent
one of £2500 a year. Clothing, household furniture, and some articles of food were indeed expensive. To Mathews, Hook wrote: "Fresh butter,
my dear fellow, is ten shillings per pound; a coat
costs thirty pounds English; a pair of gloves is
fifteen shillings." Nevertheless, within two years
Theodore was able to remit to England the sum
of £1932 4s, in full payment of his debts.

The social life of the island was surprisingly
complete. Mrs. Farquhar was able to find seven
hundred and fifty eligible women to invite to official receptions. The inhabitants were by nature
very fond of music, and there was a flourishing
theatre. Moreover: "Our races begin in July; we
have also an excellent beef-steak club; the best
Freemason's lodge in the world. We have subscription concerts, and balls, and the parties in
private houses here are seldom less than from two
to three hundred." The Mauritian misses, the
eligible ones pure French, are "beautiful and
vastly well mannered, highly accomplished, dance,
sing, draw, and play really with exquisite taste,
are truly agreeable and not *very* reserved." Lack
of reserve is an astounding thing of which to accuse the countrywomen of Paul's beloved Vir-
ginia, whose grave was shown to every visitor
to the island. One wonders further about Saint-
Pierre's heroine when Hook mentions a peculiar

custom of theirs: "They spit about the rooms; this is not agreeable at first."

The climate is tropical. To avoid "the intense heat of Christmas," the governor moves to his country house, La Reduit, up in the hills and away from the metropolis, Port Louis, for at the latter place the temperature sometimes reaches 130 degrees Fahrenheit. During the winter months of July and August, life in Port Louis runs a well-ordered round:

Breakfast at eight, always up by gun-fire, five o'clock; bathe and ride before breakfast; after breakfast lounge about; at one have a regular meal, yclept a tiffin — hot meats, vegetables, and at this we sit generally through the heat of the day, drinking our wine and munching our fruit; at five, or half-past, the carriages come to the door, and we go either in them or in palanquins to dress, which operation performed, we drive out to the race-ground, and through the Champ de Mars, the Hyde-Park here, till half-past six; come into town, and at seven dine, where we remain till ten or eleven, and then join the French parties, as there is regularly a ball somewhere or other every night: these things blended with business, make out the day and evening.

Such a life filled Theodore with great contentment.

This colony [he writes to John Elliot] is a perfect paradise — there was never anything so beautiful as the country, so charming as the climate, or so very delightful as the people — they are all gaiety and hospitality.

To Mathews he says:

In short, the whole island is like fairy-land; every hour seems happier than the last; and altogether, from the mildness of the air (the sweetness of which, as it passes over spice plantations and orange groves, is hardly conceivable), the clearness of the atmosphere, the coolness of the evenings, and the loveliness of the place itself, all combine to render it fascination. The very thought of ever quitting it is like the apprehension of the death or long parting with some near relation.

Playwriting he abandoned. He goes to the opera, he tells Mathews, and he is going to ask Fleury, the manager, to play some French pieces he (Hook) has with him. But he has "given up all thoughts of finishing my Covent Garden farce, and have returned Harry Harris the money he paid me *en avance.*" His powers of improvisation were certain to be much admired and often called for, both at the English and at the French parties. The temptation to play tricks on travellers was also too strong to be resisted. He had mapped out, for instance, an ingenious and devious route by which to drive visitors to the island through the streets of Port Louis, — a route so devised that each public building of size was approached several times from several different directions and was announced each time as a different building, — so that Port Louis for the visitor, instead of appearing what it was, a small colonial town, took on the proportions of a large city crowded with public buildings. Another joke of his is on record. He instructed the cook to gather all the noxious insects and reptiles the island possessed and to prepare them for the table in various ways. To such a repast he introduced travellers just off the ship and with stomachs still squeamish from a long sea voyage, and, as the genial host, pressed them cordially to partake of the delights of a native Mauritian repast by trying a little of this grilled lizard, or that fried snake, or this delicious stew of beetles.

As for business — oh yes, there was the treasury, of course. Well — if the government had wanted a book-keeper's clerk, they would have appointed one and not given the office to a gentleman who was above all this penny-juggling. The daily record of the state of the treasury could properly be attended to by subordinates. The office of treasurer was one of supervision mainly. It was sufficient to step into the treasury building two or three times weekly, to ask the head clerk how matters were going, to run a hasty eye over his monthly report before signing it and sending it to the governor, to keep the key of the chest when the head clerk returned it after office hours, and to know in round numbers the amount of money in that chest. Besides, in a tropical climate work has to be divided in order to be endurable. A man not inured to heat surely could not remain in Port

Louis with the thermometer registering 130 degrees. Everything, then, depended upon the honesty of the subordinates in the treasury department. Now, strangely enough, neither of Hook's two clerks was English. One of them was a negro, Allan; the other, a Frenchman, De Chaillet. The government broker was one Maure, also French. More curious still, they were appointed, not by Hook, but directly from London.

On November 19, 1817, Governor Farquhar left for a visit to England on account of his health. Major-General Gage John Hall, the commander of the troops, became governor *ad interim.* He was a military tyrant of a most autocratic stripe, and his presence in office was not long tolerated. The Earl of Albemarle, who visited the island in 1818, writes of him:

> The new functionary soon became convinced that not only his predecessor in office, but all whose duty it was to carry out the provisions of the Slave-Trade Abolition Act, were resorting to every expedient to make it a dead letter. Acting upon these convictions, Hall suspended the Chief Justice and the Attorney-General, dismissed several civil servants from their posts, and established domiciliary visits to the planters' habitations in search of newly imported negroes. Remonstrances against his proceedings by the colonists to the mother country procured his immediate recall.[1]

---

[1] George Thomas Keppel, 6th Earl of Albemarle, *Fifty Years of My Life* (1876), ii, 95.

From the beginning Hall took an active dislike to Hook. "My mind feels perfectly relieved," he wrote later to Earl Bathurst, "of that uneasiness under which it suffered during Mr. Hook's charge of the Treasury Department." One may call such uneasiness justified. Theodore was lavish with money; he was a frequenter of the race tracks; and he was somewhat undignified in his official demeanor. After Governor Farquhar's departure he foolishly purchased a house with furniture and fixtures so valuable as to bring over $13,000 at the later forced sale of his effects. On the other hand, there can be little doubt that the real cause of Hall's enmity was that Hook was a civil official. All of Hall's acts show that he had no trust in civilians — moreover, that he had little control of their actions, for they could not be ordered about as his military underlings could be. When the time came, not only Hook, but the two civil officials who worked with him, were ousted and military men substituted.

To return to events. Before Farquhar left for England in November, 1817, he appointed a committee to examine the treasurer's accounts. This body made an examination — or at any rate they officially declared, on November 19, that the treasurer's books were in order. Hook always maintained that this examination was regular in form, and thorough. Hall emphatically asserted that "Mr. Hook's *ipse dixit* was taken for the contents of the chest." But why should a committee accept the treasurer's word when the only purpose of their existence and the very object of their coming together was to verify his accounts? It is difficult to see why Hook, standing firmly by the declaration of this body, could not have refused to have any of his accounts, before those of November 19, 1817, ever examined again by any board whatsoever.

On January 15, 1818, Allan, the negro clerk, wrote to Governor Hall saying that the sum of $37,150, though received in December, 1816, had not been entered on the books. Hall at once appointed another committee (quite extra-legally, for it was the auditor general's business to investigate); but before it could meet, Allan, after giving unmistakable signs that he was mentally deranged, committed suicide. The committee, two of whom had served on Farquhar's audit board two months previously, now found a shortage of $60,000. Thereupon, writes Hook,

without question, without hearing, I was, on the first of March, 1818, dragged from my house at midnight to the common dungeons of Port Louis; but the tremendous hurricane of the 28th of February had so damaged the prison that there was no cell habitable, and at three o'clock in the morning, those who arrested me were obliged, by the merciful violence of the weather, to permit me to go in custody to the house of a friend.

After that, in defiance of all colonial law, Hall kept Hook confined for eleven days under military guard. Then he seized all of Hook's effects except the clothes he had on and sold them. Finally he released his victim under heavy bail, delivered him afterwards to military custody, and on April 18, 1818, shipped him back to England.

The passage back consumed nine months, and the ship almost foundered in the usual storm off the Cape. There was a delay of four months at Cape Town, and Hook was set free on parole. Here he met the Governor General, Lord Charles Somerset, delighted him with his sparkling improvisations, and made his famous joke in response to Somerset's inquiry whether he was returning home on account of his health — "I am sorry to say they think there is something wrong with the chest." [1]　Under way from the Cape the ship

---

[1] Albemarle, *Fifty Years of My Life*, ii, 99: "While at the Cape I became a frequent guest of the Governor General, Lord Charles Somerset, a man of considerable humour, and possessing that easy, engaging manner which seems to sit so naturally on the House of Beaufort. When I first saw Lord Charles he was full of a visit from Theodore Hook, the famous improvisatore, who had made a short stay at the Cape on his way home from the Mauritius. Dining one day at the Governor's House, Hook was asked to give a sample of his talent. He had been previously furnished with the names and peculiarities of fellow guests. For each of them he had a verse which set the table in a roar." Theodore's stay at the Cape, however, must have been saddened by the knowledge that his friend Tom Sheridan, son of the dramatist, had died there the previous year.

made yet another stop of a month at St. Helena, where Hook caught sight of the great exile.

In January, 1819, the ship reached Portsmouth, and Hook was detained there until his papers were forwarded to the Attorney-General's office. There it was found that there was no ground for criminal procedure! Theodore, now absolutely penniless, was set at large.

He was next requested to attend the sittings of the Colonial Audit Board; and from February, 1819, to August, 1823, he was obliged to appear before the board on the average of once every week: that is, he came in the morning and waited until the board found the time and disposition to call him in. Between examinations he composed abstracts of his papers, involving hours of the hardest kind of work; for every transaction which had gone through his hands during his stay on the island was exhaustively examined.

On Tuesday, June 26, 1821, the Whig M.P. for Shrewsbury, Mr. Henry Grey Bennett, the brother of Lord Tankerville, arose in the House of Commons and moved for papers "connected with the suspension of Mr. Theodore Hook, late Treasurer of the Mauritius." He was induced to withdraw his motion after an explanation by Edward Goulburn, member of the Privy Council, speaking for the government, but the distorted version Bennett gave of the defalcation did not augur well for

Hook. Some months later, on Friday, March 22, 1822, "Mr. Henry Bennett moved that the return from the Auditor's Office of the state of Mr. Theodore Hook's accounts be made forthwith." This was ordered, and the papers were presented a few weeks later; but the material was so immense that Bennett was invited to select such parts of it as he desired printed. Bennett naturally chose the most incriminating documents; these were ordered printed on the 25th of July. They occupy two hundred pages in the 22nd volume of the "Parliamentary Papers" for 1822. They consist of excerpts from the interminable examinations of Hook, of Farquhar, of Hall (now in England), and of many others, before the Board, the letters of the Board to the Lords of the Treasury, letters from the Board to Hook reproaching him for not working hard enough or attending the Board's gracious pleasure assiduously enough, and so on — the whole forming an unanalyzable mass of which this admirable Circumlocution Office might well feel proud. It is revealed, however, that the Board in October, 1821, declared Hook debtor to the Crown for over £12,000; that on November 20, the Treasury obtained a writ of extent against him; that what few possessions Hook had were taken from him and sold, thereby enriching the Royal Treasury of England by the sum of almost £60; that the Board was successful in driving its victim to desperation and to very unwise vituperation; that, finally, the cost to the Treasury of investigating this loss of, as was alleged, £12,000, was over £30,000.

The final audit seems to have been delayed until 1823, when, in August, Theodore was arrested under an Exchequer writ, and taken to the sponging house of his captor. Here in Shire Lane, in an unwholesome place in an iniquitous neighborhood, he remained month after month at great expense for miserable accommodations, almost daily expecting his release. At last, in April, 1824, Hook moved to the Rules of the King's Bench, taking a small lodging in Temple Place. Conditions here were much better, and permission to leave the prescribed district could be readily obtained.

On March 26, 1825, John Wilson Croker, Secretary to the Admiralty, after a previous unsuccessful appeal to Lushington, the head of the Colonial Audit Board, wrote a letter directly to the Chancellor of the Exchequer, reviewing Hook's case and interceding vehemently in his behalf.

If I believed Mr. Hook to be guilty of peculation [he wrote], I should never have interested myself for him. I believe him wholly innocent; but, if he were guilty, I doubt whether he has not been sufficiently punished. Twice over he has surrendered all he had in the world, even to his dressing-case; and the second time the value of the accumulated riches was under £60. Six and twenty months has he been in confinement: ten months under circumstances of discredit and disgrace. For many, the best, years of his life he has been prevented following any business or providing in any other way for present or future subsistence by the cruel occupation of endeavouring to explain to those who, he says, have as assiduously endeavored not to understand. He has lost a valuable office, and with it all hopes of estabblishment in the line of life he had adopted, and he is too old to begin anew. If he be a criminal, show me a criminal of his class who has been more punished! but if, as I believe the fact is, his imprisonment is not, and cannot legally be, meant for punishment, then, I ask you, have you a doubt that you have twice over gotten all that he had? Have you an expectation that, by breaking his spirit and destroying his health by protracted confinement, he will become better able to discharge his debt? Look at other defaulters; think of the sums they have abused! Have they pined in prison? . . . and why is this savage virtue against Mr. Hook alone? I can tell you; like a blockhead (which many a man of talent is) he mixed himself with politics. . . .[1]

It was this letter, probably, which effected Hook's release in April or May, 1826, after a confinement of over two years. But the debt to the Treasury charged to him was not stricken off; it was kept suspended over his head, the government reserving the right at any time to seize and sell whatever possessions he might acquire.

The entire course of the proceedings *in re* Hook is difficult to understand to-day. Undoubtedly

---

[1] *The Croker Papers: Correspondence and Diaries of John Wilson Croker.* Edited by Louis J. Jennings. New York (1884), i, 260 ff.

there was a defalcation; undoubtedly Theodore's incapacity and laxness contributed to it, as he was not qualified for a position requiring precision and methodical habits. Undoubtedly, too, he was officially responsible for irregularities in the treasury department. But when one turns to the specific causes of the deficit, the case against Hook does not seem black. He was charged, first, with losing money through bad financial policy. He succeeded satisfactorily in defending many of his acts under this category, but his difficulty was that the board demanded documentary evidence, whereas it must have known that, in the inevitable confusion which follows conquest, financial policy has to be largely a matter of verbal agreement and coöperation between governor and treasurer. Secondly, he was charged with a large number of minor mistakes in keeping accounts. Yet these errors of bookkeeping did not involve a large sum, and the mistakes were almost as frequently against the treasurer as in his favor; while the entire matter was hugely complicated by the presence in circulation of all sorts of constantly fluctuating media. Thirdly, there was the original matter of the fate of the $37,150 about which Allan had written to Governor Hall. Hook admitted this deficit and tried his best to trace the money. Now it is certain that he himself did not make away with this sum. All his expenditures on the island and his remittances to England were carefully checked. Certainly such a sum would never tempt him to jeopardize his splendid position. And, strangely enough, although the sum itself was not entered in the books, the premium paid for it *was* entered, and detection was thus made certain. Who did get the money then? Almost certainly De Chaillet, the French clerk. Hook later suspected him,[1] but in England he could do nothing. One cannot blame the Frenchman for robbing the English conqueror, but it is hard to understand how any English official could have appointed De Chaillet to his position.

After the defalcation was discovered, Theodore should not have been treated as he was treated. He should not have been delivered by a military officer, who did not feel that his prisoner had any rights which needed to be respected, to a Colonial Audit Board which was both judge and jury, and which was able to impose an indeterminate imprisonment upon the defendant without pronouncing his guilt. Hook should have been brought before the civil tribunal of the island and charged with certain definite offences. Only at Mauritius, the place of his alleged peculation, could either

---

[1] On the trip back from the Mauritius someone asked Hook how a certain Frenchman, an intimate friend of De Chaillet's, could enter into speculation with the Cape from Mauritius when it was known that he had absolutely no money when he left the Cape.

his guilt or his innocence have been proved. And, had all the persons concerned been apprehended (an easy matter on a small, out-of-the-way island), the real culprit would surely have been caught.

If Theodore Hook is charged with incapacity and carelessness, every other person connected with the affair must stand similarly charged. The government itself should have required a surety bond from the treasurer. Hook's two clerks, particularly since they were not his appointees, were surely liable as accessories. There was an auditor general named Dick, whose brother was deputy auditor general. One is inclined to wonder how the brothers Dick spent the long tropical days; certainly there is no record that much of their time was spent inside the treasury building. And, in the last instance, Farquhar himself was responsible for the state of the treasury, because his treasurer sent him monthly reports and was responsible directly to him. Major-General Hall did not hesitate to write to England: "A vigilant government, or an efficient auditor general, should long since have remarked this large defalcation"; and "If, my lord, I had reposed upon Mr. Farquhar's assurance, when he made the hurried and precipitate transfer of this government into my hands . . ." But even Hall's position was a peculiar one. When he assumed charge, an official committee had declared the treasurer's books in order. In short, amid this universal laxness and carelessness, it was Theodore Hook who was left holding the bag.

Why, then, was Hook the only sufferer from this highly involved business, and why did savage virtue hound him so relentlessly? Why was Bennett of Shrewsbury such a bitter foe? Croker has already given the answer — "like a blockhead he has mixed himself with politics." One sorry day Theodore began meddling in the fierce political quarrels of the time, on the side of the Tories. In doing so he made himself fair game for the Whigs. If he had but quietly waited, the case of the deficit would in all probability have been allowed to drop. It must, therefore, be concluded — although the evidence in the case of the Mauritius defalcation shows Hook to have been unfairly treated throughout — that by entering politics he brought most of his troubles in that affair upon himself.

CHAPTER V.

PAMPHLETEER, EDITOR, JOURNALIST, AND NOVELIST (1819–1841).

WHEN he went up to London from Portsmouth in January, 1819, Theodore Hook needed money badly. He immediately worked over his old play, "Black and White," which he had written for Rolls's private theatricals many years before, gave it the title of "Pigeons and Crows," and applied to Colman the younger in order to have it presented. Colman presented it at the Haymarket on August 28, 1819, choosing Liston for the comic rôle. "It is a poor piece," writes Genest; but, as it ran for twelve nights, it did bring its author a few much-needed pounds.

Hook's old friend, Daniel Terry, was now a well-established actor at the Haymarket. For Terry and for Liston, therefore, Theodore put together another play, "Exchange No Robbery; or, The Diamond Ring," acted fifteen times after August 12, 1820. It is an extremely clever farce; but, with the exception of a commonplace underplot about a diamond ring, it is not Hook's according to his own admission in the preface (it was published without his name), that the author "borrowed, or (as he had nothing to offer in exchange) more properly stole, from the play of 'He Would be a Soldier.'" This had been Frederick Pilon's last play, put on at Covent Garden on November 18, 1776, and revived there on May 16, 1794. Hook has, says Genest, "served Pilon's play as gipsies do stolen children, disfigured it to make it pass for his own." Again, however, his struggle in 1819 and 1820 to get money for the bare necessities of life must excuse him.

The last play for the professional stage with which the name of Theodore Hook was connected was a two-act farcical afterpiece, acted by Terry and others, and opening at the Haymarket on July 4, 1821. Its reception is described by the "Morning Chronicle" of July 5:

A new farce entitled "Peter and Paul; or, Love in the Vineyards," which is a translation from the French, was by no means graciously received, but it was announced for repetition this evening. It has, we understand, been imported into our language by Mr. Theodore Hook, which we think not improbable from the number of overstrained puns with which it is accompanied.

The play was never printed but there is a synopsis of it in the "Morning Post" of July 5.

From this time forward, Theodore, although he always retained a love for amateur theatricals, came gradually to have a fixed aversion for the professional stage. "He mentions in one of his last diaries," writes Lockhart, "that he had not been twice in a playhouse during eight preceding years."

As soon as Theodore arrived in London in 1819, he threw himself into politics on the side of the Tories. A bitter controversy was being waged over Sir Hudson Lowe's treatment of Napoleon. As Hook had just come from St. Helena, had gone about the island there during his stay of several weeks, and had, as he says, twice caught sight of the exile, he felt himself qualified to enter the quarrel. The result of his participation was a short anonymous pamphlet put out in 1819 by the printer, William Stockdale of Piccadilly, entitled "Facts Illustrative of the Treatment of Napoleon Bonaparte, Being the Result of Minute Inquiries and Personal Research in that Island." It is a typical Grub Street production — unfair, violent, and scurrilous. It attempts to whitewash Sir Hudson Lowe and the Tory administration; and it helps along this purpose by attacking the Whigs, Sir Pultney Malcolm, Barry O'Meara the surgeon, and, above all, by heaping taunting insult upon Napoleon, before whose utter downfall even a catchpenny pamphleteer should have stood in silence.

Hook's pamphlet, in fact, bears all the marks of being made to order. It contains minute descriptions of Napoleon's house, — Longwood, — and it gives lists of rations supplied each week to the exile and his party — matters which it is improbable that Hook could have observed for himself when on the island. It appears almost certain that this material was supplied by some member of the government — that Hook, to be more specific, was commissioned for the task by Lord Bathurst, the most prominent of the defenders in Parliament of the acts of Sir Hudson Lowe.

The tract was reviewed, unfavorably of course, in the Whig "Edinburgh Review" of July, 1819. It was replied to by Barry O'Meara, who had been attacked by it. This Irishman had been appointed surgeon to Napoleon and became one of his sympathizers. After Lowe arrived at St. Helena, O'Meara protested against his high-handed repressive acts, and was deprived, as a consequence, of his appointment and of his commission as naval surgeon. He thereupon returned to England and set about writing his memoirs. His own words tell of his reaction to Hook's pamphlet:

While occupied in preparing my Narrative and Official Correspondence for the press, and looking forward with impatient anxiety to that inquiry, which can alone enable the British nation to decide on the transactions at St. Helena subsequent to Sir Hudson Lowe's appointment and arrival there, a pamphlet has appeared under the specious title of "Facts Illustrative of the Treatment of Napoleon Bonaparte in St. Helena . . ." As this production lays claim to public attention on the score of strict veracity, while it is in reality made the vehicle of slander, calumny and misrepresentation,

I have been induced to suspend the publication of my larger work, as much for the purpose of repelling the attack which is made on my own character, as to show the nation what degree of confidence ought to be placed in statements, thus anonymously obtruded on its notice, without any other claims to credibility than those derived from plausible professions, and bold assertions totally unsupported by proofs.

O'Meara then, in two hundred pages octavo,[1] sets about refuting Hook's assertions one by one. His work is moderate and clear, and bears the stamp of truth. Unfortunately, although O'Meara may have had right, truth, and similar abstractions on his side, his opponents had political power on theirs, and Napoleon had now no rights which anyone needed to respect. When O'Meara's larger work, called "Napoleon in Exile," came out, John Wilson Croker (Secretary to the Admiralty and hence directly concerned in O'Meara's loss of his naval commission) attempted to demolish it in one of his "slashing articles" (as Disraeli was later to call them in "Coningsby") in the "Quarterly Review" for February, 1823.

---

[1] "An Exposition of some of the Transactions, That have Taken Place at St. Helena, since The Appointment of Sir Hudson Lowe, as Governor of that Island; in answer to an anonymous Pamphlet entitled 'Facts Illustrative of the Treatment of Napoleon Bonaparte.' Corroborated by Various Official Documents, Correspondence, &c. By Barry E. O'Meara. Late Surgeon to Napoleon." London, printed for James Ridgway, Piccadilly, 1819.

In 1819 and 1820 the affair on the tongues of all Englishmen was that of Caroline of Brunswick, the wife of the Regent. That notorious prince had long ceased to have any relations with her, and he had kept the child of the marriage, Charlotte, under his control. He was preparing to divorce her upon grounds of adultery, citing as evidence acts which even her best friends were forced to call indiscreet. When the old crazed king died on January 29, 1820, matters speedily became more serious, for Caroline was now Queen of England. Her husband nevertheless persisted in bringing her for trial before the House of Lords on a charge of "licentious, disgraceful, and adulterous inter- course." He failed of obtaining her conviction, and she became the "wronged mother," the "in- jured queen," the idol of the populace; whereas such ugly passions and such a clamor of execration were raised against George IV that it is surely no exaggeration to say that the fate of his throne was in jeopardy, and that popular rebellion was on the point of breaking out. The economic misery of the worker was at the bottom of such things as the Spa Fields riots, the Peterloo massacre, and the Cato Street conspiracy — causing the drastic sedition acts passed by Parliament. But the al- most universal unpopularity of the Regent fanned the smouldering discontent.

When Theodore Hook entered this affray on the side of the Tories and George IV, he exposed himself to two obvious charges: first, that, being as he was under apprehension of prosecution because of the Mauritius defalcation, he began toadying to the Tory administration in the hope of being let off; and, secondly, that, so far as prosecution for libel was concerned, it was a safe thing under a Tory régime to attack the Whigs and Queen Caroline. Undoubtedly it must be said that Hook *hoped* to curry favor with the government. Lockhart, another Tory, had observed that hope: "We used to consider him as labouring under another equally silly delusion, for to the last he clung to the persuasion that he was some day or other to be released from his difficulties by the patronage of his friends among the Conservatives." A little thought should have shown Theodore how impossible it was for the Tories to aid him. The shaky Tory administration would never dare support a man obnoxious to the Whigs; they would certainly never fight for a man under a cloud, like Hook. By the same sign they could not prevent their opponents from prosecuting a libel. Moreover, the laws of libel and of breach of privilege of Parliament were extremely stringent; the press was held in low esteem in general; and there was always a group of country members of both parties who were astonished and indignant at the idea that any newspaper had any rights whatever. The second charge is, therefore, not true, as the event itself proved.

In fact, before Hook's political writings can be fairly judged, several circumstances in his favor must be set forth. He came by his Toryism honestly. "He was from the first," writes his early friend, Sam Beazley, "enthusiastically loyal — and if during dinner a street-organ played 'God save the King,' he would insist on everybody standing up, lead the chorus, and not sit down till the anthem was closed." Now because of the political convictions both of George III and (after 1811) of his son, loyalty and Toryism easily became synonymous. And there were further considerations to strengthen the feeling. Theodore's brother had been favored by both monarchs; his brother's father-in-law was one of the Regent's closest friends. Theodore himself had been given a splendid position through the personal favor of the Prince.

Again, in supporting George IV against his Queen, Hook was on the right side. This does not mean in any way that the King's cause was just. It does mean that support of the Queen led nowhere — unless, indeed, its object was to take George IV's throne from him and thereby precipitate, perhaps, a bloody civil war. Thus it could be asserted, and with a considerable degree of correctness, that Hook was on the side of law and order, whereas the last-ditch defenders of the Queen — Whigs like Brougham, who conducted her defence, Joseph Hume, Alderman Wood, and Henry Grey Bennett — were preaching sedition and playing the dangerous game of gaining political popularity by fanning the passions of the mob.

Hook must have entered the field of politics light-heartedly enough. He had not been injured by the Whigs in 1820; there could have been no genuine personal malignity at work. Later on, naturally, the case was altered. But at the beginning, writes Lockhart,

he knew little and could have cared nothing about those who became the objects of his satire. . . . Certain men and women were stuck up as types of certain prejudices or delusions; and he set to knocking them down with no more feeling about them, as individual human-creatures, than if they had been nine-pins.

Finally, the frequency and bitterness of the attacks on the Regent and his father are notorious. "Peter Pindar" (John Wolcot), William Hone, Cruikshank, Shelley, Lamb, Hazlitt, Byron, Leigh Hunt, Tom Moore (in his "Twopenny Post Bag" and "Fudge Family in Paris"), to say nothing of the dozens of anonymous assailants — all swelled the chorus of those who, in prose and verse, in accents unhesitating, set forth their opinions of the house of Hanover. In fact, writes Huish in his

"Memoirs of George the Fourth," "Whoever has had the patience or the curiosity to peruse one half of the defamatory productions which were published against the Prince of Wales, from the year 1783 to the time almost of the Regency, will have run through a tolerable number of volumes." The attackers were bitter and personal. Shelley wrote of the sons of George III:

> Princes, the dregs of their dull race, who flow
> Through public scorn mud from a muddy spring.

Byron wrote of the unfortunate Charlotte and her father, the Regent:

> Weep, daughter of a royal line,
> A sire's disgrace, a realm's decay.
> Ah! happy if each tear of thine
> Could wash a father's fault away.

Leigh Hunt's attack on the Regent, which appeared in his "Examiner" on March 22, 1812, and caused his imprisonment for libel, is fairly well known, but it demands quotation as an illustration of the extremes to which the political writers of the day frequently went:

What person unacquainted with the true state of the case, would imagine in reading these astounding eulogies that this "Glory of the People" was the subject of millions of stings and reproaches! That this "Protector of the Arts" had named a wretched foreigner as his historical painter, in disparagement, or in ignorance of the merits of his countrymen! That this "Mæcenas of the Age" patronized not a single deserving writer! That this "Breather of Eloquence" could not say a few decent extempore words, if we are to judge, at least, from what he said to his regiment on its embarkation for Portugal! That this "Conqueror of Hearts" was the disappointer of hopes! That this "Exciter of Desire" (Bravo, Messieurs of the "Post"), this "Adonis in Loveliness" was a corpulent gentleman of fifty! In short, that this delightful, blissful, wise, pleasurable, honourable, virtuous, true and immortal Prince was a violator of his word, a libertine, over head and ears in debt and disgrace, a despiser of domestic ties, a companion of gamblers and demireps, a man who has just closed half a century without one single claim on the gratitude of his country or the respect of posterity.

In fairness to Theodore Hook the bitter tone of political controversy at the time should be remembered. Hook used the same weapons that his opponents were using; he might well hold that he was simply retaliating in kind.

In the Queen Caroline controversy, the first product of Hook's pen was the anonymous tract called "Tentamen; or, An Essay Towards the History of Whittington, Some Time Lord Mayor of London," put out by William Wright of 46 Fleet Street, in 1820. This is a satire in the form of an historical monograph written by a Dr. Dryasdust (in this case named Dr. Blinkinsop) on the legend of Whittington and his cat. Alderman Wood is Whittington, and Queen Caroline is the cat. The pamphlet ran through many editions, and it is still readable because of the boyish gusto with which Hook throws himself into the subject and deals out his vulgarities.

No one among the Whigs had more violently attacked the Regent and the Tories than William Hone. About this time Hone assailed Sir John Stoddart in a tract called "The Political House That Jack Built." A Tory writer, calling himself Dr. Slop, answered this assault in a miscellany entitled "Slop's Shave at a Broken Hone," which was printed in 1820 and also distributed by William Wright. Dr. Slop in this pamphlet names some of his Tory coadjutors in the following doggerel:

> Beware the writers in the New Whig Guide,
> And him who wrote Mat Whittington's Tentamen;
> In both their jeux d'esprit may be descried
> A hand well practised to dissect and flay men.
>
> .   .   .   .
>
> That Dr. Blinkinsop 's a knowing wight,
> (At least we think him so among the Tories)
> Well skill'd in dragging secret things to light
> And *hooking* up all sorts of awkward stories
> Which I, for one, would never wish to mention,
> But which are still by no means an invention.

Continuing, Dr. Slop names another staunch Tory pamphleteer:

> But fear no drubbing, friend, from me, much less
> From Oxford Tom my coadjutor, who
> Of this my monologue corrects the press,
> And here and there inserts a line or two.

The name here mentioned, that of "Old Tom of Oxford," appears to have been one under which several Tory writers, including Hook, wrote. Two pamphlets, both put out by Wright in 1820, cannot possibly be the work of Hook. These are "Types of the Times. By Old Tom of Oxford," and "Solomon Logwood, a Radical Tale. By Old Tom of Oxford." On the other hand, the following pamphlet is almost surely by Hook: "The New Christmas Budget. Old Tom of Oxford. London, W. Wright, 1820." It is a collection of short poems set to popular airs — all of which hold up Caroline to ridicule in no gentle or impersonal fashion. Still another pamphlet printed for Wright in 1820 is: "The Radical Harmonist; or, A Collection of Songs and Toasts given at the late Crown and Anchor Dinner. Collected by Old Tom of Oxford." This, without any doubt whatever, is the work of Theodore Hook, for several of the poems are set to the same music as, and are practically identical with, those later printed by him in his newspaper, "John Bull."

Hook may have written more pamphlets at this time, but the British Museum library holds no more which can be recognized as his. Those which have been described, with the possible exception of the "Tentamen," are sorry stuff indeed. They show that Hook, during 1819 and the early months of 1820, tasted the lowest depths of Grub Street and lived the sad life of a penny-snatching, scur-rility-dealing political hack writer.

The natural desire of the literary drudge is to establish a magazine or newspaper in order to be regularly employed and to find a constant source of income. Hook felt this desire. He turned naturally to his friends of the stage, trying to find one of them to back him in such a venture. He applied first to Elliston, and seems for a time to have persuaded him. But that actor apparently soon decided otherwise; and Theodore turned to Daniel Terry, who was willing to make the attempt.

In the spring of 1820, Hook and Terry started a small periodical which was printed by the pub-lisher Miller and was to appear monthly. It was called "The Arcadian," a reference not to Sidney but to the Burlington Arcade. Only two numbers of this magazine ever appeared, for Miller had so much difficulty in getting Hook to make up a second that he declined venturing on a third. Certainly the periodical created no interest, for Barham in 1847 or 1848 secured a number, "one of the few copies in existence," only by application to the publisher. From the selections quoted by Barham, it is evident that the "Arcadian" was of the same nature as Hook's next journalistic ven-ture, and formed a fitting prelude to it.

Hook and Terry were immediately filled with ideas for a new periodical of a violently political nature. Miller had no faith in them and was afraid of prosecution — with him, said Hook, all arguments proved "Newgate-ory." They therefore applied to another printer, William Shackell, whom Theodore already knew, for Shackell had printed several of the "Old Tom of Oxford" pamphlets. They agreed to put out a weekly newspaper, to be distributed on Saturday afternoons and dated from the Sunday. Terry seems suddenly to have dropped out of the undertaking, for the proprietorship was divided equally between Hook and Shackell — the former to have entire charge of the editing; the latter to provide the funds, do the printing, and take all the risks and responsibilities. Shackell had two subordinates, Thomas Arrowsmith and R. T. Weaver, who probably ran the presses, and he employed one Henry Fox Cooper to take upon himself the not enviable post of ostensible, or "dummy," editor. Hook's name was to remain a profound secret — the chances for this appearing bright since he had been absent from England for five years and had lived in seclusion since his return. The adoption of these many precautions shows that Hook and his associates knew the risks they were taking.

The first copy of "John Bull" came out on December 17, 1820. Only 750 revenue stamps had been purchased for the first number, but the entire edition was sold out in a few hours. The first and second numbers were kept in stereotype and were very often reprinted. By the fifth week the circulation had risen to above ten thousand copies — about twice that of the daily "Times" and practically equal to that of the very successful weekly newspaper, "Bell's Weekly Messenger." The instant success of "John Bull" was phenomenal; in fact it is unparalleled in the first half of the nineteenth century. The paper exactly caught the public fancy at a given moment.

In form the "John Bull" was not different from other newspapers. It had eight pages (daily newspapers having only four), and it sold for sevenpence. Like other papers, it reported Parliamentary news and King's Bench prosecutions, described *crim. con.* cases and the trials and executions of criminals, quoted extracts from Paris newspapers, occasionally reviewed a play, and had many advertisements. But in the original material — in the leading articles, short items, and humorous poems — the paper aimed frankly at a *succès de scandale*. This original material was all provided by Theodore Hook, the only exception being three or four articles of the utmost propriety written by his brother, James Hook, under the pseudonym of "Fitz Harding."

The focus of "Bull's" attack was the Queen. The first number left no doubt of this: "On the subject of this sickening woman we shall enter into no arguments or discussions, because they go for nothing at this period of her adventures." Moreover, her Whig and Radical adherents were warned: "Scurrility and invective, treason and blasphemy are the weapons which have for a length of time been wielded against our most sacred institutions. The retainers who are employed to fight the fight are far below our mark: — the leaders, the plotters, the hidden directors of this despoiling warfare, are our game: — we will put them up: aye, and please God! knock them over afterwards." The motto was "King and Constitution"; the politics a backward-leaning Toryism.

When "John Bull" began publication, the Queen's side was the popular one. She had retired to Brandenburgh House, where she was receiving the wives of leading Whigs, and enthusiastic deputations of tradesmen presenting memorials. Hook's purpose was threefold. He wished to support the King and his party by attacking the Opposition; he wished to frighten all ladies of quality from visiting the Queen; and he attempted to laugh the populace out of its enthusiasm for her. His tactics were to note the name of every prominent Whig and lady of quality whose name was on

the visitor's list at Brandenburgh House, and then
to rake up from all quarters every bit of calumny
and scandal — nothing was too gross — against
that man or woman, introducing it into his paper
either openly or by innuendo. He did this partly
by short items, and partly by humorous verses set
to some popular air. The latter he threw off easily,
for they were the kind of clever verses he had long
been accustomed to compose extempore at the
piano. Several of these — "Michael's Dinner,"
"The Hunting of the Hare," "Mrs. Muggins's
Visit to the Queen" — became well known. An
idea of their nature may be gathered from the following, the first three stanzas of "Mrs. Muggins's
Visit to the Queen":

Have you been to Brandenburgh — Heigh, Ma'am,
  ho, Ma'am?
      You've been to Brandenburgh, Ho?
        Oh yes, I have been, Ma'am,
        To visit the Queen, Ma'am,
    With the rest of the gallanty show — show,
      With the rest of the gallanty show.

And who were your company — Heigh, Ma'am, ho,
  Ma'am?
      Who were your company, ho?
        — We happened to drop in,
        With Gem'men from Wapping,
    And Ladies from Blowbladder Row — Row,
      And Ladies from Blowbladder Row.

What saw you at Brandenburgh — Heigh, Ma'am, ho,
  Ma'am?
      What saw you at Brandenburgh, ho?
          — We saw a great dame,
          With a face red as flame,
      And a character spotless as snow — snow,
          And a character spotless as snow.

And the first and third stanzas of "The Hunting
of the Hare" are as follows:

Would you hear of the triumph of purity?
      Would you share in the joy of the Queen?
List to my song; and, in perfect security,
      Witness a row where you durst not have been:
              All kinds of Addresses,
              From collars of S. S.'s
              To venders of cresses,
                  Came up like a fair;
              And all thro' September,
              October, November,
              And down to December,
                  They hunted this Hare!

Next in great state came the Countess of Tankerville,
      With all the sons and the daughters she had;
Those who themselves are annoy'd by a canker vile,
      Joy to discover another as bad:
              So Lady Moll came on,
              With *ci-devant* Grammont,
              And (awful as Ammon)
                  Her eloquent spouse!
              And frothy Grey Bennett,
              That very day se'nnight,
              Went down in his dennett
                  To Brandenburgh House.

"John Bull" was of the utmost service to George IV. It angered the Queen's aristocratic followers, but it frightened them as well.

There is a new paper [writes Harriet Countess of Granville, on December 22, 1820], which causes a great sensation. Its object seems to be to frighten women from visiting the Queen. Its name is "John Bull." The first victim is the Duchess of Bedford ... Lady Jersey next, very abusive, Mrs. Brougham's seven months' child. Lady Ossulston a foreigner married to a weak little lord. It is an odious publication both as to its motive and its execution.[1]

And one of the famous Creevey family, all prominent Whigs, wrote on January 15, 1821: "There is the most infamous newspaper just set up that was ever seen in the world — by name 'John Bull.' Its personal scurrility exceeds by miles anything ever written before." [2] The chief victims — Hume, Bennett, Brougham, Alderman Wood, Lady Tankerville, the Duchess of Bedford, Lady Jersey — were furious. Lady Cowper, sister of Lady Palmerston, writes in January, 1821, of the "John Bull":

I am told it is clever but very abusive, and sometimes blackguard. . . . Brougham, like a coward as he is, says blustering that he will knock down anybody who takes it in. . . . Lady Jersey is come to town furious against

---

[1] *Letters of Harriet Countess Granville, 1810–1845* (1894), i, 201.

[2] *The Creevey Papers*, edited by Herbert Maxwell (1904), ii, 1 f.

"John Bull" and all its readers, but nobody minds what she says. . . . Lady Jersey and I are apparently on very good terms, but she is in fact in a devil of a temper — finds people take in "John Bull" in spite of her and will not go to see the Queen although she has given her high authority for its being decent and proper.[1]

"Bull" accomplished another of its purposes also. It cajoled the populace out of its blind and enthusiastic devotion to the Queen. For, writes the Hon. Grantley F. Berkeley in his "Life and Recollections" in 1866:

In the columns of a new Sunday newspaper called the "John Bull," there now appeared facetious communications that did more towards re-establishing a feeling of loyalty in the public mind, than hundreds of Bills of Pains and Penalties could have done. [After "Bull's" lampoons began to raise a general laugh, continues Berkeley], those who were most severely handled by them began to move away. The great Whig families, who had supported the Queen as a party manœuvre only, rapidly withdrew. . . . The "unprotected female" cry could not get a hearing — the "injured wife" appeal only excited unpleasant retorts — and any reference to "the wronged Queen" elicited a burst of mirth. . . . Instead of being ruined by persecution, the Queen had been overthrown by puns; a threatened rebellion had been put down by a discharge of squibs.

There was certain to be talk of higher interests directing this paper which so completely served the cause of the King and the Tories. Even Lock-

---

[1] Mabel, Countess of Airlie, *Lady Palmerston and Her Times* (1922), i, 82 and 86 f.

hart relates that Walter Scott, meeting Hook in April, 1820, liked him so well that he recommended him to a "nobleman of influence and talents" who was about to establish a paper "in an English country town." Lockhart implies that the nobleman was Wellington and that the paper, perhaps, was really the "John Bull." As a matter of fact, His Grace is almost the last man with whom it would be possible to connect "Bull."

Brougham, the leading Whig, implies, in his autobiography, that the paper was inspired by George IV himself — although he does not name the "Bull," and although he exaggeratingly declares (what was not the case) that more than one paper was set up to attack the Queen:

Carlton House now took the course of filling the press with libels to deter all ladies from visiting the Queen. Papers were established with the avowed purpose of attacking every woman of rank who accepted her invitations . . . and I hesitate not to declare that this course was perfectly successful, not merely with the women, but also with their male relations, so as, to my certain knowledge, to influence their votes in both houses.[1]

But George IV had nothing whatever to do with the establishment of "John Bull." Naturally, after it appeared, he was vehemently enthusiastic about it. Croker dined with the King on Jan-

---

[1] *The Life and Times of Henry Lord Brougham, Written by Himself* (New York, 1871), ii, 318.

uary 11, 1822, and afterwards wrote an account of
the evening's conversation in his diary.

> This led him [Croker writes] to "John Bull," which,
> he said, was the only thing in political writing which
> rivalled "Anticipation" and the "Rolliad." I admitted
> that "Bull" had force and sometimes pleasantry, but
> that I thought he wanted taste, which the others pos-
> sessed in an eminent degree; the King would not agree
> in this, and went off into a dissertation on taste and
> genius. Very clever but rambling. He made some really
> just and critical distinctions, but then he, in some pas-
> sages, involved himself to a degree to be hardly intelli-
> gible. He ended, however, by saying that neither he,
> nor his ministers, nor his parliament, nor his courts of
> justice all together, had done so much good as "John
> Bull"; he stated this in a way which surprised me from
> its force and vehemence, and, let me add, exaggeration.
> He then fell upon Judge Bayley, for his sentence on the
> editors of this paper.[1]

The most likely of the place-holding Tories to
have been instrumental in the creation of "John
Bull" is the very gentleman whose words have
just been quoted — John Wilson Croker. His
participation would almost necessarily imply that
of his patron, the Marquis of Hertford, also. Now
there is no doubt that Croker and Hook met several times in 1819 and 1820, and that Theodore
looked upon Croker as his patron and advocate.
But it cannot be allowed that Croker had any interest in, or even foreknowledge of, "John Bull"
— and this for four reasons.

---

[1] *The Croker Papers*, i, 226.

In the first place, in the letter which he wrote on Hook's behalf to the Chancellor of the Exchequer in 1825, Croker says categorically:

He interested me in his case before he was ever suspected of writing a word of politics, and what he may have done in that way has been without my knowledge, and knowing his position, I should have dissuaded him from doing anything to mix himself in politics.

If Croker inspired "John Bull," he is here uttering a deliberate untruth. Such a thing is possible considering the circumstances.[1] But it has just been seen that in his private diary Croker deprecates the King's enthusiastic estimate of the paper. In the second place, at a much later date, when there was no longer the slightest reason for concealment, Hook said to Lord William Pitt Lennox, in reference to the authorship of the articles in "Bull": "Occasionally hints were given and sent me, but this finger and thumb wrote every line."[2] Thirdly, Barham writes that he has the "best grounds" for asserting that Hook and Terry alone and unaided conceived the idea of "Bull." Since Barham's

---

[1] The University of Chicago has recently acquired a number of Hook's letters to Croker. I have examined these, and intend, if opportunity offers, to publish them in the near future. They contain no indications that Croker knew about, or had anything to do with, the "John Bull" or any other of Hook's political writings — except, indeed, the Tentamen, for which he made numerous suggestions. Croker's assertion above is not, therefore, strictly accurate.

[2] Lord William Pitt Lennox, Fifty Years' Biographical Reminiscences (1863), i, 115.

father, Ingoldsby, was perhaps Hook's most intimate friend in the later years, this assertion seems
decisive. Finally, the actual circumstances of the
establishing of the paper are complete, and do not
require — do not, indeed, admit — the supposi-
tion of higher interests involved. Of course, that
the Duke of Wellington, Canning, the Marquis of
Londonderry, Hertford, Croker, and the entire
Tory party, viewed what was happening with considerable complacency does not admit of a moment's doubt.

But "Bull's" victims among the Whigs were by
no means powerless. Henry Grey Bennett had not
only the disposition but the power to strike back
on behalf of himself and the Tankervilles. It was
first necessary to discover the editor of the paper.
Bennett knew that taking a horsewhip, going to
the "Bull" offices, and asking for the editor,
would accomplish little. Indeed, a burly Irishman
had been employed to receive all inquiries with
"Oi'm th' idditer, sir." Theodore himself was
never seen anywhere near those offices; he and
Shackell met at various eating-houses, always
designated in their communications by numbers
previously agreed upon.

Bennett therefore adopted other measures. He
rose in the House of Commons on May 8, 1821,
and accused "Bull" of a breach of privilege because it asserted that he had apologized in Parlia-

ment to a member for fear of being called out by him. He succeeded in having the entire staff of the paper called before the House. But he had no success in discovering the identity of the real editor, for the defendants agreed with an alacrity indicative of long rehearsal in collusion. Seldom has simple perjury been decked in externals so mystifying and amusing as in the evasions and tergiversations of these consummate tacticians. Weaver has just bought the paper from Shackell and Arrowsmith, but no price was fixed and no money paid. He does not know where the editor lives, but his name is Cooper, and he is paid sometimes by him (Weaver), but more often by Arrowsmith and Shackell. Arrowsmith says that he sold the paper to Weaver. For what consideration? None. He owns the presses and pays the rent for the house containing them, but as a favor he allows Weaver to use them gratis. Shackell testifies that Weaver owns the paper and receives all the profits. He (Shackell) and Arrowsmith are to make good all the losses. They also pay Weaver three guineas a week for superintending the printing of his own paper. They pay Weaver's editor sometimes, too. What was that? — Yes, occasionally Shackell *does* receive the profits, but he holds them in trust for Weaver: "I presume it is common for one man to take care of another man's money." Cooper says he is the sole editor. He admits that he wrote the offending article; but he copied part of it from another paper, and made additions from general rumor. It distressed him very, very much when he discovered that the rumor was false — or, perhaps, that it was not in every detail true.

The weary inquisitors were forced to desist. Bennett moved that the public prosecutor, Scarlett, be instructed to bring these defendants before the King's Bench. The administration benches had been remarkably quiet and attentive up to this point. But now, after he had made it perfectly clear that the Tory party by no means countenanced the — the — ah — very lamentable tactics of this paper, the Marquis of Londonderry felt moved to remark that it was scarcely constitutional to worm secrets from witnesses at the bar of the House and then to use such evidence against them in a law court. What it amounted to was sending them to a court with the open condemnation of the House of Commons already branded upon them. Brougham, coming to Bennett's rescue, remarked that although this vile, unspeakable paper had outrageously insulted the dignity of the House by breathing the imputation of cowardice on one of its distinguished members, it might be as well simply to commit these persons to Newgate for breach of privilege. Sir Francis Burdett, sterling champion of free speech, pointed out that this was not a breach of privilege; it was merely a false—and not entirely false—report of a speech. Bennett then withdrew his motion. Londberry said that he could not be extremely incensed over this affront against the dignity of Parliament because he had listened in vain on previous occasions for Whig protests when libels had been poured upon the Tories; and, although, to be sure, this was not in any way whatever a party question — certainly not — yet "he would again assert that there were libels not less flagrant against Majesty itself unnoticed by the Noble Lord [Brougham] and his friends; and that in this country an attack upon the Sovereign was considered at least as atrocious as an attack upon the female character." But Parliament had to do something to avoid being laughed at. So, by a division of 109 to 23, Cooper was sent to jail to remain there till the prorogation of Parliament two months later; Weaver was reprimanded; and Arrowsmith and Shackell were discharged.

In the law courts "Bull" was frequently assailed. On February 25, 1821, he was brought before the King's Bench for a libel *on the memory of* Lady Caroline Wrottesley, born Lady Caroline Bennett, daughter of the Earl of Tankerville! [1] Weaver was fined £100; Shackell and Arrowsmith, £500, each; they were all given nine months in

---

[1] A general principle in English law at the present time is that there can be no libel against a deceased person.

jail, and were forced to find securities for good be-
havior for five years. The libel was indecent and
indefensible, but "Bull" declared that many
papers had printed the same thing and that he
alone had been prosecuted. Some time later the
same defendants were cast in heavy damages at
the suit of one Alderman Waithman. In January,
1822, they were found not guilty of a libel against
Lady Jersey, but they escaped only through a
technicality. In the same month they were prosecuted on an unbelievable charge — a libel *against
the dead Queen, Caroline!* Men like Denman and
Brougham could, as counsel for the prosecution,
say of "Bull's" attacks on Caroline: "He did not
hesitate to say that the natural consequences were
to embitter the life of Her Majesty and shorten
her days. It was not in the nature of the female
character to stand up against such repeated attacks." This when Caroline had been the subject
of official and private persecution for years, and
after she had been brought to trial for marital in-
fidelity! Conviction followed, and the suffering
trio had three more months and further fines added
to their sentences.

Bennett and his group used every means of persecution in their power. In September, 1824, the
sheriffs of London and Middlesex entered "Bull's"
offices with writs of execution for the fines for the
libels against Lady Wrottesley and Queen Caro-

line. They occupied the building for a day, despite the fact that they were shown the receipts for the payment of the fines. "Bull" made many large editorial assertions as to what he was going to do to the authors of this outrage. But he soon found that nothing could be done, because it would have been necessary to petition the Lords of the Treasury for the names of those who swore out the writs. That body would never have furnished them. In a letter to the "Morning Chronicle" the Master of the Crown Office freely admitted that these fines had been paid. The name of this gentleman was Edmund Henry Lushington; he will soon be met again as chairman of the Colonial Audit Board which tried the case of Hook's Mauritius defalcation. Thus it must be concluded about the whole miserable business of libel suits and private persecution, that, if the slanders of "Bull" are repugnant to present-day notions of decency, the Whig reprisals are equally repugnant to our sense of justice. And one is forced to admire the hardihood of Cooper, Weaver, Arrowsmith, and Shackell, all of whom endured imprisonment, paid fines, and provided peace bonds, and, in spite of offers of immunity and bribe money (Barham has it for certain that such offers were made), never suffered a syllable to pass their lips concerning the author of all these libels for which they were being punished — Theodore Edward Hook.

But there is reason to believe that the secret was not so airtight as was to be desired. It could do no harm for a few Tories like Hertford and Croker to discover the identity of the real editor. But Lady Palmerston's sister, in January, 1821 (in a letter previously quoted from), wrote quite casually:

"There is a new paper published in England, called the 'John Bull,' which makes everybody very angry. *The editor is Theodore Hook.*" The truth was probably pretty well understood — so much so that the paper on January 21, 1821, attempted the ancient ruse of printing, with a few contemptuous remarks, a pretended disclaimer from Theodore. That Henry Grey Bennett knew who the editor was, cannot be doubted. There is no other way to account for his activity in the Mauritius affair. Since the Tories dared do nothing, Hook was simply handed over to Bennett. Worse still, the head of the Colonial Audit Board and its only permanent member, was none other than the Whig Edmund Henry Lushington. If the letters and reports of this board are read, one's opinion is confirmed that Lushington knew what was expected of him, and that the investigation of Hook's deficit, after the beginning of 1821, became a piece of political and private persecution. As such many certainly viewed it at the time. "I well know that it cannot be helped," wrote Croker to Lushington on January 2, 1823. "I well know

that the Treasury *dare* not do for him what they
would do for a Whig, and I am aware of the deli-
cacy of your position, but as I believe in my soul
that he is persecuted because he is suspected of
being the writer of 'John Bull,' that alone is with
me a sufficient motive to do all I can to defeat the
unjust persecution."[1] And in the sixth number of
the "Noctes Ambrosianae," appearing in "Blackwood's Magazine" in December, 1822, the following conversation takes place between Tickler
(Robert Syme) and Christopher North (J. Wilson):

Tickler. — How despicable is Bennett's persecution
of Theodore Hook. Lord! had Hook been a Whig, like
Tom Moore, how little we should have heard of this.

North. — Why to be sure, Hook and Moore stand
precisely in the same situation — both of them clever
men — both of them wits — both of them sent out to
manage Colonial matters, — both of them meeting with
queerish underlings — both of their underlings cutting
their throats on detection — and then both of them deprived of their offices, and in arrear to the public, not
through any purloining of their own, but through circumstances which every one must regret as much as
themselves.

Tickler. — Aye, but here stops the parallel. Mr.
Moore is pitied by everybody, and no Tory ever alluded,
or will allude, to his misfortunes in the House; while Mr.
Hook is, week after week, and year after year, made the
subject of attack by all that contemptible fry of the
Bennetts, Humes, and so forth.

In August, 1821, the Queen fell ill, and "Bull"
immediately declared that he would attack her no

---

[1] *The Croker Papers,* i, 239 f.

more. Her death soon after took away most of the paper's reason for existence. But Hook and Shackell were making two thousand pounds a year each from it, and this was not lightly given up. Some attention was still paid to Whigs and Radicals, but, by the end of 1822, "John Bull" had become an ordinary Tory newspaper, never again in trouble with the authorities. It later included among its contributors the poet, Thomas Haynes Bayley, and Ingoldsby Barham.

In 1823 the prosperous "Bull" bought up some half-dozen other papers, and brought over William Maginn from Cork to conduct a Wednesday newspaper upon their ruins. The attempt failed. A literary journal under "Bull's" auspices also failed. In 1825 Shackell attempted to revive the old "European Magazine," which, however, under the editorship of Hook's old friend Dubois, quickly died a second and final death.

By 1825, as a glance at the pages of "John Bull" will show, Hook's enthusiasm had cooled. He was now the avowed editor; concealment was no longer necessary. But he was now devoting his best efforts to the writing of novels. Besides, the regularity of the labor imposed by the paper disturbed his week-end visits to the houses of the socially great. "Shackell was rather fond," writes Henry Vizetelly in a book of reminiscences in 1893,

of talking of the time when Hook would be spending the
autumn on a round of country visits to his aristocratic
friends, and he had to go and meet him regularly every
week, posting across country to some beggarly little inn
near the grand house where Hook was installed. Glad
enough at having been able to secure even these humble
quarters, he waited patiently until Hook could steal
away from his gay companions to read through the
proofs Shackell had brought with him, and discuss and
decide upon the contents of the forthcoming number of
"John Bull." [1]

And Hook's debts soon forced him to sell half his
moiety for four thousand pounds. He retained the
editorship at a salary until his death, but his income from "Bull" became very small as the circulation of the paper gradually fell away. At a
later date, Samuel Carter Hall assumed for a term
the sub-editorship. He writes: "In 1836, some
years before, and during the years afterwards, no
paragraph was inserted that in the remotest degree
assailed private character." No longer were slander and vituperation employed. Hook's advice to
Hall, "on more than one occasion while acting
under him, was to remember that abuse seldom
effectively answered a purpose, and that it was
wiser as well as safer to act on the principle that
'praise undeserved is satire in disguise.'" [2]

---

[1] Henry Vizetelly, *Glances Back Through Seventy Years*
(1893), i, 177.

[2] "Memories of Authors: Theodore Hook and His Friends,"
Atlantic Monthly, vol. xv (April, 1865).

It must be repeated, in conclusion, that Theodore Hook's plunge into base politics and his connection with the "John Bull" were not fortunate undertakings. The storm and stress period of his newspaper lasted for two years. His attacks, during this time, upon the virtue of the women who befriended the Queen were recognized as outrageous even in those days. There were worse papers, of course. Even "Bull's" enemies scarcely classed him with two malodorous publications — Bernard Gregory's "Satirist" and Charles Molloy Westmacott's "Age." "Bull" did not accept blackmail. Yet the slanders Theodore inserted in his paper were malicious enough. They directly occasioned his Shire Lane imprisonment, which permanently ruined his health. They enabled his enemies to picture him as a craven rascal dealing out blows in the dark, breathing vile slanders on happy families, toadying to the administration by defaming the opposition, and receiving in return his just deserts. They enabled men like Samuel Carter Hall, the original of Dickens's Pecksniff, to record with satisfaction things like the following:

It is said, and I believe with truth, that Sir Robert Wilson (who had almost weekly been assailed with venom) one day met Hook in the street, when a conversation to this effect took place: "Hook," said Sir Robert, "I am to be attacked next Sunday in the 'John Bull.'" "Are you?" answered Hook. . . . "It is true, however," said Sir Robert. . . . "Now mind what I say,

Hook. I know you have nothing to do with the 'John Bull': you have told me so half a dozen times; but if that article appears, as surely as you live, I'll horsewhip you wherever I find you!" The article never did appear.[1]

Thus Theodore played with pitch and he was mucked. When one sees a contemptuous reference to him, it is most probable that his connection with the "John Bull" of 1821 and 1822 is the moving cause of the critic's attitude. Theodore's friends may allege that he simply handled more ably the same weapons that all political writers then used and that the end he wished to attain demanded violent measures — but they cannot really defend his slanders. The most unfortunate aspect of the matter is that politics forced Hook to be false to his own nature. Was he hasty, rash, committing ill-judged and ill-timed acts? Yes. But bitter, rancorous, treacherous, and venomous? No. His nature was charitable, generous, and warm-hearted.

The products of Theodore Hook's pen which appeared in "John Bull" might be expunged without great loss. His "leaders" are characterized by a dogmatism, a jaunty, dictatorial cocksureness, doing duty for energy, a general absence of fair dealing, a striving for theatrical effect, a blatant speciousness, all well worked by riders of the

---

[1] Samuel Carter Hall, *Retrospect of a Long Life*, New York (1883), p. 71.

journalistic high horses of the first half of the nineteenth century; discernible alike in the pamphlet
of the scarcely literate hack and in the essay of
Macaulay. His poetic satires on the Queen and the
Whigs, although they are more clever than would
appear to one not familiar with the back-stairs
gossip of the time, have passed into oblivion with
the events they recounted. They are now (the
metaphor is trite) but the lava of a long-extinct
volcano. Nor are his book reviews and humorous
prose articles worthy of particular mention, except
the note that his political principles required him
to attack Tom Moore, Leigh Hunt, and Byron.
Politics and not literature directed his opinions in
the books that he reviewed. His "Ramsbottom
Papers" — a series of travel letters from Dorothea Ramsbottom, who saw the "Vacuum at
Rome," lived in Paris in the "Rue de la Pay, so
called from its being the dearest part of the town,"
and saw a priest "exercising the spirits in an old
lady" — contain humorous passages and proved
very popular. But Dorothea's prototypes, Wini-
fred Jenkins in "Humphrey Clinker" and Mrs.
Malaprop, are in no danger of displacement.

Theodore Hook's career as a novelist began
early in 1824.[1] Between this date and 1841, the

---

[1] It will be remembered that as a youth of twenty, in 1808,
he published his first novel, "The Man of Sorrow."

year of his death, he wrote nine full novels and
three sets of shorter pieces, and there was one collection of his brief tales and sketches. After 1824,
then, it is as a novelist that Hook's name is of most
importance to English literature. He engaged in
various other literary undertakings, but his best
efforts were devoted to the writing of novels.

In 1826 Theodore was employed by the publisher, Colburn, to compose from rough notes and
oral dictation a work entitled "The Reminiscences
of Michael Kelly, of the King's Theatre Royal
Drury Lane, including a period of nearly half a
century; with original anecdotes of many distinguished persons, political, literary and musical."
Hook had known Kelly rather intimately for
many years. The finished two-volume work received a kindly notice from Sir Walter Scott in the
"Quarterly Review." The reminiscences, in fact,
do present a good picture of the life of a singer and
actor in Italy, Vienna, and London, in the closing
years of the eighteenth century, and they are a
necessary reference when the history of the stage
or the life of an actor of the period are under consideration. But Kelly professed himself not entirely pleased. His temperament may be judged
from the complaint he made to Cyrus Redding:
"But you could not read what that rascal Hook
omitted. Why, I don't know. The infernal book-
seller employed him to put my memoirs through

the press, and he omitted things he had no right to leave out — touched his friends, I suppose." [1] Theodore had, in particular, rightly omitted a long and insipid account of how one of Kelly's friends outwitted a pursuing bailiff by digging a hole through the wall of a room and escaping into the neighboring house.

In 1832 the publisher Bentley commissioned Hook to write the life of Sir David Baird, who, in the course of one life, suffered captivity in India, was the hero of Seringapatam, commanded an English force in Egypt in 1801, captured the Cape of Good Hope from the Dutch in 1806, was involved in the Sir Home Popham fiasco at Buenos Aires, helped capture the Danish fleet in 1807, was second in command under the ill-fated Sir John Moore in the Peninsula, and lost an arm at Coruña. Such a life lends itself to vigorous narration, and Hook's two-volume "Life of General, the Right Honourable Sir David Baird, Bart." does possess considerable vigor and some dramatic passages. But this dramatic quality, combined with the purely eulogistic intention of the author, removes the work from the realm of history, as the present day knows that word. Shortly after its appearance, five letters signed "Investigator" were written to the "Asiatic Journal." These letters — which were published in pamphlet form in

---

[1] Cyrus Redding, *Fifty Years' Recollections* (1858), ii, 311.

1834 with the title "Letters Commenting upon Mr. Theodore Hook's Memoirs of the Life of Sir David Baird. By Investigator" — criticize adversely that part of Hook's biography which treats of Baird's life in India. "Investigator" — who was, almost without doubt, Lieutenant-General Sir Colin Macaulay — characterizes Hook's work as follows:

Mr. Hook's biographical memoir should have borne the title of "A Panegyric on Sir David Baird"; for such certainly has been the settled purpose of the biographer in the compilation. Like an advocate in Westminster Hall, who boldly asserts the purity and justice of his client and his case *per fas et nefas*, this biographer holds up Sir David, from his cradle to his grave, as a perfect and peerless character, and represents him to have judged and acted wisely on every occasion; while those who held opinions at variance with his, or opposed his views, — whether cabinet-ministers, or East-India Directors, or governors, or commanders-in-chief, or secretaries, or historians, — each and all without exception, were, it seems, actuated by sinister and disreputable motives.

In general, "Investigator's" comments are just. But he does not disprove Hook's specific contentions that Lord Cornwallis, by choosing Major Gowdie, and General Harris, by appointing Colonel Wellesley, on occasions when Baird was the superior and senior officer, were guilty of injustice to Baird. Hook's hero, unfortunately, was one of those Indian officers over whose heads the Governor-General, Lord Wellesley, pushed his brother, Arthur, later Duke of Wellington.

The Baird family was highly pleased with the work. They sent the biographer a letter of thanks, together with a package which he carelessly tossed into a bureau drawer. He later discovered that the package contained an exceedingly valuable diamond-studded snuff-box, which had been presented to Baird by the Pasha of Egypt. It became one of Theodore's most treasured possessions.

Colburn was the owner and publisher of the "New Monthly Magazine," which he had inaugurated in 1814 as a Tory rival to Sir Richard Phillips's Whig "Monthly Magazine." [1] It had never had an editor. But in January, 1821, the "New Monthly" came out in an altered form, with Thomas Campbell, the poet, as editor. The poet was almost ludicrously unfit for the office. P. G. Patmore writes of him in connection with this position:

In temperament indolent, capricious and uncertain, yet hasty, sensitive, wilful, and obstinate in giving his will its way; his habits of composition slow to a degree of painfulness; his literary taste refined, even to fastidiousness; and, above all, his personal position as the friend and associate of nearly all the distinguished litterateurs

---

[1] This, as we should say, dishonest practice of taking the name of a rival publication with the prefix "New," in order to share its popularity and perhaps confuse subscribers, was not infrequent then, although it was condemned by many.

of the day, and his almost morbid sensitiveness on the point of giving pain, or even displeasure to any of them; — Campbell was, and knew himself to be, the ideal of what the proffered office required its occupant *not* to be.[1]

But Colburn wanted the reputation Campbell's name would bring. Edward Dubois was even employed to assist in bringing out the first number. But the real work of editing was done by Cyrus Redding, the sub-editor. The principal contributors were Robert Hunt, brother of Leigh, Sam Beazley, and Thomas Noon Talfourd. This arrangement endured until 1830, when Redding lost his position, and Samuel Carter Hall was substituted. Campbell retired two months later, and Hall became sole editor. In 1832 Edward Bulwer-Lytton accepted the editorship, with Hall as assistant. Bulwer made the magazine intensely Liberal, frightening its aged Tory subscribers. The circulation decreased from 5,000 to 4,000, and Bulwer resigned at the end of the year, leaving Hall again in complete charge.

Theodore Hook's connection with the magazine began in 1834, with the publication of a short tale called "Magpie Castle." Very soon thereafter appeared in instalments his novel "Gilbert Gurney," and a series of sketches and stories under the

---

[1] P. G. Patmore, *My Friends and Acquaintance* (1854), i, 109 f.

general title of "Precept and Practice." In 1835 he began to write the "Monthly Commentary," a series of animadversions on passing events.

In 1836, Richard Bentley, formerly the partner but now the bitter rival of Colburn, announced a humorous magazine, or rather, a miscellany in which the humorous element should predominate, to be called "Bentley's Miscellany." This alarmed Colburn so much that he immediately sought out Hook and paid him £400 as a year's salary in advance, to be editor of a rival magazine. Of the events that followed there is only the testimony of Samuel Carter Hall, who was one of those directly interested in them. Hall, naturally enough, did not agree with Colburn's plan, for it would certainly ruin the "New Monthly" without ensuring the success of the new magazine. Colburn, half won over, went to Hook, who, Hall says, signified his inability to pay back the money, but offered to work it off as editor of the "New Monthly." Colburn agreed to this, but Hall refused again to become sub-editor. He was assured, thereupon, he says, that his title would be that of co-editor. So matters stood until, one evening, Colburn gave a dinner for the magazine's contributors. Then, writes Hall:

After dinner Mr. Forster rose and proposed the health of Mr. Theodore Hook, *the* editor of the "New Monthly Magazine." It was news to more than one of the guests. I at once said: "Forster, I can not drink that toast. If Mr. Hook is editor of the 'New Monthly Magazine,' I have no business here." Some confusion ensued, and Poole sought to pour oil on troubled waters by proposing my health in kindly and complimentary terms. But the end of it was, I received from Mr. Colburn a few days afterward a check for a year's instead of a half-year's salary. My connection with the "New Monthly" ceased, and Mr. Theodore Hook became editor of that magazine. Mr. Colburn and I parted good friends, nor had I any misunderstanding with Mr. Hook.[1]

No; the true original of Pecksniff had no misunderstanding with Theodore Hook in spite of the fact that in his memoirs he consistently belittles Hook's character. In fact, there is one small matter he has not seen fit to dilate upon. Being entirely out of a position after leaving Colburn's magazine, he accepted from Hook for a year the sub-editorship of "John Bull," but he says nothing about Theodore's kindness in creating a position for him to fill for a year while he was looking about for some other literary employment. And Hall's story sounds somewhat queer. Why should he object to the position of sub-editor under Hook of the magazine, and immediately after accept the same position under him on the newspaper? The probable truth of the matter is that Colburn, alarmed by Bentley's project, feared that the

---

[1] Hall, *Retrospect of a Long Life*, p. 184.

latter would win away the "New Monthly's" most important contributor and the country's outstanding humorist — namely, Hook; and so hastened to secure him by paying him a year's salary to edit a rival magazine. When the project was abandoned, Colburn, wishing to assure himself above all that Hook would not go over to Bentley, offered him the editorship of the "New Monthly." Hall, thinking himself indispensable, refused to accept the plan, brought the matter to an issue, and lost his position. And it would appear that Colburn and Hook did everything in their power to placate Hall.

In January, 1837, Hook's first number of the "New Monthly Magazine" appeared. The design of partially matching "Bentley's Miscellany" — the first number of which, with Charles Dickens as editor, appeared in the same month — was attempted by calling a part of each number "The Humorist." This part contained humorous poems and sketches. But the design was abandoned at the beginning of 1838. Among Hook's contributors from 1837 to 1841 were Douglas Jerrold, Captain Marryat, Leigh Hunt, James and Horatio Smith, Thomas Haynes Bayley, Poole the author of "Paul Pry," T. C. Grattan, Gleig the author of the "Subaltern," Thomas Campbell, Mrs. Samuel Carter Hall, Planché the dramatist, Horace Twiss, the Countess of Blessington, Mrs. Norton, Lady

Morgan, W. M. Thackeray, D. M. Moir, and (heavily in 1840) Laman Blanchard and Thomas Hood. Mrs. Trollope's novel, "The Widow Married," appeared in instalments, as did also the novel "Peter Priggins," which appeared anonymously both here and later in book form, but which was the work of the Reverend James J. Hewlett. In the magazine in 1837 came out Hook's "Gurney Papers," a continuation of his novel "Gilbert Gurney"; and, in 1840 and 1841, appeared another novel of his, "Fathers and Sons." He contributed also many short stories (later collected in book form with the title "Precept and Practice"), and several articles — including a lengthy one entitled "Elements of Conversation; or, Talking Made Easy," in which he poses as the master of witty repartee. After Hook's death in 1841, Thomas Hood assumed the editorship. Colburn later sold the magazine to the novelist, William Harrison Ainsworth.

The quality of the magazine did not deteriorate during Hook's incumbency as editor. The proportion of narrative material in each issue was increased, but this was certainly done with deliberation — perhaps again to match "Bentley's Miscellany." And although Hook was paid (in addition to his salary) for every one of his contributions, he did not flood the magazine with the productions of his own pen. Since the magazine circulated chiefly among old ladies and stolid old Tory gentlemen, nothing was put into any number which could possibly offend the most rigid sense of propriety. Leigh Hunt amusingly writes in his "Autobiography":

After all, swearing was once seriously objected to me, and I had given cause for it. I must own that I even begged hard to be allowed a few oaths. It was for an article in a magazine (the "New Monthly"), where I had to describe a fictitious person, whose character I thought required it, and I pleaded truth to nature, and the practise of the good old novelists; but in vain. The editor was not to be entreated. He was Mr. Theodore Hook.

The editor of "John Bull" is now the pillar of propriety!

During the last four or five years of his life, Theodore's financial affairs were desperate, and he turned to anything which would yield him a few pounds without much labor — for his time was fully taken up with his social engagements, his novels, "John Bull," and the "New Monthly." Thus he allowed several works to come out with the inscription, "Edited by Theodore Hook"; that is, he sold his name, since it had commercial value. He would also puff these works in his newspaper and his magazine. The details of this "editing" may be gathered from a letter he wrote in 1841 to Croker, concerning a biography of Townshend which neither of them had written: "The

terms you mentioned were fifty guineas for copyright (£100 being asked), with your help I might
for my name get the other £50, unless you would
put in your own, in which case my part would be
only that of master of ceremonies to introduce Mr.
Townshend to Mr. Colburn." [1] Certainly a quick
and convenient method of acquiring money at the
expense of an obscure author!

In this way Hook wrote a preface and put his
name to a translation of Dumas's "Pascal Bruno,"
published by Colburn in 1837 — although he may
also have done the translating. In 1840 his name
appeared as editor of a novel called "Cousin
Geoffrey," published by Bentley. The author,
Harriet Maria Gordon Smythies (whose name did
not appear on the work), evidently admired Hook
greatly, for the heroine of the story reads a novel
by Hook, and the author dedicated to him her
next novel, "The Marrying Man," of 1841. Theodore also lent his name in 1840 to Hewlett's novel
"Peter Priggins, the College Scout" — most of
which had appeared by instalments in the "New
Monthly." In 1841 Colburn brought out a translation of a work, very popular in France, which
purported to be the memoirs of the French actor,
Fleury.[2] To this translation, entitled (in the first

---

[1] *The Croker Papers*, ii, 196.

[2] *La Grande Encyclopédie* (article "Fleury") writes of the
work: "Un ecrivain, nommé J. B. Lafitte, a publié sous ce

edition) "The French Stage and the French People," Hook appended a few footnotes and placed his name on the title-page as editor.

Theodore Hook planned, or began, several pieces of work that he did not finish. About 1837 he put forth a prospectus concerning a "History of Hanover." It is probable that this work was suggested by Ernest, Duke of Cumberland, one of the sons of George III, who became King of Hanover in 1837, for Hook dined often with this personage. The work, at any rate, never took shape; and, writes Barham, "whether he would ever have found time, or even patience, for the research and labour necessarily involved in such an undertaking is doubtful."

When Charles Mathews died, in 1835, Mrs. Mathews turned naturally to Hook as the proper man to write the comedian's biography. Theodore agreed; he was to be paid five hundred pounds for the work. He wrote the first chapter — Barham had that chapter before him when he wrote his biography of Hook. Then, however, a difficulty arose. The busy and harrassed Theodore wished to write only the usual two-volume biography,

---

titre: 'Memoirs de Fleury, de la Comedie-Française' (1835–37, 6 vol. en -8) un livre d'ailleurs intéressant, dont il a été fait plusieurs editions. Cet ecrivain prétendit qu'il avait redigé ces memoires d'apres des notes et des papiers laissés par Fleury. Cela semble peu probable, car il est de notoriété publique que Fleury etait a peu pres illetré."

while Mrs. Mathews stood out for three volumes. Hook thereupon resigned the work into the hands of the widow. Her "Memoirs of Charles Mathews" came out in four volumes and was immensely successful. The disagreement between the two was amicable, for Mrs. Mathews in her pages shows nothing but respect and admiration for Hook.

In a letter to his friend, William John Broderip, in December, 1839, Theodore writes that he is "doing a life of Garrick"; but this work was probably never actually begun. And Hook also contemplated a history of London, or of old London buildings and streets; for John Timbs, the famous popularizer, writes that, in the sale of Hook's books after his death, "Ackermann's 'Microcosm of London,' three vols. with many plates, possessed peculiar interest from having been filled with his manuscript notes, made in 1834, when he contemplated writing an account of the streets of London." [1] Hook may have intended such a work as a contribution to the publications of the Antiquarian Society, of which he was a member.

Together with Scott, Lamb, Lockhart, and Maginn, Theodore Hook contributed to William Harrison Ainsworth's annual, "The Christmas

---

[1] John Timbs, *Anecdote Lives of Wits and Humourists* (1872), ii, 341.

Box," in 1828. His contribution was a poem called "Cautionary Verses to Youth of Both Sexes" — a punning warning to children to beware of the evil habit of punning. In 1834, Hook's friend, Henry Angelo, collected a series of stories by various hands, and published them with the title, "Angelo's Picnic; or, Table Talk." In this collection is Hook's short story "Boots," which concerns the comic mistake of an inn-keeper in believing a guest to be the Prince of Orange because of an inscription in his boots. Hook used this same incident in his novel "Gilbert Gurney," on which he was engaged just a short time later. Theodore also helped to inaugurate two magazines. To the opening number of "Sharpe's London Magazine," in 1839, edited by Allan Cunningham (and abandoned after the third number), he contributed a story called "The Splendid Annual" — a humorous account of how Alderman Scropps's wonderful year as Lord Mayor made him ever after discontented with the life of an ordinary citizen. This incident, also, Hook retold in "Gilbert Gurney." For the first number (January, 1837) of "Bentley's Miscellany," edited by Dickens, Theodore wrote a sketch of the life of George Colman the younger.

Hook's political principles and his friendships associated him with the "Quarterly Review" edited by Lockhart, "Fraser's Magazine" edited

by William Maginn, and "Blackwood's Magazine" published in Edinburgh. He had no relations with the Whig, or Liberal, "Edinburgh Review." For the "Quarterly" he wrote one, and, on
the authority of Lockhart, only one, article — a
lengthy review in 1832 of Prince Puckler-Muskau's
account of his tour in England.[1] With Thackeray,
Hogg, Ainsworth, and many others, Hook is in
Maclise's famous picture of the "Fraserians."
That Hook should have contributed to a magazine
run by his intimate friend Maginn, seems likely,
but a search through the early volumes of "Fraser's" fails to reveal anything which bears his
imprint. Likewise, Ingoldsby Barham wrote for
"Blackwood's"; and Wilson's "Noctes Ambrosianae," in that periodical, supports heartily the
"John Bull," and contains many references to
Hook — even an imaginary evening with "Mr.
Theodore" as guest (no. 45, July, 1829). But there
is no evidence of any article by Hook in that
magazine. Of course, perhaps the bulk of the
periodical articles of these years is anonymous,
and in the case of the more or less standardized
book reviews it is almost out of the question to
detect an individual hand. It is surely possible
that, between the years 1828, when his fame had
become established as a novelist, and 1834, when

---

[1] Dickens is supposed to have caricatured this prince as
Count Smorltork in the *Pickwick Papers*.

he became the chief contributor of the "New Monthly," Hook may have contributed to "Fraser's" and to "Blackwood's," as well as to other periodicals which have sunk from sight, and to the immensely popular Christmas "annuals" of various sorts.

Among Hook's papers after his death was found an envelope on which he had written "Letters to me as author of the 'Doctor.'" This envelope contained acknowledgements from Disraeli, Wordsworth, and others for presentation copies of that novel. It contained one *from Southey himself!* Ingoldsby, who investigated the matter by inquiring at the house of the publisher, Longmans, and by writing to Southey's widow, concluded that the Laureate wrote the novel (the first volume was published in 1834), but that he had never disclosed his name to Longmans; that Southey had anonymously directed that all communications respecting the work should be sent to Hook; and that Hook had nothing to do with the composition of the novel. "The reader will have observed from various passages in my father's letters," writes the Reverend Charles Cuthbert Southey,

the extreme pains and trouble he had taken to conceal the true authorship of "The Doctor"; the publication of this book, and the mystification about it, in which he contrived to involve so many people, being one of his chief sources of amusement — indeed his only recreation during his later years.

But Theodore, prince of contrivers of hoaxes, whom Southey intended to make the chief victim, did not respond to the joke; for, continues the Laureate's son and biographer:

It was hoped he [Hook] would have spoken of this hoax being passed upon him, and thus have given a fair pretext for fixing the authorship upon him. It does not appear, however, that he took up the joke with any zest, or that the matter was heard of until the letters were found among his papers after his death.[1]

The history of Southey's poem "The Devil's Walk" shows that the poet had a taste for this form of mystification.

---

[1] *The Life and Correspondence of Robert Southey*, edited by his son, Rev. Charles Cuthbert Southey (1850), vi, 337 and 339.

CHAPTER VI.

SOCIAL LIFE (1819–1841).

WHEN Theodore Hook returned to London in January, 1819, after his absence of over five years, his father was still playing the organ at Vauxhall. It was not until the summer of 1820 that the old composer retired from the exertions of a long and busy life, and went to spend his remaining years across the Channel in Boulogne. Without doubt Theodore crossed to see him before his death in 1827 — in fact, Mrs. Ramsbottom's adventures in France were certainly suggested by her creator's own experiences there. After the composer's death, his widow returned to England, but her relations with her stepson seem to have been neither extended nor friendly.

For a period of about four years after his return from Mauritius, Hook felt his position keenly and endeavored to avoid all except a few tried old friends. He lived during this time at various places and in considerable obscurity. He did not take up residence again in Charlotte Street, Bedford Square, where he had passed his boyhood. The Colonial Audit Board was frequently at a loss where to find him; it most frequently directed its summons to Kentish Town. From his lodgings at this place, Hook wrote to Mathews in 1822: "Owing to my hurried circumstances, I have been very little here of late, and next week propose quitting it altogether." He next moved to Somers Town, and here he remained until his arrest in 1823.

While he was living in almost friendless obscurity in Somers Town, he formed a connection with a young woman which endured until his death. She always remained faithful to him, and she was the mother of his five children. The connection was thus a marriage in fact, and Hook should have added legality to it by going through the marriage ceremony. For he felt the obligation he had assumed. Lockhart, upon inspecting Hook's manuscript journal, or diary, writes of the years after 1819, that his "affections were twice during the period deeply and seriously engaged," but that on each occasion "there occurred something to press on him the claims of that which, as he words it, 'He felt to be, yet could not bear to call, his home.'" Since he was unwilling or unable to abandon his mistress, he should, indeed, have married her. As it is, the most that can be said for him is that what he did was certainly not unknown or greatly reprobated then, and that he did not outrage popular opinion, as Shelley and Byron did, by any public display.

In truth, Theodore Hook was not a ladies' man. Before his departure for Mauritius he had experienced several affairs of the heart. Two of these early attachments were more serious. "One of them," writes the author of a sketch of Hook's life prefixed to Colburn's edition of his novel "Fathers and Sons,"

was the beautiful daughter of a retired actor, whose suppers in those days were celebrated for the wit which sparkled at the table — and the other was the daughter of a gallant deceased general whom he had met during a visit at Taunton. The former was afterwards married to a member of a noble house, and still lives the ornament of the circle in which she moves; and the latter became the wife of one of our celebrated legal characters, who has since been sollicitor-general and a judge, and has now been dead some years. Taunton will long remember the period of this courtship; for his mad pranks and his facetious sallies kept the whole town alive during the time he was one of its denizens.

Attracted and smitten young Hook may have been in these cases. But, considering his extreme youth at the time and his lack of a steady occupation, it is hard to believe that he had contemplated marriage. In fact, to repeat, it is difficult to associate Theodore with amatory adventure of the romantic variety. He respected women of position, and he entertained them pleasantly in the presence of their men. But they almost invariably distrusted and disliked him, and were not at all disposed to coquette with him. Perhaps women are instinctively suspicious of clever and witty men; perhaps they did not understand his jokes; perhaps they thought him an unsettling influence upon their men. As for Theodore himself — he much preferred the easy manners of the dining-room after the ladies had retired.

During his confinement at the squalid Shire Lane sponging house, where his bailiff had the interesting name of Mr. Hemp, Hook's constant visitor was William Maginn. It was through this intelligent but improvident and intemperate Irishman that Hook probably did most of his communicating with Shackell about "John Bull" — for Maginn had been brought over from Ireland by "Bull." This Shire Lane confinement permanently ruined Theodore's health, for he took no exercise and he indulged heavily in alcoholic liquors. "He came out," says Lockhart, "pale and flabby in the face, and with a figure fast tending to corpulence."

After his discharge from custody in the spring of 1825, he engaged a house at Putney and remained there during two very happy years. He began gradually to emerge from his seclusion — to recover old acquaintances and to acquire new ones. He was beginning to be sought out, not only for his unrivalled powers of entertainment, but as a popular and successful novelist, and as the undoubted, if unconfessed, editor of an influential

Tory newspaper with a large circulation. The lazy days in company with an intimate friend on the Thames — the fishing, the rowing up to Ditton, the stops at the ale-signs — must have been doubly sweet after his long confinement. His money was rapidly accumulating, for his income, from 1824 to 1828, could hardly have been less than three thousand each year.

But he made a mistake — another mistake. After Walter Scott had won his first successes, he began to buy up poor land at high prices and to erect the money-absorbing Abbotsford. In 1827, Theodore Hook, similarly situated, decided to move to the heart of London and set up a fashionable establishment. There is no greater curse for a man of sanguine temperament than to have thrust upon him for a few years a large yearly income. Of course, there was little reason for Hook to attempt to save money even if he had possessed the disposition to do so. The government always held over him the overwhelming Mauritius defalcation. At its pleasure, at any time, his belongings could be seized and sold for the benefit of the Treasury. Should he have tried to pay back his deficit to the government? He could never have amassed twelve thousand pounds. If he had tried to pay all he could, would the government have cancelled the remainder? They would perhaps have wished to do so, but the wish could never have been carried out because of the Whigs. Moreover, to expect Hook, with two years of imprisonment still rankling within him, to become a humble debtor, is to ask too much of human nature. And to pay even one pound would have been an admission of guilt.

The London house that Theodore selected was No. 5 Cleveland Row, just opposite St. James's. Sir Sidney Smith, the naval officer, had lived there in 1810. It was the property of Lord Lowther, but the lease was owned at this time by the novelist, Captain Marryat. After taking up residence here, Theodore launched himself into society. He was rapidly elected to the most notable of the many clubs which were being, or had just recently been, organized. He became one of the founders of the Garrick Club, and he belonged to the first generation of the Athenæum.[1] He was elected to the famous gambling club, Crockford's, and to the Tory Club, the Carlton. He himself gave many dinners and frequent entertainments, and No. 5 was visited by numerous fashionable callers.

The rent Theodore paid for his Cleveland Row dwelling was £200 a year. He also laid out several thousand in furniture. And he began collecting dozens of useless and expensive pieces of bric-à-

---

[1] He is prominently mentioned in Mr. Humphry Ward's *History of the Athenæum* (1926).

brac like the following, described after his death
in Robins's auction catalogue:

369. A pair of handsome large eau de Cologne bottles
and stoppers, with bronze Gothic stands.

390. The Piping Boy, a truly delicate and beautiful
carving in ivory, most elaborately finished, with marble
plinth and glass shade.

441. A magnificent and richly chased silver candela-
brum, scroll branches for 4 lights, 23 inches high.

462. A pair of elegant plated ice-pails, handsomely
chased with vine leaves and grapes, silver shields and
borders.

These purchases, added to the magnitude of his
current expenses, soon brought him into debt,
from which he never emerged.

Theodore remained in Cleveland Row until
1831, when he found himself forced to curtail expenses. He therefore retired to a pleasant house
at Fulham, with a garden on the Thames, very
close to Putney Bridge and Fulham Road. He
gave up entertaining all except a few intimate
friends and neighbors, but he still accepted invitations to the houses of the fashionably great. At
Fulham he remained until his death in 1841 —
indeed, after that, for he was buried in the church-
yard not a stone's throw from his house.

An effort must be made to sketch those qualities
which established Hook as the social lion of his
day. To recount the spontaneous jokes of a wit!
It is like rising at seven o'clock in the morning to

remember the sparkle of last night's assemblage
— to recall the gay and well-fed throng, all tem-
peramentally attuned to the animation of the improvisatore, urging him on by their delighted
applause, watching the play of his features,
catching his sly references to every slight event of
the evening. Spontaneity is the essence of this:
the spirit gone cannot be recovered. *Recepto dulce
mihi furere est amico*, says Horace; but when the
charmed circle of friends (that necessary background of true humor) is not there, when the pale
ghost of the foolishness appears in print, then the
casual reader may say: "The man was a buffoon.
Poor Yorick was only a buffoon." Theodore Hook
had no Boswell. Not many of any company that
he delighted voiced sentiments which are audible
to-day. Of those who did, the greater part is content to record its surprise, its unbelief, the incredible nature of the performance. There are a
few who attempt to remember particular sets of
verses. But one becomes painfully aware through
the differing accounts they give of the same incident that much of the reconstruction is the memoir writer's own. There is a case in point. Barham, quoting from "one who was present," tells
of a party at a country place at which Hook was
giving an improvised performance. Dawn was
breaking, and the subject "good night" was given
him. A little boy was standing by the piano.

Hook turned to him with an expression of "deep pathos" and sang:

> But the sun see the heavens adorning,
> Diffusing life, pleasure, and light!
> To thee 't is the promise of morning,
> To us 't is the closing "Good night!"

In the "Atlantic Monthly" of April, 1865, Samuel Carter Hall describes the same incident, and says that the concluding lines were:

> For you is the dawn of the morning,
> For me is the solemn good-night.

And he adds in a footnote: "Mr. Barham has a confused account of this incident. He was not present on the occasion, as I was, standing close by the piano when it occurred." In his "Recollections and Reflections," published in 1872, J. R. Planché describes the incident, affirming that the lines were:

> You laugh! and you are quite right,
> For yours is the dawn of the morning,
> And God send you a good night!

He continues:

Other versions of this remarkable incident are in print, but I have confidence in the accuracy of my own for one particular reason. Supposing that I had imperfectly heard the words, I could not have mistaken the emphasis in their utterance, and the fervour with which God's blessing was invoked upon that beautiful and joyous boy could not by any possibility have accompanied such words as "For me is the solemn good-night," nor the applause that followed, loud and long, been caused by so melancholy a farewell.

The foundation of Hook's powers was a ready perception, a consuming curiosity, and a keen sense of the ludicrous. He was thoroughly alive to everything about him. "Nothing in the shape of absurdity ever escaped his observant eye," asserts the memoir writer, Mrs. Houstoun.[1]

As I was walking one night with Theodore Hook from the play [writes Henry Angelo], passing along Coventry-street, a sewer was being repaired at the time. Several men with lighted candles were below, at a considerable depth, and were busily employed at work. At the top was a railing over the cavity where they descended, and a crowd standing around. Theodore Hook, not preferring to make any inquiries of them, had placed his head over the rails, calling out, "What are you about? What are you looking for?" when those at the bottom, much engaged, and not willing to answer his repeated calls, replied, "We are looking for a seven-shilling piece, which perhaps you want more than we do," to the no small amusement of the bystanders.

That is the spirit of Theodore reduced to its elements: the observation, the scent of the ridiculous, the fresh touch in the commonplace situation. It was this spirit which, in the old days, made him stop the pompous old gentleman promenading slowly down the street with "I beg your pardon, sir, but pray may I ask, are you anybody in par-

---

[1] *A Woman's Memories of World-Known Men* (1883), p. 108.

ticular?" In 1827 the boyish impertinence has largely disappeared. The old spirit is now usually manifest in quips and puns, in quickness of repartee, in the art of narration, in dexterity of extempore composing. With it went, according to the testimony of those who knew him at all, a bubbling good humor which took away all possible sting from whatever he said.

The old composer, his father, had taught him the art of the quip and the pun. Theodore's days and evenings with his friends were spent in continuous practice of the art: they matched jokes, good and bad, during the entire time they were together. Some specimens of Hook's talent have been preserved. He once presented to the inveterate snuff-taker, Edward Cannon, a snuff box on which was inscribed "Non sine pulvere." His epigram on the legal action brought by a certain lord against one Cumming for defamation, but later abandoned, was:

> Cease your humming,
> The case is "on";
> Defendant's Cumming,
> Plaintiff's — gone!

When the famous duel between Thomas ("Anacreon") Moore and Jeffrey of the "Edinburgh Review" had been stopped by the police, who found that the pistols were not loaded with ball, Hook wrote:

When Anacreon would fight, as the poets have said,
　A reverse he displayed in his vapour,
For while all his poems were loaded with lead,
　His pistols were loaded with paper;
For excuses, Anacreon old custom may thank,
　Such a salvo he should not abuse,
For the cartridge, by rule, is always made blank
　Which is fired away at Reviews.

Hook and a friend, writes Barham,

were walking in the neighbourhood of Kensington, when
the latter, pointing out on a dead wall an incomplete or
half-effaced inscription, running "Warren's B—," was
puzzled at the moment for the want of the context.
" 'T is *lacking* that should follow," observed Hook in
explanation.

Henry Angelo writes:

Being fond of the arts, and particularly of caricatures, I had by me a great number of Rowlandson's, to
one of which I was puzzled to give a name. The subject
was an old man at breakfast, seated near the fire, his
gouty leg on a stool, and the kettle boiling over; the
water is falling on his leg, and he is ringing the bell. The
room door is open behind him, and a black servant is
kissing the maid, who is bringing in the toast. I requested Theodore Hook to write a title to it, and he put
"chacun à son gout."

A considerable part of Theodore's humor, then,
consisted of the pun. A considerable part of any
witty repartee is certain to consist of puns. The
pun, too, was then in favor — not frowned upon as
now. And, after all, he was not that contemptible
beast, your inveterate, hard-working, "professional" punster.

The great (indeed, the only) merit of a pun [he writes in "John Bull" in 1823] is its undoubted originality — its unequivocal novelty — its extemporaneous construction and instantaneous explosion. [As for the] regular, hard-going, thick-and-thin punster [he] is the dullest and stupidest companion alive, if he could but be made to think so. He sits gaping for an opportunity to jingle his nonsense with whatever happens to be going on, and, catching at some detached bit of a rational conversation, perverts its sense to his favourite sound, so that instead of anything like a continuous intellectual intercourse, which one might hope to enjoy in pleasant society, one is perpetually interrupted by his absurd distortions and unseasonable ribaldry.

Thus, while James Smith, Sam Beazley, Horace Twiss, as well as many of the society wits like Sam Rogers, Jekyll, and Luttrell, could think out their puns at home and utter them when abroad, they all hesitated to enter into competition with Theodore on any occasion when they were not prepared, for he was the ever-ready, spontaneous joker. Indeed, Hook's only undoubted superior at the play on words was that prince of the pun, Tom Hood.

As a *raconteur* of the amusing and absurd incidents which he himself had "staged," Theodore Hook had no equal in his day. Among the best of his stories is his account of his explanation of the identity and functions of the various court officials at the trial of Lord Melville, to a mother from the country and her eight-year-old child. Barham recounts many more; unfortunately they do not admit of condensation, for the humor of them lies mainly in the expansion of each minute incident. "We have seen him," Lockhart declares, "in company with very many of the most eminent men of his time; and we never, until he was near his end, carried home with us the impression that he had been surpassed" — the only occasions being the two times he dined with Sydney Smith at a date when Theodore was so close to death that alcoholic stimulants alone sustained him. Very seldom did anyone attempt to compete with Hook, and the impression that the spectator who did not know him received was that of Grantley Berkeley, who thought that Hook was "a terrible bully over other wits." [1]

Lockhart, anxious for the honor of Scotland, tried a contest once, of which the editor, William Jerdan, who was present, wrote down an account:

Peter Robertson, now Lord Robertson, and an honoured judge of the supreme Court of Session in Scotland, was long acknowledged as the Edinburgh Premier in the social Court of Humour and Facetiae, and was at this period on a visit to London. In London the supremacy of Theodore Hook in convivial intercourse was equally established, and a plan was arranged, not a disagreeable one in any respect, that the heroes of the North and South, the modern Athens and the modern Babylon, should be pitted against each other at a dinner-party in

---

[1] *My Life and Recollections*, iv, 10.

Albemarle Street, Mr. Murray [1] holding the lists, and giving a hearty welcome to all the lucky comers, about a dozen strong. Mr. Lockhart was second to his countryman, Lord Peter, and Mr. Milnes, of the Woods and Forests, appeared as the backer of King Theodore; or rather, I should say, these were their respective bottle-holders, as long as either combatants or seconds could manage to hold a bottle. During dinner the conversation was lively and sparkling, and Hook's wonderful ready wit carried all before it. He was in high feather, inextinguishable and inexhaustible. It seemed as if the Scotchman had a very poor chance; and would be what the jockeys term nowhere. But Mr. Lockhart was an abler tactitian and knew better. He suffered Hook to expend some of his brilliant fire, and after the cloth was removed, brought out his man. He gave us at due intervals a Gaelic sermon without a syllable of the Erse language, an Italian operatic scena without a word of Italian, and post-prandial speech after speech of military, political and other characters, to which bursts of extorted laughter did homage for their racy performance and extraordinary ingenuity. . . . Stimulated by this most amusing display, Hook was primed in superb trim to answer the calls for various improvising interludes, and never afforded more entertaining proofs of his marvelous talent in this, I was about to say art, but in this astonishing natural gift. Flash upon flash burst upon every man at the table — his own backer and the Woods and Forests were glorified in a superb vein of satirical ridicule, nor did the Scots artist and his Scot supporter escape scot free from the scoffing criticism of the pseudo-provoked flagellator. . . . It was truly a day to be marked with a white stone. I shall never spend the like again, and so, I doubt not, will respond the

---

[1] The famous publisher, John Murray, owner of the "Quarterly Review," which Lockhart edited.

voices of those who yet remain, and who helped to con-
tribute to, and partake of, this memorable enjoyment.[1]

As an English improvisatore Theodore was
unique.

As far as our knowledge goes [says Lockhart, who had
heard him many times], England never had a really successful performer in this way except Theodore Hook.
. . . When the call was well-timed and the company
such as excited his ambition, it is impossible to conceive
anything more marvelous than the felicity he displayed.
. . . About the complete extemporaneousness of the
whole there could rarely be the slightest doubt; if he
knew who was to be there, he might have come provided
with a few palpable hits — but he did the thing far the
best when stirred by the presence of strangers, and . . .
the staple was almost always what had occurred since
he entered the room — what happened to occur while
he was singing.

If the company was, for the most part, strange,
Hook would seat himself at the piano, ask for the
name of each guest, and immediately compose to
some popular tune a quip upon each name, or
avoid it with a pun. Thus Mr. Winter was served
as follows:

We have next Mr. Winter, assessor of taxes;
I'd advise you to pay him whatever he *axes*,
Or you'll find, and I say it without any flummery,
Though his name may be Winter, his actions are *sum-
mery.*

---

[1] *The Autobiography of William Jerdan* (1852–1853), iii.
18 ff.

A young Dane, Mr. Rosenagen, had a name difficult to manage:

> Yet more of my muse is required,
> Alas! I fear she is done;
> But no! like a fiddler that's tired,
> I'll *Rosen-agen* and go on.

At other times Hook would call for a subject. "But as often," says Barham,

as a subject impossible in any way to have been anticipated, was proposed by one of the company, generally the most incredulous, and with scarce a moment's consideration, he would place himself at the piano-forte, run over the keys, and break forth into a medley of merriment, of which, unhappily, no idea can be conveyed for the benefit and conversion of the sceptic.

At a dinner given by Frederick Mansell Reynolds, the subject "cocoanut-oil" (a substitute for kerosene) was given him. During an evening at William Jerdan's someone suggested "Edmund Yates's big nose."

To any one else [writes Samuel Carter Hall] such a subject would have been appalling: not so to Hook. He rose, glanced once or twice around the table, and chanted (so to speak) a series of verses perfect in rhythm and rhyme: the incapable theme being dealt with in a spirit of fun, humor, serious comment, and absolute philosophy, utterly inconceivable to those who had never heard the marvellous improvisator, — each verse describing something which the world considered great, but which became small when placed in comparison with "Yates's big nose"! It was the first time I had met Hook, and my astonishment was unbounded. I found it impossible to believe the song was improvised; but I had afterwards ample reason to know that so thorough a triumph over difficulties was with him by no means rare.

Horace Twiss, at the time of the question of the admission of the Jews to Parliament, suggested the unpromising subject "the Jews." After it had been given him, according to the account written by Fanny Kemble, the actress, Hook

shrugged his shoulders and made a discontented grimace, as if baffled by his theme, the Jews. However, he went to the piano, threw back his head, and began strumming a galloping country-dance tune, to which he presently poured forth the most inconceivable string of witty, comical, absurd allusions to everybody present as well as to the subject imposed upon him.[1]

Charles Greville wrote in his diary for August 13, 1834:

Dined at Roehampton yesterday with Farquhar. Mrs. Norton and Mrs. Blackwood and Theodore Hook dined there among others. After dinner he displayed his extraordinary talent of improvisation, which I had never heard but once before, and then he happened not to be in the vein. Last night he was very brilliant. Each lady gave him a subject, such as the "Goodwood Cup," the "Tithe Bill"; one "could not think of anything" when he dashed off and sang stanzas innumerable, very droll, with ingenious rhymes and excellent hits, "his eye begetting occasion for his excellent wit," for at every word of interruption or admiration, every look or motion, he

---

[1] Francis Ann Kemble, *Records of a Girlhood*, New York (1879), p. 171.

indulged in a digression, always coming back to one of the themes imposed upon him.[1]

One night, at the house of Lord William Pitt Lennox, Hook was given as his subject the name of a young woman, Jane Cox, and he composed about twenty stanzas thereon. In 1866, in one of his many gossipy books of memoirs, Lennox tried to reconstruct these verses. In these reconstructed stanzas, one may be certain, of course, that there is a great amount of material invented by Lord William himself. But since he had heard Hook many times, and at least knew the spirit of the improvisatore's performances, it is interesting to look at a few of the stanzas:

> While straying alone on the shore
> A picking of weeds from the rocks,
> I beheld (I ne'er saw her before)
> The charming and pretty Miss Cox.

> I followed this grace to a door,
> Where she gave to the rapper some knocks;
> She entered; I dared do no more,
> But learn that her name was Miss Cox.

> There is sugar that grows in the West;
> There is rum in the ships in the docks;
> But none of these equal at best
> The sweetness and spirit of Cox.

> There are lovers who say, yet won't do,
> (The *nihil praeterea vox*);
> But such is not he who would sue
> For the lily-white hand of Miss Cox.

---

[1] *The Greville Memoirs*, edited by Henry Reeve (1875), iii, 118.

When the moon is all bright in the sky,
What delight under cover of *nox*
Just to walk and to talk and to sigh,
With that charmer, the lovely Miss Cox!

The young Roman virgin when press'd,
Used to blush, and to whisper out "Mox."
How truly would that man be bless'd
Who could get such an answer from Cox.

To church let me lead her, and there,
With a service the most orthodox,
Put an end to this teasing affair
By changing the name of Miss Cox.[1]

Not the least part of the improviser's accomplishment was his ability to take advantage of every interruption that occurred while he was at the piano. He was one night at the home of Mrs. Norton, the beautiful daughter of the ill-fated young Tom Sheridan, and was singing about "Nelly" (Lady Dufferin) and "Cosy" (Lord Albemarle). During the performance, Lord Castlereagh, thirsty after the long debate in the House on the Beer Bill, came in quietly and went to take a glass of brandy. Interrupting his song:

If any one here is stupid or prosy,
He should just take a lesson from Nelly and Cosy,

Theodore turned on the newcomer:

Hallo! my Lord "Cas," what do you do here?
With your brandy and water instead of your beer?[2]

---

[1] Lord William Pitt Lennox, *Drafts on My Memory* (1866), i, 279–282.

[2] From Albemarle's *Fifty Years of My Life*, ii, 267 ff.

The eternal readiness of the man amazed the poet, Sam Rogers.

Words [he writes] cannot do justice to Theodore Hook's talent for improvisation: it was perfectly wonderful. He was one day sitting at the pianoforte, singing an extempore song as fluently as if he had the words and music before him, when Moore happened to look into the room, and Hook instantly introduced a long parenthesis,

> And here's Mr. Moore,
> Peeping in at the door.[1]

Of entire evenings with Theodore Hook, there are very few records indeed. T. Ashton Baylis, his neighbor at Fulham, once jotted down a rambling record of two evenings. The first was a dinner party at Hook's Fulham cottage.

Lechmere and myself and Crofton Croker[2] dined with Theodore Hook on Sunday the 15 December, 1839 at half-past five o'clock. We had for dinner mock turtle soup — fried soles — boiled beef and brace of pheasants with plum pudding. We staid till half-past one o'clock. Hook's conversation full of wit from beginning to end. He said he was in reality a very shy and nervous man, and mentioned as an instance of it, that when I asked him to take Lady Whitmore down to dinner on an occasion of his dining at Pryorsbank, he said he asked himself what he could possibly talk to her about, and that he felt embarrassed and very awkward about it. He said the feeling of juvenility and youth was very

---

[1] G. H. Powell, *Reminiscences and Table-Talk of Samuel Rogers* (1903), p. 227.

[2] Thomas Crofton Croker, the Irish author and antiquary — not John Wilson Croker, Hook's patron, the Secretary to the Admiralty.

strong in him. He still fancied himself a boy, and that
sometimes he was on the point of making an observation
but checked himself, fancying that his age and experience did not entitle him to make the remark.

The second evening described by Baylis was the
already-mentioned evening, one week previous,
when Hook had been asked to take Lady Whitmore down to dinner. The host on this occasion
was Baylis himself.

Mr. Hook dined at Pryorsbank with Lady Whitmore,
Sir George, Captain and Mrs. Stopford, Mr. and Mrs.
Nugent and [Crofton] Croker on Sunday, the eighth of
December. He sang two extemporaneous songs of about
twenty verses each. Betted with Lady Whitmore that
he would make Captain Stopford laugh after the ladies
left — the which he did — and Lady W. lost. Mr. Hook
said that for two years he slept in the same room with
Lord Byron — who called himself Bӯron and not Bȳron,
as he was popularly called. After we had drunk wine
till ten o'clock, Theodore Hook said, "Now we'll order
in the ham, spirits and hot water and begin the evening." He told us [that] the anecdote in Gilbert Gurney
of the Prince of Orange and the boots happened to himself at the Clarendon Hotel at Leamington when he
went to visit his sister[-in-law] there. Mr. Broderip
was admiring the boots before the fire at Brighton
— looked inside — saw the name of the Prince of
Orange. O'Shaugnessy made the boots. On calling on
him who had disappointed him in getting his boots
made, O'Shaugnessy apologized, saying he had been to
take leave of his brother from whom he had just parted
— having been hung that morning at Newgate —
offered the boots, fitted — and brought them away.
[He said that] after assisting Sir Martin A. Shea in dis-
tributing prizes at the Royal Academy where he went

instead of dining at Lord Harrington's, he went to the Athenæum — on asking the little waiter what he had to pay — "Six shillings," says the man. "What for?" says Theodore H. "Six glasses of brandy and water." [1] When elevated with liquor, he said he had a great enmity to turnpikes, and that once in coming home he broke the turnpike at Queen's Elms. He said that he had lived in his house seven years [2] and never had the curiosity to go into his kitchen or wine cellars. His magnificent dog, Belle, the gift of Lord Hertford, he seemed exceedingly fond of. If he said, "Ah, Belle, you don't love me," the huge black animal, with the most intelligent eyes I ever saw out of a human being's head, would immediately spring upon him, put his fore legs round his neck and commence kissing and fondling him. He showed us the different portraits of him, and amongst them that taken by Count D'Orsay, which he considered the best. "I think D'Orsay's the best," he said, "and perhaps it might be; but I loathe him." I thought his portrait was still to be taken. While his portrait was being taken, Lady Blessington observed: "Now, Alfred [D'Orsay], you see it is of no use your attempting to take his likeness, for you observe he is looking all the while at Lady —." But Count D. observed: "Then bring Lady — round here and I shall have him in perfection." Croker observing that the person who built Hammersmith Bridge caught cold and died, Hook observed, "Then he abridged his life." [3]

---

[1] Perhaps a reference to the fact that Hook's favorite table was called "Temperance Corner" because the diners at it always facetiously affected to call for lemonade or to be persistently ignorant of the nature of the liquid they were imbibing.

[2] His Fulham house, to which he had moved in 1831.

[3] This account by Baylis in his handwriting is in the British Museum and has never been published. I have taken some liberties with punctuation and have guessed at several illegible words.

Baylis's sketchy account presents a picture of Theodore at ease among good friends and neighbors. But when distinguished strangers or men of great literary note were among the company, his efforts were far more brilliant. What was probably the most notable of Hook's evenings has fortunately been rescued from oblivion by William Jerdan and, in a lesser degree, by Lockhart. The occasion was a dinner given by Frederick Mansell Reynolds. Jerdan and Lockhart were both among the guests.

I never saw Hook [Jerdan begins], often as I have seen him in his hours of exuberant humor, in such glorious "fooling" as on this occasion. From his entrance to his departure his countenance beamed with overflowing mirth, and his wonderful talent seemed to be more than commonly excited by the company of Coleridge, whom, I think, he had never met — at any rate never met with his legs under the same mahogany before.

Theodore's inspired outbursts came in steady succession. The company soon began to break all the wine glasses. Amid the hubbub and confusion, Coleridge's sonorous voice was heard declaiming on the extraordinary ebullitions of Hook: "I have before in the course of my time met with men of admirable promptitude of intellectual power and play of wit, which as Stillingfleet tells,

'The rays of wit gild wheresoe'er they strike';

but I never could have conceived such amazing readiness of mind, and resources of genius to be poured out on the mere subject and impulse of the moment." Having got the poet into this exalted mood [continues Jerdan], the last of the limited wine-glasses was mounted upon the bottom of a reversed tumbler, and, to the infinite risk of the latter, he was induced to shy at the former with a silver fork, till after two or three throws, he succeeded in smashing it into fragments, to be tossed into the basket with its perished brethren. It was truly bang-up philosophy, and, like all such scenes, may perhaps appear somewhat wantonly absurd in description (for the spirit which enjoyed them cannot exist in the breasts of readers); and I have a letter of Lockhart's alluding to the date of our witnessing the roseate face of Coleridge, lit up with animation, his large gray eye beaming, his white hair floating, and his whole frame, as it were, radiating with intense interest, as he poised the fork in his hand, and launched it at the fragile object (the last glass of dinner), distant some three or four feet from him on the table ... Hook, after dinner, gave us two of his usual extemporized songs, one of them characterizing all the "present company," no one excepted, and few, if any, were spared the satirical lash; so cleverly applied that Captain Harris could not credit that the whole was not preconcerted by Mr. Lockhart, Hook, and I.

Theodore demanded that Captain Harris name a subject, and he gave "cocoanut oil." Immediately Hook composed fifty or more stanzas on the subject —

and all this in versification which might have been taken in short-hand and published verbatim. Great was the astonishment and admiration of Captain Harris, largely shared even by those who were best acquainted with the improvisatore's most successful displays of that marvellous faculty. Coleridge was in the seventh heaven, and varied the pleasures of the evening by some exquisite recitation, as well as humorous stories of Southey, Wordsworth, and other brother bards.

After the party, writes Lockhart, he and another friend walked home with Coleridge, On the way, the poet delivered "a most excellent lecture on the distinction between talent and genius, and declared that Hook was as true a genius as Dante — *that* was his example." [1]

Can it be said at the present day that Theodore Hook was the greatest of England's professed wits and (to avoid all labored distinctions between wit and humor) humorists? The question is, it is to be feared, insoluble. Undoubtedly, men like Tom Hood, Douglas Jerrold, and Sydney Smith were superior to Hook in certain aspects of wit and humor. Hook left hardly any humorous (non-political) verse on the basis of which he might be compared with Hood and Jerrold. If Theodore, then, were to be awarded the primacy, it would be largely because of the ebulliency, the explosive nature, the spontaneousness of his witticisms. But alas! he had no Boswell. His quips, puns, and *facetiae* have come down, when they have done so at all, by the doubtful medium of the memoir

---

[1] The account of this evening is taken chiefly from William Jerdan's *Autobiography*, iv, 230–237. Lockhart gives an account differing in some particulars. The incident of the walking home with Coleridge comes solely from Lockhart. Jerdan walked home with the Brompton waiter hired for the occasion.

writer, in practically every instance writing many
years after Hook's death. In such a case, not only
is the reproduction likely to be almost entirely the
memoir writer's own, but one may be sure that the
quips he remembers are those which appealed to
his own sense of humor — the range of the humor
is thus exceedingly restricted. After all this filtra-
tion there can be little wonder that the product
is usually flat, that much of it is punning, —
and not very good punning, — and that it frequently bears the weight of the traditional British
heaviness.

But no matter. As an English improvisatore,
Theodore Hook stands alone. His performances
were praised with amazement and delight by men
of judgment and eminence, — men like Leigh
Hunt, Campbell, Coleridge, Rogers, and Lockhart,
— men who were by no means predisposed in his
favor. Lockhart rarely let himself go; he surely
cannot be accused of consistent overpraise. But
here is what Lockhart — in one of the finest passages he ever wrote — says of the wit of Theodore
Hook:

He was as entirely, as any parent of *bon-mots* that we
have known, above the suspicion of having premeditated
his point; and he excelled in a greater variety of ways
than any of them. No definition either of wit or humor
could have been framed that must not have included
him; and he often conveyed what was at once felt to be
the truest wit in forms, as we believe, entirely new. He

could run riot in conundrums — but what seemed at
first mere jingle, was often perceived, a moment after,
to contain some allusion or insinuation that elevated the
vehicle. Memory and knack may suffice to furnish out
an amusing narrator; but the teller of good stories seldom amuses long if he cannot also say good things.
Hook shone equally in both. In fact, he could not tell
any story without making it his own by the ever-vary-
ing, inexhaustible invention of the details and the aspects, and above all, by the tact that never failed to
connect it with the persons, the incidents, the topics of
the evening. Nothing was with him a patch — all was
made to assert somehow its coherence with what had
gone before, or was passing. His play of feature, the
compass and music of his voice, his large and brilliant
eye, capable of every expression from the gravest to the
most grotesquely comical, the quiet aptness of every
attitude and gesture, his power of mimicry, unrivalled
but by Mathews — when to all this we add the constant
effect of his innate, imperturbable good humour — the
utter absence of spleen — and ever and anon some flash
of strong sterling sense, bursting through such an atmosphere of fun and drollery — we still feel how inade-
quately we attempt to describe the indescribable. The
charm was that it was all Nature, spontaneous as water
from the rock.

In 1825, Coleridge wrote to Thomas Hood concerning a recently published work of the latter.
Coleridge did not like it — "least of all, the title,
Odes and Adresses to Great Men, which connected
itself in my head with Rejected Addresses, and all
the Smith and Theodore Hook squad." It is not
difficult to enumerate the members of the "Theodore Hook squad" for they were almost always to

be found in each other's company. A stranger meeting Hook rarely failed to meet also others of the "squad" at the same time.[1]

Among the intimate group, then, that surrounded Theodore Hook, were, in the first place, the brothers, James and Horatio (called Horace) Smith. James knew Hook very early — perhaps when the latter was only ten or eleven years old.

---

[1] Of interest in connection with the subject of Hook's acquaintances is a volume in the Harvard University Library entitled *The Literary Blue Book, or Kalendar of Literature, Science, and Art, for MDCCCXXX.* London, Marsh and Miller, 1830. This is a directory of living authors, artists, etc. In this copy Theodore Hook, apparently about 1835, wrote a few marginal comments — that he wrote them is proved by the handwriting and by the comment after his own name. His observations which concern literary names are as follows:

BAYLEY, THOMAS HAYNES: "An extremely good fellow with an extremely handsome and agreeable wife. A talented writer."

BEAZLEY, SAMUEL: "Very clever and my friend."

BLESSINGTON, LADY: "Gay and vivacious."

BURY, LADY CHARLOTTE: "An old friend full of talent."

CAMPBELL, THOMAS: "Clever but maddish."

CROKER, JOHN WILSON: "Taken altogether, the cleverest man I ever knew."

D'ISRAELI: "Clever."

HARNESS, REV. WILLIAM: "Good. My schoolfellow."

HILL, THOMAS: "Pooh pooh."

HOOK, THEODORE: "That's me."

LOCKHART: "Very superior."

LUTTRELL: "Most agreeable."

MARRYAT: "One of our best novelists."

MAGINN: "Full of talent and learning."

MOORE, THOMAS: "A very delightful man."

After the M's, Theodore tired of his diversion.

He mixed much in society and had a name as a wit. Horace wrote several novels; his "Brambletye House" (1826) is still remembered — but hardly read. The brothers made their great literary sensation with their "Rejected Addresses" of 1812. This thin volume is one of the two or three best parodies in English literature. It was received with tremendous acclaim. Theodore Hook's "address" in this volume was written by Horace. It is called "Punch's Apotheosis," and it is a parody of Theodore's Haymarket farce manner. It is, however, one of the least successful "addresses" in the group — not to be compared for an instant with those ascribed to Coleridge, Wordsworth, or Scott. Later in life Horace wrote a book of reminiscences, "A Graybeard's Gossip About His Literary Acquaintance," which has much to say about Hook.

Samuel Beazley (1786–1851) has already been met as a friend of Theodore's boyhood. He was by vocation an architect; but his preference was literature, and he wrote a few short-lived farces. He was, according to Ingoldsby, "one of the most good-humoured lively companions in the world."

Edward Dubois (1774–1850) has been mentioned as the editor of Tom Hill's "Monthly Mirror," and as assistant to Campbell in the task of getting out the first number of the re-animated "New Monthly Magazine" in 1821.

He was a lawyer by profession; and, writes a brother member,

in addition to being a recognized patron of literature, performed judicial functions in a small debts court, in a street leading out of Holborn, called the Court of Requests, but his duties never seemed to give him anxiety or to affect his cordial good temper. His house formed a fair example of the hospitality of a former generation.[1]

Since 1813, Charles Mathews, the comedian, had made a trip to America, had been injured in an accident, and had been foolish enough to sign a very disadvantageous theatrical contract. He was, about 1830, a busy man at the height of his career — perhaps the greatest English comedian of all time. But he and Hook still called frequently on each other, and met often at the "Garrick" and the "Athenæum." Mrs. Mathews's "Memoirs" of her husband bear abundant testimony to the closeness of the friendship. In 1834, when husband and wife departed for a second tour of America, Theodore wrote to them: "Assure yourselves that, however chequered my life may have been, and however much we have been separated by circumstances, the early feelings of friendship and attachment are still fresh in my heart."

Theodore knew Daniel Terry before 1813, but it was after his return from Mauritius that the

---

[1] Sergeant William Ballantine, *Some Experiences of a Barrister's Life* (1882), i, 110. Meeting Dubois, Ballantine also met Hook, Ingoldsby, Hill, and the Smiths.

two became particularly close friends. It has been related how Terry acted in and brought out Hook's last three plays; how the two collaborated with the "Arcadian"; and how the idea of the "John Bull" was worked up between them. Terry's name disappears rather mysteriously from connection with "Bull," but it must have done so by his own wish, for he and Hook were always warm friends. Whenever Scott made a trip to London, he of course talked with Terry. Thus Hook first met Sir Walter through Terry, not through Lockhart.

Tommy Hill, the little old dry-salter, "rosy as an abbot," had been the genial host at the "Sydenham Sundays" during the old days. His theatrical journal, the "Monthly Mirror," became in the later days somewhat of a joke, for Dubois so filled it with neighborhood gossip and references to events known only to a few, that it must have made strange reading for the uninitiate. Hill had also collected a respectable library of rare editions. But a business misfortune deprived him at one stroke of most of his money, and he moved from Sydenham to modest quarters in London. He was the good-natured butt for the jokes of the group. They made good-humored fun of his reputed great age, his insatiable curiosity, and his renowned "pooh, pooh!" His friendship with Hook was never interrupted.

Hook had met Richard Harris Barham during his brief residence at Oxford. The acquaintance was renewed when Hook took the lease of No. 5 Cleveland Row, just opposite St. James's, where Ingoldsby, who had taken orders, came regularly as one of the priests of the Chapel Royal. From then on, writes Richard Harris Dalton Barham, the son of Ingoldsby, Hook found in the author of the immensely popular "Ingoldsby Legends," "to the last a very sincere friend, and, in literary matters, an honest and perhaps not altogether injudicious adviser." The son's biography of his father is crammed with references to Theodore, for Ingoldsby's diary tells of meetings, dinners, evenings of amusement, and long fishing trips on the river.

Edward Cannon had been the Prince Regent's chaplain when Hook had made his acquaintance in 1811. He soon fell into disfavor both with the Regent and with Mrs. Fitzherbert. Few indeed except intimate friends, who knew that it was merely his manner, could endure Cannon's blunt, undiplomatic, outspoken directness. He was a wit of the caustic variety, extremely bibacious, and, although there is no record that he took his clerical duties lightly, he was surely a strange churchman even in the secular days before the Oxford Movement. He made some attempts at humorous verse, but he usually responded to the calls of his friends after dinner with the recitation of a Robin Hood ballad.

It has been related how William Maginn came over from Cork in 1823, to edit a paper to be run in connection with the successful "John Bull." Hook and he were intimate associates for a number of years afterwards, but they gradually drifted apart. "Subsequently," writes Lockhart, "they were separated by circumstances; but their mutual kindness seems never to have been disturbed." Maginn was for long time the editor of "Fraser's Magazine," in which, in 1834, he wrote a very pleasant and friendly account of Theodore — No. 47 in the well-known "Gallery of Literary Characters."

Stephen Price fairly certainly belongs to the Hook squad, for he was regularly present at dinners and entertainments given by other members of the group, and he belonged to the Garrick Club. He was an American whose interests ran to the turf. For a time he took over the lease of the Drury Lane theatre. He it was who brought over from America the recipe of what became known as the famous Garrick punch: "pour half a pint of gin on the outer peel of a lemon, add lime juice, sugar, a little maraschino, a pint and a quarter of water, and of soda-water two bottles."[1]

---

[1] Recipe quoted from T. H. S. Escott, *Club Makers and Club Members* (1914), p. 257.

William Jerdan had been a reporter for various papers before becoming editor of the "Literary Gazette." He gained a considerable reputation in his day; it is hard to see why — perhaps because his editorial approbation was much courted by rising young writers. His one literary discovery of note was "L. E. L." whose talents he first brought to public notice. He knew Hook well, and had heard his extemporaneous performances often, as the "Autobiography of William Jerdan," written in 1852, records.

Lord William Pitt Lennox was the third son of that Duke of Richmond who, as Governor General of Canada, died of hydrophobia from the bite of a fox. Lord William's mother gave the famous ball on the eve of the battle of Waterloo. Lord William first met Theodore at a party given by Ingoldsby, about 1827. "From that period," he writes, "until his latest hour, I was constantly in the habit of meeting him both in town and country houses, where he was always the life and soul of the party." Lennox's long life, with his parties of friends and his sporting interests, seems to have been ideally pleasant. In his old age he began to write his recollections in many thin, repetitious, and gossipy volumes.[1] These contain abundant references to Theodore Hook.

---

[1] *The Story of My Life* (1857), *Fifty Years' Biographical Reminiscences* (1863), *Drafts on My Memory* (1866), *My Recollections* (1874), and *Celebrities I Have Known* (1876–1877).

The Smiths, Beazley, Dubois, Mathews, Terry, Hill, Ingoldsby, Cannon, Maginn, Price, Jerdan, Lennox — these men, then, belong to the inner circle of Hook's friends. They were a highly sophisticated, citified group. They were all members of the Garrick Club; they knew London thoroughly; they were familiar with the theatre; they had, as reporters for newspapers or editors of periodicals, a wide literary acquaintance. Some of them essayed humorous verse, and they all made some pretensions to wit. They liked to drink, to eat well, and to exchange stories (not necessarily indecent) after dinner; they were all convivial, extremely good-humored, and very informal in their habits. When Lockhart went to London as editor of the "Quarterly" in 1825, Walter Scott, as a zealous father-in-law, gave him some advice.

When all was finally settled, or even before [writes Lockhart's biographer, Andrew Lang], Sir Walter advised Lockhart to "take devilish good care of your start in society in London." Especially he was counselled not "to haunt Theodore Hook much. . . . He is 'raffish,' *entre nous*." Again, "You will have great temptation to drop into the *gown and slipper* garb of life," which Sir Walter hated with a righteous hatred, "and live with funny, easy companions," such as Theodore Hook and Maginn.[1]

---

[1] Andrew Lang, *Life and Letters of John Gibson Lockhart* (1897), i, 373.

Perhaps Scott's epithets are as good as any others — the "raffish," "gown and slipper" Theodore Hook squad.

There are several men who are not of Hook's group, but who are more or less closely connected with him.

Samuel Carter Hall (1800–1889), an Irishman, after a youth spent as a reporter, and after much distress caused by the failure of an "Annual," finally became the editor of one of the first art periodicals in England, the "Art Union Monthly Journal," later called the "Art Journal." His pretensions to a knowledge of art were laughable, even for these pre-Ruskin days; but his self-esteem was in good order and made him many bitter enemies. Grantley F. Berkeley, for instance, writes of him: "This is the gentleman who sometimes seeks to entertain an audience by relating what he thinks of his most celebrated contemporaries — it would entertain them still more could they hear what his distinguished contemporaries think of him." Hall has already been met as the sub-editor of the "New Monthly," and, for a year, of "John Bull." He had a talented Hibernian wife who wrote novels. In his later days he began writing his memoirs — "Memories of Authors" and "Retrospect of a Long Life." His assertions concerning literary men whom he knew, including Hook, are by no means to be believed without independent testimony. Hall was, in fact, a grandiloquent "bounder," and the character of Pecksniff, whose prototype he was, peeps out throughout his works. His artistic principles may be illustrated by the impression he received from the living-room of Theodore's Fulham cottage:

The only room of the cottage I ever saw was somewhat coarsely furnished: a few prints hung on the walls, but there was no evidence of those suggestive refinements which substitute intellectual for animal gratifications in the internal arrangements of a domicile that becomes necessarily a workshop

— whatever this juxtaposition of words may mean!

James Robinson Planché, playwright and theatrical manager, is perhaps now best remembered as the librettist of Von Weber's "Oberon." In his "Recollections and Reflections of J. R. Planché," published in 1872, he describes his meeting and acquaintance with Theodore:

I had often met Hook in society without being introduced to him; but our acquaintance and intimacy dated simultaneously from the evening of a dinner at Horace Twiss's in Park Place, St. James's. . . . Mr. John Murray (the great Murray of Albemarle Street), James Smith, and two or three others, remained till very late in the dining-room, some of us singing and giving imitations. Hook being pressed to sing another of his wonderful extemporary songs, consented with a declaration that the subject should be John Murray. Murray objected vehemently, and a ludicrous contention took place, during which Hook dodged him round the table, placing chairs in his path, which was sufficiently devious without them, and singing all the while a sort of recitative, of which I remember only the commencement:

"My friend, John Murray, I see, has arrived at the
    head of the table,
And the wonder is, at this time of night, that John
    Murray should be able.
He's an excellent hand at a dinner, and not a bad one
    at a lunch,
But the devil of John Murray is that he never will pass
    the punch."

[Planché continues]: From that day to the latest of his life, Hook's attachment to me was so remarkable, that, knowing his irresistible passion for hoaxing and practical jokes of all descriptions, I was at first a little alarmed occasionally at the peculiar and marked attention he paid to me, accompanied as it was by respect, which from one of his age and celebrity was as singular as, if sincere, it was flattering. That it *was* sincere I had many gratifying proofs, some of which I still treasure, in his handwriting.

Yet the playwright does not belong to the inner group of Theodore's friends.

Thomas Haynes Bayley (1797–1839) wrote poetry for "John Bull" and for the "New Monthly." He was a dandified sort of person, whose extremely moderate poetic talents were devoted to the writing of boudoir or hurdy-gurdy ballads, such as "I'd be a butterfly," and "Oh no, we never mention her." Hook, in 1829, intro-

duced him to Ingoldsby as follows: "Barham —
Mr. Bayley — there are several of the name; this
is not 'Old Bailey,' with whom you may some day
become intimate, but the gentleman whom we call
'Butterfly Bayley.'"

In order to end the list in a strong major key,
the name of William John Broderip (1789–1859)
has been reserved to the last. After 1835 he was
the most sincere and dependable of Hook's friends.
Broderip was of the firm of Powell and Broderip,
solicitors, and he later became a magistrate in the
Thames Police Court. He was an excellent naturalist, and a Fellow of the Royal Society; he
formed the Zoölogical Society; and he wrote many
zoölogical articles for the "New Monthly" and
"Fraser's" — which were later collected and published as "Zoölogical Recreations" (1847), and
"Leaves from the Note-book of a Naturalist"
(1852). He constantly advised Hook in pecuniary
affairs, although toward the end nothing but a
miracle could have extracted Theodore from debt.
William Broderip was a thoroughly estimable and
upright man.

There were a number of men of letters with
whom Hook was well acquainted, but hardly intimate. Richard Brinsley Sheridan and George
Colman the younger, he knew early in life. He
knew both of them well, but his attitude toward
them was naturally that of an awe-struck pupil

toward his master. Thomas Campbell and Leigh Hunt were associates of the Sydenham days. When Lockhart got to London, he did not heed Sir Walter's injunction strictly, for he soon got to know Hook. "Our acquaintance with him," Lockhart writes in 1843, "commenced twenty years ago, and had long been familiar, but it never reached intimacy." No one, it is certain, is going to accuse Lockhart of a tendency to form extreme intimacies with anyone.

Of Hook's literary acquaintances — of the men whom he met and talked with occasionally — a few only can be marked out for mention, because it may safely be said that, with only a very few exceptions, he had met and knew every man of letters of his time. The Garrick and the Athenæum were the literary clubs, and Hook belonged to both. He was a famous diner-out, and was to be met at the dinner tables of literary men. He was the editor of a periodical to which some of the most distinguished writers of the day contributed. He was a novelist of reputation. He attended the meetings of the contributors to "Fraser's." He came to the notable literary gatherings at the publisher Murray's place at 50 Albemarle Street: "Theodore Hook," writes the publisher's biographer, Samuel Smiles, "came to Murray's dinners again and again. He was the soul of wit and humour, sparkling in repartee, and genial in manner and conversation."[1] Thomas Hood contributed to the "New Monthly" and succeeded Hook as editor. To that magazine John Forster was an important contributor when Hook took it over. He, as has been recounted, proposed a toast to Theodore on that occasion; according to Hall, the two soon disagreed. Laman Blanchard (1804–1845) was a verse writer for the magazine. Cyrus Redding had been sub-editor during Campbell's time, and knew Hook and his friends — "a set of wits among whom I felt like a fish out of water." Sergeant Talfourd, the biographer of Lamb, had been connected with the "New Monthly" before its rejuvenation under Campbell. Lamb himself met Hook at least once, but apparently not through the author of "Ion."[2] John Poole, author of "Paul Pry" and "Little Pedlington," wrote for the magazine and knew Hook well. Honest Allan Cunningham dined occasionally at

---

[1] Samuel Smiles, *A Publisher and His Friends* (1891), ii, 424.

[2] George Daniel, *Love's Last Labour Not Lost* (1883), pp. 14 f. Lamb was at the old Queen's Head hostelry at Islington: "It was here that he chanced to fall in with that obese and burly figure of fun, Theodore Hook, who came to take a last look at this historical relic before it was pulled down. Hook accompanied him to Colebrooke cottage which was hard by. During the evening Lamb (lightsome and lissom) proposed a race round the garden; but Hook (*à cochon à l'engraisse*, pursy and puffy, with a nose as radiant as the red-hot poker in a pantomime, and whose gait was like the hobblings of a fat goose attempting to fly) declined the contest, remarking that he could outrun nobody but 'the constable.'"

5 Cleveland Row. Theodore was, of course, acquainted with his publishers, Henry Colburn and Richard Bentley. The latter belonged to the Garrick. In April, 1820, Hook first met Walter Scott through Terry. Their second meeting Sir Walter has recorded in his "Journal" under the entry of November 11, 1826: "Croker came to breakfast, and we were soon after joined by Theodore Hook, *alias* "John Bull"; he has got as fat as the actual monarch of the herd." This taking on of flesh had been caused by his imprisonment. Scott, though he did not approve of Hook as a companion for his son-in-law, yet thought well of Theodore's literary abilities — for his journal entry of February 21, 1828, reads:

Last night after dinner I rested from my work and read the third part of "Saying and Doings," which shows great knowledge of life in a certain sphere, and very considerable powers of wit, which somewhat damages the effect of the tragic parts. But he is an able writer, and so much of his work is well said, that it will carry through what is manqué.

The place *not* to look for Theodore Hook is Holland House, the stronghold of the Whigs. Liberal and Conservative did not then mix in society. "Tory politicians of the orthodox kind," writes Mr. Lloyd Sanders, "were scarce birds at Holland House." [1] Samuel Rogers, Luttrell, —

The Holland House Circle (1908), p. 292.

author of the "Letters to Julia," — Sydney Smith, Thomas Moore, Hallam, Macaulay, and (at an earlier date) Byron, were the chief of those who regularly frequented the place. Hook knew Rogers and Moore almost intimately. But as a Tory his cue was to ridicule both in "John Bull." He fathered a lot of mediocre puns and epigrams on Rogers,[1] and he wrote parodies of Moore's drawing-room songs. As Theodore was an intimate of Croker's, Macaulay's words in his journal in 1858 are understandable: "I see the merit of the novels of Theodore Hook, whom I hold in greater abhorrence than even Croker, stuffed as those novels are with scurrility against my political friends." [2] If it did not savor of sacrilege to accuse Macaulay of not having *read* some particular thing, one would without hesitation pronounce him ignorant of Hook's novels, for, although "John Bull" in its time was stuffed with scurrility against Whigs, the novels are singularly free from references to contemporary politics.

To come now to Hook's aristocratic acquaintances. Their number was surprisingly large. His diary, writes Lockhart,

---

[1] P. W. Clayden in his *Rogers and His Contemporaries* (1889), ii, 131 f., gives an account of the matter scarcely fair to Hook. Rogers was by no means an innocent victim.

[2] G. O. Trevelyan, *Life and Letters of Lord Macaulay*, New York (1876), ii, 386.

came to contain an array of names which, after some observation both of him and of London, it surprised us to go over. Long before the close it included various members of the royal family — numerous representatives of every rank in the peerage — with few exceptions, all the leading politicians on the Tory side — not a few of their conspicuous opponents in both houses — a large proportion of what attracted most notice at the time in the departments of art, literature, and science — and, lastly, whatever flaunted and glittered in the giddiest whirl of the *beau monde*.

A brief mention, therefore, of a few of these friends is all that is possible.

Theodore's sponsor was John Wilson Croker. The two were regularly seen together; the relation between them was one of deep and honorable friendship. Croker is, wrote Hook, "taken altogether, the cleverest man I ever knew" — and Theodore must be allowed to be no mean judge. At Croker's residence in Kensington, he was a frequent visitor. There he met many of the Tory politicians and their families, and delighted and amazed them all with his extemporaneous performances. There Mrs. Croker, a rather formidably religious lady, frequently tried her hand at reforming him — a story pertaining thereto being told by Mrs. Houstoun:

I recollect . . . a rather comical anecdote told me by James Smith . . . and which is illustrative of Mrs. Croker's earnest but futile efforts to "reform" one of the most graceless of her husband's guests. It was the after-dinner hour, and when the ladies were on the point of what is called "retiring"; consequently the excellent lady could hardly have chosen a less propitious moment in which to work, or rather, attempt to do so, a miracle on the sinner by her side. After several intellectual efforts to engage her neighbour in *serious* talk, she, with a sigh that sounded almost like one of despair, said, "There are but three words, Mr. Hook, which a believing man should, at such a time as this, have on his lips and in his heart." "And what are they, pray? — 'Pass the bottle,' I conclude," retorted the audacious wit, as he quietly suited the action to the word.[1]

Croker's fate has been curious: his entire position in history has been given him by his bitterest political opponents. Macaulay regarded him with a fierce and unreasoning hatred, but Croker had the better side and gave the better argument in the House of Commons, and his "Boswell" is by no means as bad as Macaulay represents it. In "Coningsby," Disraeli makes Rigby (Croker) the unspeakable toady of Monmouth (Hertford), but Croker's letters to Hertford are the addresses of a gentleman to a gentleman. It is true that Croker managed Hertford's huge estates and helped keep in order the seats in Parliament that he controlled. But he received no money for this, and he was only moderately mentioned in Hertford's will. His "slashing articles," as Disraeli calls them, show a dogmatic antipathy to the newer school of poetry, and he fought to the last ditch against the

---

[1] *A Woman's Memories of World-Known Men*, p. 116.

Reform Bill — both of which mean that he was a thorough Tory, like Sir Walter Scott. Wellington brought Croker forward; the ill-fated Perceval gave him his position as Secretary to the Admiralty. He held the post for twenty-two years. His personal qualities were probably not engaging. But he was a good friend to Hook at a time when Hook most needed a friend. His intercession at the Exchequer rescued him from the indeterminate sentence of imprisonment the Audit Board saw fit to inflict. Hook was indebted to Croker for a multitude of kindnesses. Theodore knew it, and Theodore's relatives knew it. On August 27, 1841, Theodore's nephew, the Reverend Walter Farquhar Hook, began a sad and affecting letter to Croker with the following words:

Although you have been duly informed of my poor uncle Theodore's death, I cannot refrain, as the eldest of his surviving relatives, from writing to you to say that I remember with gratitude that he was indebted to you for almost everything in life. When he was under circumstances of the deepest depression, you were the person who helped him; and when all the world was frowning upon him, in you he found a patron and a friend. Many years have passed since these things occurred, but my grateful admiration of your conduct was strongly excited in my youth, and I have not forgotten those feelings now that I am past my meridian. Your name is sometimes remembered in my prayers as the benefactor of one most dear to me.[1]

---

[1] *The Croker Papers*, i, 239 f.

To picture Hook, as Disraeli does in "Coningsby," as Croker's buffoon whom he exhibited on occasions, is to utter a ridiculous slander.

Croker's influence probably caused Hook to be elected to Crockford's and to the Carlton Club. The former was a gambling house which provided excellent dinners gratis to players, and which had a very distinguished list of members — including the Duke of Wellington, Count D'Orsay, and the future Napoleon III, then an exile. The Marquis of Hertford's place in Manchester Square knew Hook's regular visits. Hertford he had known before his departure for Mauritius. But the "gentle Marchesa" had eloped with another. To Hertford's country house at Sudbourne, in Suffolk, Hook naturally came more than once. Thomas Raikes, the society diarist, wrote on October 2, 1831, at Hertford's, that "Theodore Hook is of the party here." With Charles Manners Sutton, the Speaker of the House, who later acquired the usual peerage and retired to the other house as Lord Canterbury, Hook shortly after his return to England struck up a warm acquaintance. The two were seen so often together that they became the subject of a friendly caricature by H. B., a well-known cartoonist of the time.

Although Hook abjured the professional stage after 1821, he still engaged in private theatricals among his distinguished friends. "We have on our table," Lockhart writes, "several light and easy little melodramas which he composed at the request of the late amiable and excellent Marchioness of Salisbury, for the amusement of Hatfield House." And Lockhart thinks it amusing that Hook's property man at these entertainments was "that grave presbyterian, Sir David Wilkie." The actors were people of rank and fashion. Among them, writes the Earl of Albemarle,[1] were "Lady Salisbury, our hostess; Lord and Lady Francis Leveson Gower, afterwards Lord and Lady Ellesmere; Lord Morpeth, afterwards Lord Carlisle; Mrs. Robert Ellison, sister of Lord Rokeby; Mrs. Robert Ellice; Sir George Chad; and Lord Normanby's brother, Colonel, afterwards Sir Charles Phipps." And the same writer continues:

The pieces performed were French vaudevilles adapted to the Hatfield stage by Theodore Hook. . . . On one grand occasion, the Duke of Wellington, then Prime Minister, almost every member of the Cabinet, and nearly the whole of the *Corps Diplomatique* came from London to witness our performances. . . . The festivities closed by a sumptuous banquet. Theodore Hook, in unusually high force, astonished the company by his wonderful improvisations.

It would be practically impossible to record the great number of fashionable places at which Theo-

---

Fifty Years of My Life, ii, 249–252.

dore was an occasional guest. But there were certain places at which he was a regular and frequent visitor. The salon of the famous Lady Blessington was one of these. She, it will be remembered, was one of the contributors to the "New Monthly" during Hook's editorship. She attracted to her gatherings practically all of the prominent men of letters of London. Another group among whom Hook was often present gathered at the residence of General Phipps, Lord Normanby's brother. Theodore dined frequently at Lord Harrington's, where the Duke of Wellington and other leading Tories often assembled. He went many times to Charles Kemble's, where Fanny Kemble saw and heard him but did not like him. He is often mentioned, also, as a guest of Mrs. Norton, the beautiful daughter of Tom Sheridan, the short-lived son of the dramatist. "At Mrs. Siddons's receptions," writes A. G. L'Estrange, in his biography of the Reverend William Harness, "Mr. Harness became acquainted with Theodore Hook, who was then in general request in fashionable and literary society." Theodore went to these receptions the more readily because he was certain to find Horace Twiss there. A stimulating and convivial evening was then certain, for, in addition to being Mrs. Siddons's nephew and an M.P., Horace was a wit of considerable reputation. Finally, Hook was often present at the dinner table of the Duke of

Cumberland, who, at the death of William IV, became King of Hanover. It was the suggestion of this personage, probably, that caused Theodore to formulate plans for a "History of Hanover."

On the question of Hook and his aristocratic friends there are certain to be voices raised in judgment. "Sad vision," laments R. H. Horne in his "New Spirit of the Age," "of a man of genius, as Hook certainly was, assiduously pickling his prerogative and selling his birth-right for the hard and thankless servitude of pleasing idle hours and pampered vanities." In the same vein Charles Knight's "Popular History" has it that Hook "was, we trust, the last of that race of authors who, without being the hired servants of the great, found a place at their tables for the sole purpose of contributing to their amusement, like the jesters of the Middle Ages." These two writers, it is certain, knew very little about Theodore Hook. But the question they raise may as well be disposed of finally.

In the first place, Hook loved to frequent the circles of the great. He accepted other invitations, of course; he was seen just as often at the tables of the burgher class, and far more often at the centre of his own intimate literary circle. But, no doubt, he was proud of his wide fashionable acquaintance and of his distinguished friends. There is considerable pride and complacency, for instance, in what he writes in a letter to his neighbor, T. A. Baylis: ". . . I am unable to promise inasmuch as during the Christmas week I am engaged to an annual visit to Elvaston Castle to meet the Duke of Wellington, who takes that in his way to Belvoir, whither he annually goes on the 4th of January, being the D. of Rutland's birthday." [1] But, after all, this is pardonable. Certainly there is nothing *necessarily* disgraceful in his acceptance of the invitations of the great, and in his pride at knowing them.

In the second place, there is nothing necessarily disgraceful in the fact that he was in universal demand as a dinner guest at places of fashion. True, he was not invited because of his rank or title. He was sought after because of his sparkling wit and his unique gift of improvisation. The hostess angled for him because his presence assured the success of her party. To the guests he was a hugely entertaining fellow. The fact that his wit made him a much-desired guest does not *necessarily* mean that he was looked upon as a sort of music-hall performer.

The question, then, seems to resolve itself into this: when in company with the titled and the great, was he servile? Disraeli and Thackeray (as will be seen later) said so; but their testimony

---

[1] From a MS. letter in the British Museum.

must be ruled out, for they made the assertion in novels where the cast of characters called for a sycophant's part for Hook. If he had been a toady, surely the memoirs of those who knew him — particularly Whigs like Leigh Hunt, Moore, and Rogers — would have recorded this fact. But there is no indication in the memoirs of the time, written by men who knew Hook personally, — whether they liked him or not, — that he was a servile and hired jester. There is, on the contrary, plenty of evidence asserting the direct opposite — that Hook was extremely tender of his dignity and was indignant when he suspected that he was being imposed upon. He was not a tuft-hunter, writes Barham; he was *tuft-hunted.* Declares Lockhart: "He was never servile." "I will tell one incident about Hook," writes the Reverend J. Richardson:[1]

It shows the happy sarcasm in which the man could convey rebuke, and it may be a warning to certain "lion hunters" of the present day to abstain from their pursuit of animals which are furnished with teeth as well as with the capacity for astonishing without frightening their admirers. In the meridian of his reputation, Hook was incessantly worried by Albina, Countess of Buckingham, with cards for "coffee at nine o'clock," but never with an invitation for the more genial hour of six, at which last-mentioned hour the dinner on her ladyship's table was most punctually served. It may be supposed he never accepted the invitations for nine,

---

[1] *Recollections* (1856), ii, 151 f.

and to avoid their continuous recurrence for the future, returned an answer to the last: — "Mr. Hook presents his compliments to the Countess of Buckingham, and has the honour to inform her ladyship that he makes it an invariable rule to take his coffee where he dines."

The truth is that Theodore was pestered with invitations to parties, and, when present at them, with exhortations to "one song more." And it was a weakness in him to accept them as often as he did. This social life took too much money. He adopted the scale of expenditure current in aristocratic circles. He lost a lot in gaming to men who considered him an admirable mark — for a temperament like Hook's is fatal to a gambler. Unlike his aristocratic associates, he had no income independent of his literary work. As a result, he began to get money on promises to write, to turn his hand to anything that would bring him a few pounds without much labor. He sank into hopeless debt and galling misery. He began to sustain his social talents upon the stimulation of alcohol. But none of this need be regretted. Without a circle around him of admiring auditors, without an intellectual and elegant audience upon whom to exercise his wit — this man would not have been Theodore Hook. And his constant association with the titled great sets him apart from practically all other literary men of the day. Practically none of his fellow writers — be they great or small in talent — had the *entrée* into the highest society that Hook enjoyed. He was rightly proud. For the writer of the sketch of his life prefixed to "Fathers and Sons" says truly enough that "by the brilliancy of his wit, his convivial powers, and his agreeable manners, he quickly enjoyed a position in society that few literary men, by profession, have ever obtained."

After 1839 Hook was a mere caricature of himself. Richardson presents an affecting picture of him.

Almost the last time [he writes] I had the pleasure of meeting Theodore Hook was towards the conclusion of his earthly pilgrimage. It was at Vauxhall on the occasion of the ascent of a balloon. I met him in the fireworks ground of those gardens in which he had enjoyed so many pleasant hours, and met so many pleasant friends since departed. I could not help being struck with the alteration of his appearance from what it used to be in his best days. It was evident the hand of death was upon him, and that all he could expect was to linger for a few months on the stage on which he had been so conspicuous and so admired an actor. What made his situation the more to be deplored was the necessity which the uncompromising admiration of his friends forced upon him of acting the part of a lion, when his mental and physical powers were equally incompetent to the task of supporting the character. He was pestered to the last by importunities from persons who gave dinners to honour their parties by his presence, when his faculties for "roaring," or for keeping "the table in a roar," were too feeble to support his reputation without the aid of stimulants to fire his flagging wit and rouse his torpid humour. But his fame was at stake, and . . .

he was fain to draw that inspiration from brandy which he had originally derived from the unassisted powers of nature. . . . The spontaneous combustion which had once flashed forth like lightning was burnt out, and little of the fire of former days remained in the ashes.

His condition was realized by those who knew him, and who knew him at his best. The men who published their diaries and wrote their memoirs in the eighteen-seventies and eighties knew Hook only during the last pathetic years. Accordingly, their words are only too often something like this: Society has changed greatly since the late thirties of this century. When I was a young man just entering London society, it contained some wild and dissipated characters. For instance there was Theodore Hook, of flaming red face and corpulent body — and so on. They did not know Theodore Hook; they saw only his shell.

The end was not far off. Hook's last diary entries, as given by Lockhart, are remarkable for their morbidity and gloom. Cirrhosis of the liver was already far advanced. He struggled to keep up until the first week in August, 1841. Then he took to his bed, and died on the 24th of that month, in the presence of his nephew, Walter Farquhar Hook.

There is one final observation to be made about this life. Theodore Edward Hook *knew* London. He knew its summer gardens and its theatres; he wrote its plays; he had been smiled upon by its ruler; he held a position from its government; he edited one of its newspapers; he knew the Grub Street life of its pamphleteers; he had been in its prisons; he edited one of its notable magazines; he was invited to the tables of its middle classes, its burghers, its men of letters, and its titled great. Apparently none of its manifestations escaped his eye — and it was an observant eye. He loved its society, its dinners, the great current of its social and intellectual life. In the midst of the life he loved, then, it is fitting to take a last view of him, through the eyes of his intimate friend, William Maginn, who, in April, 1834, wrote beside Maclise's picture of him in "Fraser's" the following words:

He has just descended from the grand vestibule of the Athenæum, where he has been enjoying Praed's rhymes of the morning, a well-cayenned mutton chop, and a glass of the Murchison sherry; forthwith he will glide round the corner . . . and esconce himself in the small oratory of the Carlton dining-room, there to refresh body and mind with another chop, another bumper, and another squib. Theodore will then be primed to shine in the Conservative circle above stairs, bright over all the other luminaries of the gang, until it be time for him to doff his knowing surtout and appear in finished grace, the full-figged swell of the eight o'clock board, whether in Piccadilly, in Palace Yard, or in Privy Gardens, or beneath some less stately roof, more worthy to ring with the trumpet notes of honest laughter and the linked sweetness long drawn out of "one cheer more" — the delighted and delighting guest of some huge-paunched alderman, red-gilled archdeacon, or gorgeous widow. . . . Peace and jollity go with him, wherever he is this evening destined to prick his turbot-fin, lap down his magnum, exhibit the splendid *tabatière* of the Capitan-Pacha, and shower wit and fun and conundrum about him — like a fountain of Vauxhall fire, radiant but harmless! Peace be with the most un-envious of satirists, the kindest-hearted of libellers, the most sincere, steadfast, unflinching champion of the long cork, and the alliance of Church and State.

CHAPTER VII.

HOOK'S NOVELS.

I. Publication.

THE first series of Theodore Hook's "Sayings and Doings: A Series of Sketches from Life" was published by Colburn and Bentley, and appeared on February 21, 1824. The three volumes contained four stories: "Danvers," "The Friend of the Family," "Merton," and "Martha the Gypsy." "Merton," the longest of the four, was a rewriting of his first novel, "The Man of Sorrow," which he had published in 1808 under the name of Alfred Allendale. It had attracted so little attention at the time that Hook did not hesitate to use the plot again — to use, as he wrote to Colburn, the incidents of this boyish story, of which "I was very soon heartily ashamed," as a "skeleton to fill up with better matter."

The success of the series was very great. It was reprinted three times before the spring of 1825, and Hook received two thousand pounds as his share of the profits. A "Blackwood's" reviewer wrote of it: [1]

---

[1] Vol. xv, p. 334 (March, 1824).

There is an air of *savoir vivre* about it, which marks it as the composition of a man who has moved in all the various circles which he describes — an air which cannot be picked up by the uninitiated, no matter with what assurance they may affect it.

Colburn readily undertook to publish a second series. Accordingly, three more volumes, the second series of "Sayings and Doings," appeared on January 26, 1825. Again there were four stories: "The Sutherlands," "The Man of Many Friends," "Doubts and Fears," and "Passion and Principle." For this series Colburn paid Hook a thousand guineas, and later, when its success became apparent, he added sums of £200 and £150. In the February "Blackwood's Magazine" Timothy Tickler (the pseudonym of Robert Syme) wrote sympathetically of Hook and his work: [1]

His tales, then, came before the public with two decided claims to popularity. Their materials were drawn in no trifling measure, and were supposed to be entirely drawn, from what he himself had actually witnessed among some of the most talked about circles of London life; and they were written in a style distinguished by several most attractive qualities. There are plenty of people who can, even in these plotless days, invent far better plots for stories than Theodore Hook. There are plenty who can command passions and feelings higher, far higher, in class, than those he wishes to meddle with. . . . But who is he that has touched with equal skill the actual living, reigning follies of the existing society of England, or rather, say we, of London? Who is he that

---

[1] Vol. xvii, pp. 221 f.

glances over the absurdities of the actual, everyday surface life of our own day with so sharp and quizzical a pen? And who, finally, contrives, by general lightness of touch, facility of transition, careless recklessness of allusion, and perpetual interspersion of really masterly paragraphs of humorous description, to make all the world forget the absurdities of plots, which are not even in many instances, very new, — the uninteresting characters of a hero and heroine, — the farcical extravagance of a thousand of his incidents, — and, we must add, the highly reprehensible tone in which he treats throughout many matters of no ordinary importance? All the world answers — NOBODY. Here stands the great Theodoro, and here standeth he alone.

The third and final series of "Sayings and Doings" was put out by Colburn and Bentley, on January 29, 1828. It was in three volumes, but it contained two stories only: "Cousin William; or, The Fatal Attachment," and "Gervase Skinner."

Hook's next work of fiction was the full three-volume novel "Maxwell," brought out by Colburn and Bentley on November 15, 1830. Hook earned a thousand pounds by it — and this sum was the usual payment made him for each of his full-length novels. In September, 1831, during one (No. 58) of the "Noctes Ambrosianae," Timothy Tickler speaks again of Hook's qualities as a novelist as they are further demonstrated by "Maxwell":

Confound haste and hurry! What else can account for Theodore Hook's position? Who that has read his

"Sayings and Doings," and, above all, his "Maxwell," can doubt, that had he given himself time for consideration and correction, we should have been hailing him, ere now, *nem. con.* as another Smollett if not another Le Sage? Had he, instead of embroidering his humour upon textures of fable, as weakly transparent as ever issued from the loom of Minerva Lane, taken the trouble to elaborate the warp ere he set about weaving the woof — which last could never have been any trouble to him at all — upon what principle can any man doubt that he might have produced at least one novel entitled to be ranked with the highest? Surely sheer headlong haste alone — the desire, cost what it may, to fill a certain number of pages within a given time — could ever have tempted such a writer, one whose perceptions of the ludicrous have such lightning quickness, into tampering with such materials as make up, without exception, his serious, and above all, his pathetic scenes. Those solemn commonplaces produce the same painful sense of incongruous absurdity which attends the admixture of melodramatic sentimentalities in a broad farce at the Haymarket. Loves and tears, and grand passions and midnight hags, and German suicides alongside — *parietibus nullis* — of his excellency the Governor-General, and Mr. Godfrey Moss! What would one say to Julia de Roubigné, spun thread about in the same web with Humphrey Clinker?

In 1832 the firm of Colburn and Bentley was dissolved, Bentley buying out Colburn. Thus Hook's three-volume "The Parson's Daughter," which made its appearance on May 2, 1833, was published by Bentley. On November 24 of the same year, Whittaker and Company printed three volumes entitled "The Widow and the Marquess;

or, Love and Pride." This work consists of two distinct and unrelated stories by Hook — one about a widow and a theme of love, the other about a marquess who is the personification of pride.

Hook's achievement as a novelist is characterized by Allen Cunningham in an article written for the "London Athenæum" in 1833.[1]

It would not be easy [he writes] to find another artist with ability equal to Hook's for discussing the good and evil, the passions and affectations, the fits of generosity and settled systems of saving, the self-sufficiency and the deplorable weakness, the light and darkness, the virtue and the vice, of this prodigious Babel. The stories which he tells might be invented with little outlay of fancy, for the best of them are far from being either clear or consistent; but the characters which live and breathe in them, would make the narratives pleasing, though they were as crooked as the walls of Troy.

After Hook had become a contributor to Colburn's "New Monthly Magazine," he wrote for it his novel "Gilbert Gurney," which appeared by instalments during 1834 and 1835. When the work came out in book form, printed by Whittaker and Company, on November 30, 1835 (dated 1836), it contained eight additional chapters. The novel was very favorably received; and as soon as Hook became editor of the "New Monthly," he

---

[1] "A Biographical and Critical History of the Literature of the Last Fifty Years."

began a continuation, or sequel, which appeared by instalments in 1837 and 1838, under the title of "The Gurney Papers," and which was published in three volumes by Colburn (who had returned to the trade) in 1839, as "Gurney Married: A Sequel to Gilbert Gurney."

In 1836 a "New Monthly" reviewer wrote of the author of "Gilbert Gurney": [1]

Mr. Hook will not, we suspect, give himself the trouble to construct a regular story. His connected sketches — his keen satire, which, keen as it is, he manages most admirably in nine cases out of ten to blunt with his natural good-nature — his absurdity — his whim — his drollery — have always *told* so well, that he has been too indolent to call up the higher powers of his mind: he has not wanted them, and so suffers them, perhaps too quietly, to "sleep on and take their rest."

In the same year this reviewer writes again: [2]

Mr. Hook is a writer who belongs emphatically to the world as it is. His animated sketches are the clear reflections of what he has seen. He gives us the living English manners, from high to low, as they now exist.

On March 15, 1837, Bentley brought out the novel "Jack Brag." It occasioned an unfriendly estimate of Hook's talents in the "Westminster Review" in 1838. [3] The article reads in part as follows:

---

[1] Vol. xlvi (1836, i), p. 53. S. C. Hall may have written it.
[2] Vol. xlviii (1836, iii), p. 234.
[3] Vol. xxviii. The extracts are from pp. 175 and 182 f.

But without the fact that he began his career as a writer of farces — not even a play-wright, but a *farce-wright*, making burlettas, strings to hang catches upon, and the lowest sorts of comic pieces, provided according to rule, with forced incidents, *outré* characters, and all the commonplaces of outraged oddity, the reader could not see the origin of the characteristic which gives to this writer the position he occupies as a comic literary artist.

[And again]: We pass over a serious but minor fault with which he is chargeable, his failures in the delineation of good characters: we forgive him that he never sets out with a virtuous man or woman, but he leaves them weak or wicked enough at last: that his good heroes invariably break down long before the third volume, and are generally imbecile to immorality: . . . that, in short, the only way he has of persuading the reader his characters are good, is by telling him they are so, and never allowing them to do anything afterwards.

Hook's next novel was "All in the Wrong; or, Births, Deaths, and Marriages," published by Bentley and appearing on March 18, 1839. It was the least popular of all his works of fiction. The publisher offered only £600, and the work barely paid expenses.

The three volumes put out by Colburn in 1840, with the title "Precept and Practice," were a collection of twenty short stories and sketches, all of which had been written by Hook for the "New Monthly" during several years. This magazine, in 1840 and 1841, contained instalments of another novel by editor Hook — "Fathers and Sons." The final number came out after Hook's death, but it appears certain that he had entirely completed the work before he died. It was published in book form by Colburn, in 1842, with a preface containing a good biographical memoir of the author.

On the 29th of July, less than a month before Hook's death, Ingoldsby Barham saw him for the last time. They spoke on that occasion about his "novel 'Peregrine Bunce,' then going through the press, but which he never lived to complete." It is indeed plainly evident that the last four chapters of Hook's last novel are the work of another hand. The novel, "Peregrine Bunce; or, Settled at Last," was published by Bentley in 1842.

It is apparent that contemporary criticism — of which the foregoing extracts may be called representative — had fairly definite opinions about Theodore Hook's abilities as a novelist. He was accused, first, of undue haste and carelessness. Next, he was praised for the number and variety of his descriptions of London life; it was recognized that he is primarily a realist, and most felicitous when recounting, humorously or satirically, the scenes in the society in which he himself moved. Again, it was held that he frequently mars his accomplishment by introducing the frothy unrealities of farce. Finally, it was asserted that he is unable or unwilling to construct a plot good enough to hang his realistic scenes on. The plots he does employ are old and insipid; they involve colorless heroes and heroines whose characters often break down before the conclusion of the story. These judgments by critics of Hook's day are all fundamentally sound. They form a natural basis for any present-day discussion of Hook's novels.

There need be no debate about the first of the charges against Hook. He wrote far too hastily and rapidly. Extemporaneous conception and execution were integral parts of his nature. Barham asserts that the idea and plan of the "Sayings and Doings"

were struck out during the sitting of a sort of "John Bull" conclave, held at Fulham, at which Terry and Mr. Shackell were present, and had origin in a suggestion of the latter; delighted with the anecdotes of colonial life which his friend was pouring forth, he conceived that they might be turned to better account than the mere entertainment of a dinner party, and hit upon the title, at which Hook caught with eagerness.

Yet this initial enthusiasm met impediments. Hook was the editor of a newspaper and was soon to become editor of a monthly periodical; he was in demand as a diner-out in literary and aristocratic circles, and he began to receive numerous invitations to country houses. To write forty volumes of fiction in seventeen years could be accomplished, under these conditions, only by lengthy and forced spurts of writing in which any thought of revision was out of the question. For example, Samuel Carter Hall, acting editor of the "New Monthly," when "Gilbert Gurney" was appearing therein, writes:

The part for the ensuing number was rarely ready until the last moment, and more than once at so late a period of the month, that, unless in the printer's hands next morning, its publication would have been impossible, I have driven to Fulham to find not one line of the article written: and I have waited, sometimes nearly all night, until the manuscript was produced.[1]

It is true that other novelists besides Hook composed with startling rapidity. Ballantyne published four full-length novels by Lockhart in as many successive years. The speed with which a Waverley Novel took shape is proverbial. "In these days," writes (presumably) Hook himself in "John Bull" of February 6, 1841, "ladies and gentlemen, not contented with writing three or four novels in their lifetimes, go to work upon as many at once." That Hook was then following what he considered the custom of novelists of his day, is shown by a portion of his letter to Broderip of December 31, 1839:

Nonsense as it is I do — I have too much to do — but I have several cogent reasons for doing as much as I can. I have in hand a novel for Bentley ["Peregrine Bunce"], a novel for Colburn ["Fathers and Sons"]; I

---

[1] "Memories of Authors," *Atlantic Monthly*, xv, 483.

am editing a work for Colburn [Fleury's memoirs], I am editing a novel for Bentley ["Cousin Geoffrey"]; I am doing a life of Garrick; I have undertaken to edit another work for Colburn; I edit the New Monthly and write in it, and ditto the Bull; and I have but one head and two hands.

In view of the practice of other novelists, Hook's breathless haste does not mean that he (as the phrase goes) prostituted his pen. During the last fevered years, from 1838 to 1841, he did indeed perform any odd job which would pay enough to silence his most insistent creditors. Yet even these last years saw no deterioration in the quality of his novels. "Fathers and Sons" of 1840 is not more hurriedly or carelessly written than "Maxwell" of 1830. Nor can it be said that the desire to pick up a few shillings drove him into the field in 1824. At that time he needed no money. He had been for three years in receipt of £2000 annually from "John Bull," and he was in jail, where opportunities for lavish expenditure were limited. Moreover, he had no reason, in 1824, to anticipate large returns from writing novels. His first venture, in 1808, had been a a total failure.

II. Plots

"Give me a story to tell and I can tell it, but I cannot create," Hook said once. Give him a framework, a plot, and he was able to fill it with scenes and characters taken from life. From what source could he speedily acquire a plan for his tales? A natural impulse caused him to turn again to the stage and press into service his experience in writing farces. In his preface to the first series of "Sayings and Doings" he remarks that the French have long been accustomed to write "short dramatic pieces, in which they have illustrated or exemplified the truth of old sayings." It was from these pieces, he writes,

that I first caught the idea of noting down what I saw passing in society, in order to judge, by the events of real life, the truth or fallacy of those axioms, which have been handed down to us with a character for "usefulness and dignity" as conducive to the understanding of philosophy, of which they are the very remains.

I have for many years watched the world, and have set down all that I have seen; and out of this collection of materials, I have thrown together a few historic illustrations of quaint sayings, the truth and sagacity of which the characters introduced by me have unconsciously exemplified in their lives and conduct; and which I have the small merit of bringing to bear, after long observation, upon the axioms affixed to each tale.

Thus each of the ten stories in the three series of "Sayings and Doings" is to illustrate some general moral observation or "saying." The objection to such a plan is obviously this: either the tale is constructed to fit the moral — in which case it is certain to be mutilated by the plan to which it must conform; or the moral is constructed to fit the tale — in which case the moral is either inapplicable or unnecessary. Hook's stories by no means escape this dilemma.

Three of the tales are, in fact, completely ruined by the plan they are forced to follow. "Danvers," the first story in the first series, must illustrate the saying: "Too much of a good thing is good for nothing." Consequently, when the happy and contented middle-class lawyer suddenly finds himself possessed of an immense fortune and is impelled to seek social and political prominence, it follows that on every occasion his money proves a curse to him, and he is swindled, duped, and cheated. The plot of "Gervase Skinner," the last tale of the third series, is intended to exemplify the principle of "penny wise and pound foolish." It is thus certain that every time this miserly country squire tries to save a shilling, he will lose many pounds, and be subjected, in addition, to a highly disagreeable experience. But the extreme expression of the idea is furnished by "Merton," the third story of the first series. The "doings" of Merton are to illustrate the "saying," "There's many a slip 'twixt the cup and the lip." So then, his house burns down just after the insurance on it has expired. He buys a lottery ticket and it wins the grand prize — but he has lost the ticket. When he is tried for murder, every bit of circumstantial evidence is against him, although he is entirely innocent. The clergyman is just uttering the words which will unite him with the heroine when she is taken from him. On a dozen different occasions he just misses meetings with his beloved which would have cleared up all his difficulties. And when he finally emerges from his troubles and is able at last to rush to her arms — she is dead!

In brief, the principle of a "saying" illustrated by "doings" is fatal to any realistic purpose. If every act of a helpless main character is made to point a moral, the result cannot be called "sketches from life." Fortunately, a few of the ten stories rise above the limitations of the plan, so that the moral affixed to them seems an artificial addition. Such tales, since they are not damned at the outset, have some chance of success. Fortunately, too, Hook soon began writing full-length novels. He found himself obliged to abandon a plan which could not possibly be applied to a three-volume novel. Yet in 1833 he returned to the idea once more in his shorter story "The Marquess," which is to exemplify the saying, "Pride goes before a fall." Every one of the acts of the Marquess of Snowden is dictated by his excessive pride, and results in his humiliation.

A second and even worse heritage came to Hook's prose fiction from the farce stage. Several of the tales in "Sayings and Doings" adopt the farce structure in its entirety, so that they are in effect stage pieces with all the characteristics of Hook's Haymarket farces. Emphasis is placed on action and complication, which go forward by scenes and conversations, and at every important turn of the story the improbability and extravagance of farce are given free control. The characters in such tales become the usual farce types, endowed with stock "stage business" attributes. In "The Sutherlands," in the second series, there are two brothers, one generous, one miserly. Both, by a combination of farcical circumstances, are brought to grief by their marriages. In "The Man of Many Friends," also of the second series, the young man is in London on the road to ruin, the easy prey of a group of unscrupulous hangers-on. The old man, his uncle, seeing the state of affairs, sets up a rival establishment and wins away the pretended friends, who see fresh prey before them. Thus the young man, seeing his beloved uncle apparently in the same state in which he himself had recently been, has his eyes opened to the real characters of the sycophants who had surrounded him. In "Doubts and Fears," the young man is in love with a fair unknown. The old man, doubting her respectability, endeavors to dissuade him, only to find that the girl is his own daughter. There is also a go-between (the Phormio of this Terentian plot) upon whom the action hinges.

It is obvious, surely, that such a complete adoption of the farce framework is ruinous to a story. A minor farcical incident or character in a humorous story is one thing. But an entire farce plot and a complete cast of farce characters is decidedly another thing. For farce characters are regularly ticketed automatons, and farce action is a collection of arbitrary and selected incidents, amusing because of coincidence, whimsicality, or bewildering complication. Into such a mould no fusion of realistic characters and scenes can be poured. That Hook did not recognize this fact shows how pronouncedly his early farce writing had marked him. His adhesion to the unfortunate principle was tenacious. Farce dominates his shorter story, "The Widow," of 1833. It disfigures also three of his full-length novels — "Jack Brag," "Gilbert Gurney," and "Peregrine Bunce." Remarkably enough, in his remaining three-volume novels, the plots of which were borrowed but from a different source, there is very little farcical incident. The author avoids it and does so consciously and studiously. At one place in his "Fathers and Sons" he writes:

Now these two letters lay upon Mr. Grindle's table together, ready for folding, putting in envelopes, sealing and directing; and it is not quite impossible that the reader may think, that in the pure spirit of farce, it would be quite allowable . . . that George Grindle in his agitation . . . might put the two letters in the wrong covers, and so create scenes of infinite embarrassment and distress. *But no — in real life these fortunate mistakes seldom, if ever, occur.*

What other source was there from which a plot might be acquired? There was the picaresque story, which, indeed, can scarcely be said to possess a plot at all. For it demands only a *terminus ad quem* and a set of loosely connected incidents leading the action in a leisurely manner toward that terminus. Smollett, writes Professor George Saintsbury in the preface to his edition of "Roderick Random,"

seems to have had little positive invention, and he did not care to bestow any pains on the constructive part of his stories. Most of them, indeed, begin in a sufficiently orthodox manner with the birth, and end in an equally orthodox manner with the marriage, of the hero. But the intermediate progress is altogether of the "go-as-you-please" order.

Theodore Hook was likewise unwilling or unable to construct a well-knit plot. The picaresque plot, it would seem, was thus well adapted to his temperament and capabilities. It is true that after Smollett's death the novel of comic incident suffered a half-century of eclipse. But there were signs, in the early twenties of the nineteenth century, of its emergence from oblivion. In 1821 there began to appear Pierce Egan's immensely popular "Life in London," the story of the boisterous adventures of Tom, Jerry, and Bob Logic.

J. J. Morier's "Hajji Baba," of 1822, recounts the escapades of a Persian Gil Blas. In France, in the same year, appeared Paul de Kock's "Mon voisin Raymond," and everyone in England who could read French at all devoured (in the privacy of bedroom or boudoir) the works of this prolific scribbler.

Theodore Hook made three experiments with this type of almost plotless story — "Jack Brag," "Peregrine Bunce," and "Gilbert Gurney." The results are highly disappointing; two of the three are essentially failures. What caused their failure, it has already been noted, was the author's complete surrender to farce. Jack Brag, the vulgar and boastful son of a tallow chandler, is a toad-eating parasite who attempts to imitate people of rank and position, and force himself on their society with inflated self-confidence. His efforts are invariably defeated. Peregrine Bunce is a miserly and mean-spirited Cœlebs in search of a rich wife. Every one of his woddings results to his own discomfiture. These two plots are legitimate enough for stories of the "Gil Blas" type. They make but one demand of the author — yet that demand is a stringent one. The main character, the *picaro* himself, must be a real person. He must have the consistent impulses of a genuine man. If the *picaro* — Gil Blas, Don Quixote, Roderick Random, Hajji Baba — meets this requirement, it

scarcely matters how many farce characters he encounters in his travels or how many farcical scenes
he enacts. If he does not meet the requirement,
the story is a failure, even as Hook's "Jack Brag"
and "Peregrine Bunce," which present the spectacle of a stock farce character set into automatic
motion through a series of vaudeville acts, all of
which terminate in the same manner, and most of
which are frothy and unreal farce.

Illustrations of this situation may be picked at
random almost anywhere in either novel. In
"Jack Brag" the widow Dallington and her sister,
Blanche Englefield, are in love, respectively, with
Sir Charles Lydiard and Frank Rushton. Sir
Charles cannot muster up sufficient courage to
propose; Rushton, on the other hand, is too im-
petuous. Now enter Jack Brag. The ladies lead
him on. He proposes to both of them; both accept
him. The suitors are aroused. There is much
complication, the result of which is that the ladies
achieve their purpose: Lydiard is emboldened;
Rushton's ardor is moderated. Brag is exposed,
ridiculed, and turned out. The whole incident is
pure farce (copied from the "Merry Wives of
Windsor"), with characters distorted into the
artificial contrasts demanded by the situation.
And Jack Brag, instead of being a vulgar and in-
sinuating *picaro*, is only a colorless, helpless go-
between. Worse still, Hook is occasionally capable

of destroying what little interest adheres to each scene by announcing the result before relating the incident — as in the following instance: "It was a short time after this that Mr. Brag was called upon to perform a feat for the amusement of his aristocratic friends, which, however powerful the effect it actually did produce, terminated in a manner less agreeable to the actor than to the audience." [1] It is difficult to regard leniently the failure of these two novels. A man of Hook's experience in society must have had continually before his eyes a dozen *genuine* Jack Brags and Peregrine Bunces.

"Gilbert Gurney" is considerably better. It is tarred with the same stick, to be sure. Why should the course and the sentiment of the entire story be jolted in order to introduce the episode in which the father of the heroine gets Gilbert drunk at one o'clock in the morning, and calmly proceeds to wish upon the befuddled young fellow, despite his confused protests, the hand of the heroine — calling her out of bed for that purpose? But even such a capitulation to farce, although it injures the character of the really estimable heroine and leads the story into a blind path, cannot jar Gilbert Gurney himself into the shadow world of farcical extravagance. Gilbert remains a real youth —

---

[1] Professor Wilhelm Dibelius cites this passage in his *Englische Romankunst* (ii, 262).

and the reason is not far to seek. For the young Gilbert is the young Theodore Hook; the story is essentially autobiographical. When Gilbert reaches one of the four or five crises of his youthful life, he acts as Theodore did when faced with the same problems. Thus the novel possesses a living character and a solid substratum of reality. Around such a framework can readily be built comic scenes and characters. They can never stray far into the realm of cheesecloth, for the living Gilbert is always there to breathe into them some of his own vitality.

In dozens of places in his novels Theodore Hook proclaims that he is a realist — that he is faithful to the actualities of life and scorns the extravagances of the romance writer. In "The Friend of the Family," for example, he writes the following:

. . . and although some part of the occurrences which took place may appear to some of my readers as are determined upon having nothing but truth in my sketches, somewhat romantic, they are nevertheless copied from nature, and will be found upon inquiry to be only some of those "curious coincidences" which daily occur to every one of us, upon which we always exclaim, "If this were put into a novel, it would be called improbable and absurd."

In "The Parson's Daughter":

"It won't do, Charles. I rejoice to see your spirits return; but drowning a whole family to give me a peerage, is rather too romantic — it is carrying the joke too far; it would not be tolerated even in one of Colburn and Bentley's namby-pamby novels."

In "Fathers and Sons":

It is no easy matter, whatever people may think of it, to describe the heroine of a simple story. To authors who deal largely in silken tresses and melting eyes, soul-fraught intelligence of expression, and a gentle mixture of roses and lilies by way of complexion, cherries for lips, and pearls for teeth, it may be a work of equal facility and felicity; but to plain-speaking, or rather plain-writing persons, who endeavor to describe with something like accuracy, scenes and circumstances as they occur, and put down upon paper the impressions which they themselves receive from the works of nature, it is far different.

It would thus appear that Hook studiously avoided all connection with romance. Yet romance was the dominating force in English fiction during the first quarter of the century. It seems strange that a novelist in need of a plot should not have gone to the innumerable romances of the day in search of one. It is true that, with the exception of two slight tales dashed off for the "New Monthly," Hook made no trial of the historical novel, which, in 1825, under the leadership of Walter Scott, was the favorite type of romance. Nor was he attracted by the Gothic romance with its elements of the supernatural and the horrible. The Ann Radcliffe type of novel was out of date when Hook began to write fiction. He made one attempt at the supernatural, however, in his brief tale, "Martha the Gypsy," the last story of the first series of "Sayings and Doings." It is the account of the disastrous fulfilment of a curse pronounced by an evil-looking old gypsy woman upon a gentleman who had refused her demand for alms. The instincts of the realist betrayed Hook so far that he attempted to place this tale against a background of broad daylight and the busy streets of the London of 1820![1]

But in addition to these two special types of romance, there were the romances proper — those whose background is not some historical period, and which do not emphasize the supernatural or the terrible. There were great numbers of works of this nature during the first two decades of the century. The proverbially infamous Minerva Press turned them out by dozens.[2] In quality they were undistinguished if not entirely poor,

---

[1] Dibelius thinks (*Englische Romankunst*, ii, 242) that Hook's novel "Maxwell" was influenced by Ann Radcliffe. In this novel an apparently fearful mystery hangs over the story. It is revealed finally that the body of the unjustly condemned merchant, Hanningham, had been brought from the gallows to the surgical laboratory of the physician, Maxwell, and had been restored to consciousness there. To suspend an apparently supernatural mystery over a story and to give a rational explanation of it at the end was, of course, the stock in trade of the woman novelist.

[2] Thomas Rees, *Reminiscences of Literary London*, New York (1896), p. 87: "The 'Minerva Press,' by Wm. Lane, in Leadenhall Street . . . was noted for the number and variety of books, called novels, which were continually produced and distributed to all the circulating libraries in the country. From ten to twenty pounds were the sums usually paid to authors for those novels of three volumes. The Colburns and Bentleys drove this trash out of the market."

and time has obliterated them. Lists of those who wrote them can easily be compiled from the book reviews of the periodicals of the time, but the names in such lists will strike few responsive chords in the memories of present-day readers. There were, to mention a few, Mary Charleton, Sarah Wilkinson, Agnes Musgrave, Francis Lathom, Mrs. Hofland, Mrs. Pilkington, "Mrs. Bridget Bluemantle," "Anne of Swansea," "Rosa Matilda," and (perhaps a point or two higher in the scale) Laetitia M. Hawkins, and Regina Maria Roche. It may be observed that these writers (as well as their readers) were chiefly women.

The plots of these romances were all very much alike. The same materials were used over and over again. It is no great task, then, to discover what was perhaps the favorite one among the three or four standard plots used regularly by the romance writers. Its nature is well illustrated by Regina Maria Roche's "Clermont," of 1798. The plot of "Clermont" is this:

Madeline Clermont is the daughter of a noble old man who is leading a rustic life but who has evidently seen better days. One evening she meets De Sevignie, an excellent young man. He is attired as a peasant, yet he seems, from the distinguished cast of his features and the elegance of his deportment, to be of a more elevated origin. The two fall in love. But De Sevignie cannot push his good fortune because of the mystery surrounding his birth and station. He does not even confide his difficulties to Madeline, but retires to solitude in grief.

Madeline leaves her retirement and comes into the world under the aegis of a countess. This worthy woman dies suddenly, after entrusting Madeline to the care of her daughter, Madame D'Alembert, an unfortunate lady who has a deeply villainous husband. When he sees Madeline, he wishes to win her. Consequently, he removes his wife from the scene, announces her death, and confers with his equally villainous father. The two know some secret involving Madeline's father.

The elder D'Alembert seeks out Clermont, proclaims his son a widower, proposes in his son's name for Madeline's hand, and hints that it will go hard with Clermont if his desire is not gratified. Clermont is not averse to the proposal. He does not know of De Sevignie's love; nor is he aware that young D'Alembert's wife is still alive. But Madeline instinctively scorns both the D'Alemberts. She is threatened thereupon with the ruin of her father. Distracted at this prospect, she is inclined to yield. But her love for De Sevignie induces her to make an attempt to free herself. She flees with her father to Paris, is deceived by those she trusts, and finds herself in young D'Alembert's power. She refuses his dishonorable proposals, and he prepares to use force. But at the "crucial moment" she is rescued by De Sevignie, who has followed her. It is discovered that the secret imperilling Clermont — a charge of murder — is untrue, and that Clermont himself is of noble birth. De Sevignie, too, proves to be a lost heir.

This is a very old plot — an adaptation of the "exile and return" theme of mediaeval romance. The formula it follows is simple: the heroine loves the hero, but for some reason he must temporarily retire from her presence. The way is thus made clear for the entrance of the villain, who begins to persecute the heroine. The villain must be disposed of before the two lovers can be united.

Theodore Hook must have considered this plot a very satisfactory one indeed, for he employed it in twelve of his novels and shorter tales — comprising fully two thirds of his work as a writer of fiction.[1] It may thus be called his standard plot. Was his adoption of it successful? It is true that the frequency with which he used it seems a mistake. Yet it may be contended that Jane Austen wrote her novels according to a formula [2] without having it held against her. The question of the success of Hook's standard plot resolves itself into this: can a realist use such a romance plan as a framework for materials drawn from real life? Can this romance plot be given a realistic setting? Thus stated, the question becomes even more definitely resolved. The romance formula demands certain characters to carry on its action. Will these characters endure transplantation from romance to realism?

---

[1] He used it in four shorter stories: *The Friend of the Family, Passion and Principle, Merton,* and *Gervase Skinner;* in three volume-and-a-half novels: *Cousin William, The Widow,* and *The Marquess;* in five "three-decker" novels: *Maxwell, The Parson's Daughter, Gurney Married, All in the Wrong,* and *Fathers and Sons.*

[2] Upon first meeting B, A does not like him; but meeting him under different circumstances, and after a certain lapse of time, she does like him.

III. CHARACTERS.

In examining the major characters of Theodore Hook's novels, little attention need be given those which illustrate the two ideas that he brought over from the minor theatre. The first of these, the idea of "doings" illustrating a "saying," renders impossible, if rigidly applied, any sort of character portrayal. Thus Danvers, Merton, Gervase Skinner, and the Marquess are helpless ciphers, doomed at every turn to act so as to exemplify a formula. The second idea, the bodily transference of a one-act farce from the stage to prose fiction, is likewise fatal to character creation. For in farce the major characters become types — the young man, the old man, the go-between. The few individual qualities of such characters are dictated by the events in which they take part. In "Doubts and Fears," for example, the situation requires Sir Harry Dartford, the respectable parent type, to play also the part of the attempted seducer of the innocent heroine. Can such a character be made plausible? The attempt is not made; Sir Harry is described as

the most thoughtless, extravagant, profligate creature upon earth. . . . Volatile and hare-brained as a boy of twenty; the most eccentric, grave, gay, lively and severe person imaginable — full of all sorts of abomination and indiscretion, but with such a heart!

This is not a character at all. It is a peg on which to hang two opposing and contradictory qualities demanded by the action.

It has already been remarked that two of Hook's three novels of comic incident are failures because of his inability to make the central figure of each a living character. At the beginning of "Jack Brag" and of "Peregrine Bunce," the title-rôle character is presented, fitted with one weakness, one piece of stage business — and sent forthwith through a series of farcical scenes in each of which his one weakness causes his downfall, the last one being overwhelming. Peregrine Bunce had an initial shyness which

was by no means unprepossessing, inasmuch as it passed for that which goes far to win a well-bred woman: a respectful deference, which, when he once felt that he liked and esteemed those with whom he was living, wore off — the chilling mist in which at the outset he appeared to be enveloped, was dissipated as he warmed in society; while his excessive devotion to what he was pleased to call "the fair sex" was never in the slightest degree diminished by his own secret good opinion of himself in the art of gaining their hearts and affections.

This one characteristic Bunce unfailingly exhibits. He (and Brag likewise) remains, therefore, a stage figure playing the part of dupe in a succession of short farce scenes.

"Gilbert Gurney," it has also been noted, is vastly better than "Brag" or "Bunce," because

the main character seems drawn from reality. In
his diary Hook speaks of his writing of it as "working on my life." Gurney, in fact, is Theodore with
a few fictional alterations. Gilbert was born in the
same year and same month with Lord Byron —
January, 1788; Theodore was born in September,
1788. Gurney's first farce was damned; Hook's
was a fair success. The practical jokes that Theodore committed when a youth are, in the novel,
given to a character named Daly; hence Gilbert is
less active and mischievous than Theodore was.
Both have elder brothers, but Gilbert's is in India.
Gilbert marries; Theodore did not. Yet one feels
distinctly that Hook identified himself with his
character, and that in creating Gurney, he lived
over the exciting moments of his own youth.

The major characters of those stories in which
Hook uses his standard plot, borrowed from romance, require a somewhat more extended consideration.

It will be remembered that the major characters
in Mrs. Roche's "Clermont" are the hero and
heroine, the parent, and the villain. The plot in
which these characters act makes several demands.
The hero must retire temporarily from the scene;
the villain must be plausibly introduced; and (if
the story is to contain a proper element of sus-
pense) his chances of success in coercing the
heroine must appear good. The romancer meets

these demands by the use of well-tried and generally accepted conventions of romance: the peerlessly beautiful and persecuted heroine, the scrupulously honorable hero, the noble but victimized father, the black villain. She uses the "lost heir" motive to explain the hero's temporary retirement; she gives the villain power over the parent by employing the "mysterious crime" theme.

Such characters and such themes are accepted as characteristic of romance. If the romance is a good one, the reader willingly suspends disbelief. But a realist can have nothing to do with them. When Theodore Hook took over the romance plot, he had to find realistic motives for the characters. He most frequently adopted the motive of parental authority — the hero is forced to retire because the parent of the heroine commands her to marry the villain. That authority is exercised with varying degrees of rigor. In "The Marquess," and "Fathers and Sons," for instance, the parent is a tyrant who will endure no opposition to his will. In "The Widow" and "Passion and Principle," the parents urge the heroine to marry the villain, but they do not attempt to coerce her. In "Maxwell" and "Cousin William," the heroine chooses the villain practically of her own volition. Moreover, in many of the stories, Hook makes the villain's success appear probable by actually allowing him to marry the heroine.

These motives, which Hook substituted for the unreal formulas of the romancer, are real enough. Parental authority — as it existed in Hook's day, at least — forms a sufficient cause for the retirement of the hero and the introduction of the villain. Again, in a day when divorce was a long, costly, and uncertain business, involving also loss of caste, the marriage of the heroine and the villain was surely occasion enough for the hero's discouragement and the villain's apparent triumph. Indeed, the idea of such a marriage is strikingly opposed to the romancer's conceptions. It means that the heroine, when she finally marries the hero, will be a widow — a situation breaking sharply with the romancer's constant and fervent cult of virginity.

So far as substituting realistic motives is concerned, Hook's adaptation of the romance plot seems successful. But the effect of this substitution upon the major characters has still to be considered. In what state do the hero and heroine, the parent and the villain, of the romance, find themselves in Hook's novels?

In Mrs. Roche's romance, the father of the heroine, Clermont, is a noble old man somewhat helplessly at the mercy of circumstances. But in Hook's standard plot such a passive rôle is impossible. The action turns on parental authority. The parent favors, and usually commands, the marriage of the heroine and the villain. Now, since this marriage is desired neither by the heroine nor by the hero (who are obviously created for each other and who have the reader's sympathy), and since it is in reality an ill-assorted match, there is no help for the parent. When he asserts his authority, he takes upon himself the qualities of a villain. Hook is obliged to picture the parent, therefore, as a military tyrant (Colonel Bruff in "Fathers and Sons"), as a titled egotist (the Marquess), as a hopelessly impractical old twaddler (the schoolmaster Rodney of "Passion and Principle"), as a coldly calculating, mercenary woman (Mrs. Franklin of "The Widow" and Lady Frances Sheringham of "The Parson's Daughter"). Such characters are difficult to portray; it is hard to make the reader believe in them. For very frequently their decision seems utterly unreasonable, their motives lame, and their other acts out of harmony with their blind insistence upon an obviously unsuitable marriage. A good example of this is Colonel Bruff of "Fathers and Sons." He agrees with Sir George Grindle to marry his daughter Jane to Grindle's son George. Jane has fallen in love with Frank Grindle, Sir George's son by his second marriage, but Bruff refuses to allow her to marry Frank instead of George. Hook sees the lameness of Bruff's motive:

Many people may, and perhaps will think, whatever Bruff's anxieties about the baronetcy might be, that if it could be shown to him that the alternative between his daughter's marrying the one son or the other of Sir George Grindle, was her happiness or misery, no man could be so obstinate and obdurate, considering how slight the difference between their fortunes apparently was, to hesitate which course to pursue.

He has therefore to assert repeatedly that Bruff is a martinet who fixes his mind according to his whims and is immovable to entreaty. Yet Bruff's other acts deny this characteristic, for he is, in general, easily swayed by those about him. Thus he takes over the qualities of a villain at the price of losing congruity as a character.

Mrs. Roche's Madeline Clermont is a true heroine of romance. Her figure, her features, her disposition, her poise, her delicate air of languor, are all lovely beyond comparison:

Her eyes, large, and of the darkest hazel, ever true to the varying emotions of her soul, languished beneath their long silken lashes with all the fire of animation; her hair, a rich auburn, added luxuriance to her beauty, and by a natural curl gave an expression of the greatest innocence to her face; the palest blush of health just tinged her dimpled, fair and beautifully rounded cheek; and her mouth, adorned by smiles, appeared like the half-blown rose when moistened with the dews of early morn.

When Hook's heroine appears, she is perhaps not so ecstatically described, but she is always a compound of almost all the female perfections. Yet

when she begins to take part in the story, her
chances of remaining on her lofty pedestal are
slim. Her character, in fact, fluctuates inversely
as does the character of her parent. When he
tyrannically compels her to accept the villain,
then she need exhibit only the passive qualities of
the persecuted female, and the perfections with
which her creator endowed her can persist unim-
paired throughout the story — except, indeed,
that her spineless acquiescence arouses the reader's
impatience. But in those stories in which the
parent employs methods less rigorous than com-
pulsion the heroine's character begins to suffer.
For in such cases parental authority does not completely motivate the hero's retirement and the
villain's temporary success; the heroine must also
bear part of the blame. It is true that the earnest
wish of a parent is not to be lightly disregarded.
But it is also true that by consenting without real
coercion to marry one man when she loves another, such a heroine commits a great wrong. Instead of being helpless, she is culpably weak.

The complete fall of Hook's heroine occurs in
those stories in which the father only mildly urges
his wishes, for then her proposed marriage with the
villain is practically of her own choosing. Hook
tries, indeed, to excuse these heroines by showing
them more or less at the mercy of untoward circumstances. But he loses patience with them,

nevertheless. When Kate Maxwell, forbidden to marry her true love, drifts into a marriage with a dishonest stock-broker, Hook sneers at her: "When it is recollected that the swain had reached his forty-fourth year and the nymph her twenty-fifth, some allowance may be made for the unsentimental considerations which filled the mind of the latter." And when Caroline Crosby of "Cousin William" deserts the one she loves and marries another, she regains her hero only at the cost of becoming an adultress and suffering an unhappy fate as a terrible example of "conflicting passions and strong feelings, acting upon an ardent mind, uncontrolled by principle, and unfortified by religion."

The romancer's hero exists practically unchanged in Hook's novels. He is amiable and honorable, but he has no active rôle to play. When he learns that the heroine is intended for another, he has merely to retire and wait for an interval until the situation clears itself. Then he can step forward and claim his beloved. If there is a difference between Hook's hero and the hero of romance, it is that the former, since he exists in a background of realistic motives, seems even more pathetically helpless.

The villain in "Clermont" possesses a nature of unrelieved blackness and infamy. He pursues the heroine relentlessly because the pursuit is part of

his villainous nature. Such a character may exist
in a romance, but it is difficult for a realist to trans-
port him to nineteenth-century London and to explain his impulses and motives realistically. When
Hook's villain first appears there is no doubt of his
character. A dishonorable or infamous past is
regularly created for him, and he is obviously far
inferior to the hero. But he is rarely actively
wicked during the course of the story. He does not
persecute the heroine. He will marry her willingly
enough, but the burden of blame for that ill-
advised match rests on the shoulders of the parent,
or, indeed, of the heroine herself. In short, the
villain is relieved of his villainy; his character
gains greatly by being transplanted to a realistic
setting. For example, George Grindle of "Fathers
and Sons" has a bad past record. He has ruined a
confiding and innocent young woman. Yet his
conduct throughout the novel is decent enough.
His worst faults are that he is a dandy — a class
B dandy — and that his company becomes bore-
some:

Yet there was, in point of fact, more *in* George
Grindle than he would permit you to think. He affected a sort of childish manner of speaking, and talked,
as we have already seen, in a phraseology peculiar to a
certain, and certainly not the best, clique; and although
there was a quaintness and oddity in its style . . . it
grew tiresome by constant practice.

The conclusion cannot be doubtful. Theodore Hook's attempt to use a romance plot in a realistic story is not a success. He did indeed discard the traditional formulas of romance and substitute genuinely real motives like parental authority. But he failed when he tried to make the major characters of the romance act amid realistic surroundings. Then the noble father became a tyrant, the heroine toppled from her pedestal, the amiable hero became more helpless, and the villain lost his blackness. To atone for this general pejoration, this reduction from type to anomaly, these characters acquire no compensating reality. They are no longer of the romance, because they have lost their conformity to type; they are not drawn from life, because they are composed of conflicting, incongruous impulses. They have been taken out of romance, but they have not been admitted into realism. They are in a state of suspension between the two.

The search for characters drawn from real life leads one, therefore, to the minor characters of Hook's novels.

When the reader is introduced to Hook's minor characters, he learns that they regularly possess certain peculiarities. Thus Dr. MacGopus of "The Parson's Daughter":

The Doctor had his peculiarities. . . . In the first place, the Doctor uniformly differed in opinion with every body round him.

In the same novel there is Miss Jarman:

> There was one peculiarity for which she was rather remarkable: — with every disposition for conversation, . . . she had not the faculty of recollecting any thing in the world which she wished to remember.

There is Mrs. Rodney of "Passion and Principle":

> Mrs. Rodney was a pattern of excellence, but she had a few peculiarities; — one consisted in always speaking the truth and the whole truth, regardless of circumstances or consequences; and the other in never permitting any human being to be happy or comfortable under any circumstances whatever, at the same time wishing them with all her heart to be both.

Moreover, the reader soon learns that it is by these one or two peculiarities, and by them alone, that the character is to be recognized at all future meetings.

Now this method of portraying characters is clearly the method of "humours." On the English stage the practice is as old as Ben Jonson. The "humour" itself is defined by Congreve, in his well-known essay on comedy, as a "singular and unavoidable manner of doing or saying anything, peculiar and natural to one man only; by which his speech and actions are distinguished from those of other men." In the farces of the eighteenth century, characters with "humours" were not uncommon. The plays of Colley Cibber, the elder Colman, Foote, Peake, and others are comedies of situation, the main action of which is carried on by major characters who are not eccentric in dress, manners, or actions. But there is frequently some other character whose function is to give expression to one or two personal eccentricities. He is a low comedy character, with one or two pieces of stage business. As a farce writer Hook knew these caricatured characters well. They appear in his own farces. In "The Soldier's Return," for instance, there is a character named Rocket, who has two peculiarities: he dresses so that no one would suspect him of being a gentleman (for he really is one), and he has the habit of showing his erudition by giving short biographical sketches of all the famous men whose names happen to be mentioned in conversation.

Moreover, these "humorous" characters had entered the novel before Hook's day. Tobias Smollett first brought them in. Fielding, in his preface to "Joseph Andrews," declares firmly against "burlesque" characters. Sterne's creations are of a different mould. But in Smollett's novels there are a fair number of "originals" — of characters eccentric in appearance and action. In "Ferdinand Count Fathom" there is Captain Minikin. He has two "humours":

The captain's peculiarities were not confined to his external appearance; for his voice resembled the sound of a bassoon, or the aggregate hum of a whole bee-hive, and his discourse was almost nothing else than a series of quotations from the English poets, interlarded with

French phrases, which he retained for their significance, on the recommendation of his friends, being himself unacquainted with that or any other outlandish tongue.

After 1770, characters with "humours" continued to appear occasionally in the novel. There are a number in Fanny Burney's novels, several (like Miss Bates) in Jane Austen's, and a few (like the Dominie Sampson) in the Waverley Novels.

When Theodore Hook used "humorous" characters in his novels, he was thus by no means an innovator. As a writer of farces, he had before him the example of the farce stage, which had long known these characters. As a novelist, he was faced by the example of Smollett, who first demonstrated that such characters could be used in prose fiction. Yet Hook's achievement was considerable.

The objection which the realist can urge against the "humorous" characters of the farce and against many of those in Smollett's novels is impossible to confute. It is that real people are not simple formulas; they cannot be reduced to two or three peculiarities. When real people do possess eccentricities, these do not appear in everything they say or do. The idea of "humours," the realist will say, thus involves caricature and exaggeration. This is particularly evident when the "humours" ascribed are far-fetched and extravagant — as in practically all low-comedy characters on the stage, and as in many characters in Smollett's novels — notably, perhaps, Pallet and the physician in "Peregrine Pickle," and Commodore Trunnion in "Roderick Random." Characters like these are confessed burlesques. They are artificially constructed; there is no real substance in them. In pure farce they are permissible, but they damage any novel which attempts to portray real life.

Theodore Hook's practice takes away much of the force of this objection. He created fully two hundred minor characters with "humours." In Smollett's novels there are no more than forty (and many even of these are only doubtfully "humorous"). When only a few of these characters appear in a story, each one is brought too definitely before the eye of the reader. There is a tendency to compare him with characters not supplied with "humours," or to take him apart from his surroundings and observe how he is constructed. Under such scrutiny his artificiality becomes apparent. But when, as in Hook's stories, multitudes of eccentric characters are present, the effect is different. Each one is a minor character. He is never long enough in any one scene for his artificiality to appear. Moreover, he lives and interacts with many others of his kind. The reader's attention rests on the group, not on the individual personage. And the impression given by the group — which can be very large because its members are not presented at full length — is real. The characters seem to supplement each other, to form a lifelike confusion in which the individual member, composed as he is of unique and unvarying qualities, nevertheless stands out distinctly. A character with "humours" does not easily pass from the memory. Again, if there are large numbers of minor characters, the "humours" can scarcely be extravagant or grotesque. The author will remain perforce near the norm of human experience, and select for "humours" those slight eccentricities which real people possess and which everyone observes in distinguishing one person from another.

Hook improves the caricatured character in another way as well, and again his achievement consists in going beyond and perfecting the example of Smollett. On perhaps a dozen occasions the older novelist, when introducing an "original," not only names his "humours" but appends a detailed description of his external appearance. Thus Ferret of "Sir Launcelot Greaves":

The solitary guest had something very forbidding in his aspect which was contracted by an habitual frown. His eyes were small and red, and so deep set in the sockets, that each appeared like the unextinguished snuff of a farthing candle, gleaming through the horn of a dark lanthorn. His nostrils were elevated in scorn, as if his sense of smelling had been perpetually offended by some unsavoury odour; and he looked as if he wanted to shrink within himself from the impertinence of society. He wore a black periwig as straight as the pinions of a raven, and this was covered with a hat flapped, and fastened to his head by a speckled handkerchief tied under his chin. He was wrapped in a greatcoat of brown frieze, under which he seemed to conceal a small bundle. His name was Ferret, and his character distinguished by three peculiarities. He was never seen to smile; he was never heard to speak in praise of any person whatsoever; and he was never known to give a direct answer to any question that was asked; but seemed on all occasions, to be actuated by the most perverse spirit of contradiction.

Hook has a far greater number of such descriptions than has Smollett. He almost always accompanies his minor characters into the scene with detailed descriptions of features and dress. For example, there is Jim Salmon of "Jack Brag":

At this moment Jim made his appearance, dressed in a tight, light green coat, and a buff waistcoat, with striped blue and white cotton trousers, made tightish to his plump figure, a coloured check handkerchief round his neck, and a white hat stuck on one side of his head, with a bunch of whitish-red curls sticking out from under it.

There is a dishonest lawyer in "All in the Wrong":

Brimmer Brassey was a stirring person, and likely to make himself and his principal popular amongst the Radicals. He was always over-smartly dressed; his countenance was florid, edged with much black whisker; he wore his hat — a silk hat — on one side of his head; a coloured handkerchief round his neck; a chain, questionable as to metal, by way of guard to an equivocal watch, over a velvet waistcoat. He was well able to drink punch, weak or strong, hot or cold, as the case might be, at any time, and in any quantity; smoked cigars if desired, and went the whole length of pipes if necessary; was upon intimate terms with several of the actors of the minor theatres; sang songs which were not in print; told anecdotes which astonished the natives; had a friend who benevolently lent money to anybody, upon the least imaginable security; and in fact was the most accommodating person in his peculiar line of the profession to which he did not do too much honour.

And there is Mr. Misty of "Peregrine Bunce":

Mr. Christopher Sugg Misty was a little, thin, wiry elderly gentleman, with a prodigious large head, on which the bump of benevolence was very strongly developed. His eyes projected like a lobster's; he had two big red ears which stood out on either side his head like the paddle-boxes of a steamboat; and he had lost all his front teeth, with the exception of two black stumps, which whenever he happened to smile, lent peculiar sweetness to his simper. . . . He wore black shorts and gaiters; a black coat singularly eccentric in its fit, and luxuriant to excess in point of skirts; a white, thickly padded neck-kerchief, in which his chin was deeply imbedded; and an old-fashioned gold watch, nearly as large as a warming-pan, whose chain and seals went dangling half-way down to his knees.

It is obvious that these descriptions greatly increase the effectiveness of the method of "humours" by reducing further the realist's contention concerning the artificiality of the method. For even though it is admitted that a "humorous" character, regarded by himself, is only an animate formula, yet it can truly be contended that minute descriptions of his appearance bind him closely to reality. It is impossible not to believe in the genuineness of people minutely described as Hook describes them. For it is immediately evident that these descriptions are drawn from observation — are modelled after people Hook knew well.[1] And for the number and variety of them Hook's wide-observing eye must receive praise. He sets forth clergymen, soldiers, foreigners, noblemen, rich citizens, school teachers, dandies, tradespeople of all sorts, scheming hypocrites, dowagers, servants, children, actors and actresses — a great section of the society of his day stands out in vivid clearness.

When these minor characters associate with the various major characters of Hook's stories, how do the two agree? The minors fare best when they are given a free hand. In "Gilbert Gurney" the only major character is Gilbert himself, and he, it has been remarked, is somewhat inactive, although he remains real. In this novel, then, the lesser people have full sway. They are present in numbers; they are very well depicted; and the incidents in which they engage are almost always genuinely comic. In "Jack Brag" and "Peregrine Bunce" the actions of the minors are restricted by

---

[1] The original can in many cases be named. Lady Cramley of *Fathers and Sons* is the novelist, Lady Morgan; Old Nubley of *Gilbert Gurney* is Lord Worcester; Godfrey Moss of *Maxwell* is the Reverend Edward Cannon; Hull of *Gilbert Gurney* is old Tommy Hill of the Sydenham Sundays.

their being forced to act in scenes of frothy farce with the unreal Brag and Bunce. Occasionally they find themselves alone; then the scene which results is vivid. Notable among such scenes is that on Jack Brag's yacht, in which the very point of the situation is that Brag sits in astounded silence in the background, while his guests, utterly ignoring his existence, devote themselves to conversations with each other.

But it is in those novels and tales in which Hook employs his standard plot, of romance origin, that the difficulties of the minor characters are the greatest. For this plot does not require the agency of minor characters; the entire action is carried out by the principals. The minors have nothing to do; they are an unnecessary side-show to the main performance. The strictest care must be exercised to prevent them from getting in the way of the action of the story. Worse still, they differ from the major characters in kind. The latter are formless creatures, composed often of contradictory qualities. Their color is pale, and they seem to have only a two-dimensional existence. The minors, on the contrary, have vivid and sprightly qualities, and possess a three-dimensional reality because they have been taken from life. The result is a noticeable duality, a distinct cleavage, which injures these stories markedly. The reader receives as a total impression the sense of a commonplace plot with unreal principals, in the midst of which, and totally unconnected therewith, arises a set of vividly portrayed minor characters who are looking in bewilderment for something to do.

IV. BACKGROUND.

Theodore Hook's prose style — perhaps because of the speed with which he composed — is an undistinguished medium of expression. His sentences are usually long and involved, with much doubtful grammar and much repetition of phrase and thought. The motion of the narrative is slow and leisurely. Yet sometimes the situation in the story excites its author to the temporary acquisition of what may be called energy — as, for instance, in the following passage from "Maxwell":

Eight o'clock arrived — it was dusk — the dinner was done — overdone — waiting: the servants had twice been into the drawing-room to know if they were to wait any longer. At five minutes past eight a knock and ring announced an arrival, and a yellow postchaise, come through from Liphook, drew up at the door.

"There they are, by jingo!" said Hanningham, jumping up and running, or rather tumbling down stairs to receive the visitors.

"Mercy on us!" said Mrs. Hanningham — not quite relishing the enthusiasm which her husband displayed upon the occasion of Miss Maxwell's arrival, and resolving to treat her with a proportionable degree of coolness, so as to mark her disapprobation of his conduct.

"Up stairs — up stairs!" she heard Hanningham say; and then followed the noise of kissing — extremely tantalizing, and not, as she thought, altogether called for under the circumstances. "Up stairs — take care — mind the corner — there, up with you — Oh, never mind the things — up with you."

And amidst all this jumble of words, and scuffling and scrambling, and pushing and thumping, who should rush into the drawing-room to the astonishment of Mrs. Hanningham, but old Mr. Wilson, the agent from Fayal, and his charming daughter.

Hook's earlier stories, particularly his three series of "Sayings and Doings," are marked with the stereotyped moral *obiter dicta* which were part and parcel of romance. Stale and feeble reflections, intended to serve as a commentary on the action in progress in the story, are inserted at regular intervals with an almost mathematical precision. Thus one reads:

The richest gem in the universe would have less effect upon the heart of man than one tear of affection shed for him by the woman he loves, and who, he thinks, loves him.

But the great Disposer of events heard the prayers of his sorrowing servants, and rescued them from the snares which the wicked had laid for them.

And this was the being whose happiness, whose fame, whose very existence, perhaps, was to be endangered by the malicious insinuations of a demon in human shape!

Death, relentless death! before whose unerring dart the great, the good, the virtuous and the wise, alike must fall.

These things are signs of degenerate and moribund romance. They are a heritage from Leadenhall Street. Hook took them over probably because, at the beginning of his career as a novelist, he thought the reader had come to expect and demand them. He discarded the worst of them as he gained experience, but he adopted nothing genuine in their place. There is, consequently, little philosophical background to Hook's novels — little intellectual depth or subtlety.

Politically, it has been seen, Hook was a genuine and ardent Tory. Surprisingly enough, his novels contain very little direct and open party eulogy. With the exception of a few sugary panegyrics on the Duke of Wellington and one or two slighting allusions to Lord Brougham, there are almost no references to contemporary politicians. Toward politics, indeed, there is an almost American cynicism. In "The Marquess" Hook writes of 10 Downing Street: "There is a fascination in the very air of that little *cul de sac*, — an hour's inhalation of its atmosphere affects some men with giddiness — others with blindness, — and very frequently with the most oblivious forgetfulness." There is an election scene in "Danvers" which is a picture of unconcealed bribery by both sides. The Whig candidate is indeed shown as a hypocrite and a demagogue. But the Tories dishonestly allowed Danvers to pour out money in what they knew was a hopeless contest. When "All in the Wrong" was written, the Reform Bill had passed and the Whigs were in power. Yet the election in this novel is still a financial business, although the bribery is carried on with more adroitness and circumspection.

Theodore Hook's Conservative principles are, however, evident in his general attitude toward society. He is clearly an advocate of the old order of things, of the landed aristocracy and the High Church, and an opponent of the "howling liberty boys" and Methodists.

One hears a vast deal [he writes in "Fathers and Sons"] of . . . the "equality" of human beings . . . but high-sounding as all these very cheering, consolatory, and encouraging preachments and speechifications may be, in point of fact when tested by practice, they are so much nonsense, because, although men and women may be universally constructed alike (each in their kind), the disparity of their qualities and qualifications is too evident to require a moment's consideration.

Even the blustering Radical feels this. For, writes Hook in "Passion and Principle":

The stubborn, high-spirited, independent Briton . . . who rails and blusters at his betters, and thinks it the birthright of an Englishman to be discontented, and to proclaim his discontent at every possible opportunity, is, when the test is applied, the most fawning sycophant upon the face of the earth.

Everyone should remain in the place for which nature intended him. The misfortunes of Dan-

vers all arose when he attempted to push himself
into aristocratic society, where he was not only an
annoyance to those about him, but became himself miserable. Incumbent upon the higher members of society is necessarily a *noblesse oblige:*
"There is nothing more absurd, nothing more re-
pulsive, than false pride; and the leading characteristic of a truly noble mind is kindness towards
and consideration for our inferiors." But this
kindness must not extend to intimacy. To become
intimate with servants may do very well "in
America, indeed, where colonels drive stages and
judges keep alehouses," but not in England. Caroline Crosby of "Cousin William" made a confi-
dante of her maid, Davis, and the consequence was
ineffaceable sin. Squire Harbottle of "The Parson's Daughter" and Colonel Mortimer of "All in
the Wrong" also met disaster by confiding in servants. One should help the poor and unfortunate
by unostentatious charity. But one should be
careful not to give to them too freely. Danvers
thus mistakenly indulged them. And what was
the result? "The poor of the neighbourhood were
actually in arms against him because the beer
which he gave to them in charity was not of the
first quality of ale, and a report had been spread
. . . that the soup was made of dead dogs because
it happened not to be turtle."

As for the English aristocracy, it is the *crème de la crème*. "When," Hook writes in "Passion and Principle,"

the number of the aristocracy of this country is calculated, and the constant watch kept upon all its actions duly considered, I am apt to believe that the vices of the higher grades, however much more exposed to view, will be found infinitely fewer in proportion to their numbers, than those of middling society; in the classes below mediocrity it will not be thought too severe (since the statement is founded upon observation) to say, that those virtues for the absence of which the great are most satirized, are beyond all measure rare.

From Hook, consequently, one need expect little humanitarian sympathy with the downtrodden, or interest in their lives and problems. The reader does not become, like Oliver Twist, familiar with the "cold, wet, shelterless, midnight streets of London; the foul and drowsy dens, where vice is closely packed and lacks the room to turn; the haunts of hunger and disease, the shabby rags that scarcely hold together." On the other hand it by no means follows that every lord is a model of excellence. In "The Marquess" the titled principal character is brought to grief at every turn, and Lord Elmsdale is beaten out in the contest for the heroine by the tutor, Burford. In "Cousin William" appears the Earl of Leatherhead: "The yahoo was of the equestrian order — no less a personage than an English earl." Even in "Passion and Principle," where the aristocracy is most markedly exalted, Major General Brashleigh is set down as a contemptible martinet, and it is intimated that the governor-general of India promotes officers under him chiefly according to the beauty and accessibility of their wives.

There is another reason for Hook's emphasis on high society. At the beginning of his efforts as a novelist he was attempting to write "fashionable" novels. He assumed a deliberate pose. He set himself up as the delineator of the arcana of fashionable society — as the man of *ton* perfectly at home in the most snobbish and esoteric circles.

His pose has a double aspect. He adopts, for one thing, a tone of fastidious despair and humorous scorn toward the dinners, affairs, and customs of the middle class — toward the *Kleinbürger* who attempt to imitate their betters. This attitude is particularly evident in the three series of "Sayings and Doings." In "Danvers," the first story of the first series, one reads:

This sounds strange, but it is true, and I and every other man who mixes in society perceive it, that wealth, inordinate and immense as it may be, cannot give the tact, the manner of doing things. In the midst of the golden dishes and golden vases, there is always some mistake at such dinners, some little blunder which neither the master nor the mistress of the house can hope to rectify on any future occasion, not being conscious of any thing wrong: for instance, the butlers stand looking at each other, in attitudes with dishes in their hands, waiting for signals, and hesitating where to

put them down: then there is always a dreadful uncer-
tainty about the wine; Lunel is detected in a long-
necked bottle up to his chin in an ice-pail, presuming to
do duty for St. Peray, absent without leave; the claret
is frozen hard, the Hock left luke-warm, and common
red port put down upon the table as if people were to
drink it; the fish is generally doubtful; the *entrées* cold,
and the soufflets flat and heavy: while the want of regularity in the dinner pervades even the guests, and one
has perhaps to sit opposite to two or three odd-looking
persons (connexions of the family who *must* be asked)
with coarse neck-cloths and great red hands, with gold
rings upon the fingers; people who go the horrid lengths
of eating with their knives and calling for porter. In
short, there is always some drawback, some qualifier in
the affair, which it would be difficult distinctly to de-
fine, but which invariably gives the *air bourgeois* to all
the attempts of upstart wealth to imitate the tone and
manner of the aristocracy of our country.

Think of descending even lower in middle-class
society and of attempting to sit through the
"heavy details of a plebeian dinner" — such as
the one in "The Man of Many Friends":

To grace the board, there was, first, a tureen filled
with stuff, made at a neighbouring pastry cook's (sent
home in a copper pan, upon the head of a dirty boy in a
linen jacket, with a paper of sweet cakes under his arm),
called mock-turtle — a glue-like mixture, illustrated
with dirt boluses, much in use amongst modern Goths:
secondly, the head and shoulders of a cod-fish, as large
as a porpoise; nad a haunch of mutton, kept till half
putrid, decorated with a paper ruffle, to look, and, if
possible, smell like venison. The second course consisted of three twice-roasted pigeons, ambushed in
parsley, some limp jelly, some sky-blue blanc-mange,
and a huge fruit-pie covered with crust!

And imagine a gentleman attempting to endure a *parvenu* reception, such as that in "Merton":

... gold and jewels, and greengage-coloured velvets, and crimson and fringe, and flounces and tassels, and tawdry necklaces and ear-rings, abounded; but the girls perked themselves up, and wriggled themselves about, and rapped their partners' arms (for they danced quadrilles after the manner of Almack's), and gave themselves all the little coquettish airs of their superiors. But the rooms, somehow, smelt badly; they had no more idea of *Eau à bruler* than they had of nectar; and the people drank hot punch, which was handed about in little tumblers by under-sized livery servants in cotton stockings and without powder; in short, it was altogether vastly oppressive.

Another aspect of Hook's "fashionable" pose is his presentation at length of the "silver fork" details of exclusive social circles. He entered here what was essentially a new field for the novelist, and the success of these descriptions doubtlessly explains the great popularity of the three series of "Sayings and Doings." Not only is the reader introduced to fashionable balls and receptions — any butler or waiter could describe those. In Hook's pages one becomes familiar with the intimate family life of lords, the pomp of bejewelled dowagers, the officers' mess of regiments, the legal bickerings attending the marriage of titled lovers, the purchase of immense estates, the political manoeuvrings of high-placed politicians. And there could exist little doubt in the reader's mind that the author had seen and experienced what he set forth. The manner is too sure and easy; the handling of the details reveals too practised a touch. That air, a "Blackwood's" reviewer truly wrote of the first series of "Sayings and Doings," "cannot be picked up by the uninitiated, no matter with what assurance they may affect it."

In his "Popular History of England," Charles Knight feels moved to write:

> Hook was almost the last of what was called the "silver-fork school." It was a school that flourished before Reform-bills and railroads; and its disciples long persisted in their ignorant endeavor to paint the domestic life of the flourishing citizen as uniformly vulgar, and in their base delineations of the struggles of honest poverty as revolting and disreputable. Every invention of industry, every social arrangement, which had a tendency to put high and low on a level of convenience and comfort, was hateful to such writers and to their fashionable admirers.

Passing over the other mistakes and extravagances in this curious collection (itself a pose struck by a popularizer of literature), let it be said only that the most naïve misconception is that fashionable novels were read by "fashionable admirers." They were written instead for the apprentice and the mantua-maker. When Hook pilloried the *parvenu* and emphasized the silver forks, he was adopting a pose as deliberately as did the Grub Street writer who was paid twenty pounds for writing a fashionable novel for the Minerva Press.

Hook had known the great and was soon to know them again. But when he began the "Sayings and Doings" he was in jail as a public defaulter. It is amusing to picture Theodore, after a light "regale" of perhaps bread and cheese, and beer brought in by a strolling pot-boy, sitting down in Mr. Hemp's reception room (which was comfortable enough, Hook said once, "barring the windows") to heap scorn on vulgar plebeian dinners!

Moreover, Hook's fashionable pose is evident only in the "Sayings and Doings" and in "Maxwell." After 1830, several circumstances combined to cause him to drop it. He foresaw, probably, that the popularity of the novel of fashion was soon to wane. He had won fame as a novelist in his own right; he no longer needed to court favor by imitation. Most important of all, in the early eighteen-thirties he reëntered society. After invitations to the houses of the great had become usual affairs, Hook ceased to boast about his aristocratical leanings and no longer posed as a "genteel" writer. Intimacy had bred, not contempt surely, but better taste. He still describes the haunts of the fashionable, but he no longer enters them merely to parade his knowledge of silver forks. Again, the Tory attitude of class separation is still there. But the honest, unpretentious member of the middle class is now scarcely ever held up to ridicule. Now it is the hypocrite, the upstart, the hanger-on of the great, who become the objects of humor and satire. The heroes and heroines are regularly of the middle class; the point of the story is very frequently the victory of true love over wealth and rank.

If Hook's moral *obiter dicta* are taken over from romance, if his Tory principles are those regularly held by members of his party, if his pretensions to snobbery constitute a deliberately assumed pose soon discarded — then these things are shells. The kernel must lie beneath them.

It is when Theodore Hook describes the exterior aspects of the London life of his day that he has found his true subject. His novels are filled with minute descriptions of the manners, the things, the outer appearances of contemporary English life. The social range of these word pictures is very broad; it extends from the upper-high to the lower-middle and servant classes. His description, in "The Marquess," of the visit of the king to Lionsden Castle has not one false note; that of the contents of the bureau drawer of Gubbins, a third-rate governess, in the "Man of Many Friends," is an excellent accumulation of characteristic detail. In the geographical range of his scenes, Hook wisely restricted himself to places he knew well — Brighton, Oxford, Leamington, Somersetshire. The island of Mauritius does not enter the picture, but the passage to the Madeiras is twice set forth, and "Passion and Principle" ends with the description of a typhoon off the Cape of Good Hope. But, after all, Hook is primarily the London Englishman. The metropolis forms the centre of all his stories; the characters either remain in London or come there for part of the tale.

Perhaps most frequently of all in Hook's pages are descriptions of dinners. And there is justification for this, he writes, because

eating is the universal employment of our countrymen; and, as has been before observed, so much time is devoted to the operation, and occupied by it, and it is, in fact, so vitally interwoven with English society, that to give anything like a faithful sketch of passing events, dinners must be served up on paper as well as in parlours.

Hook delights in describing middle-class dinners to the last intimate detail — the most elaborate of them occurring in "Maxwell" and in "Passion and Principle." He likes also to introduce with comic results a vulgar person into an aristocratic dinner. There is a good example of this in "Jack Brag," and an even better one in "The Marquess." He will give you every conceivable part of a dinner-party — the half-hour of constraint before, the entry into the dining-room, the courses of the dinner, the wine-drinking, the conversation before and after the retirement of the ladies, the coffee in the drawing-room.

About balls, "Peregrine Bunce" has this to
say:

Balls all over the world bear a strong family likeness
to each other; more especially in England, where to
have seen one, is pretty nearly to have seen all. Rooms
lit up to an excess, so that not a single wrinkle under a
would-be juvenile dowager's eyes shall escape scrutiny;
floors chalked to represent flowers, fruits, and leaves —
most appropriate winter devices; benches, chairs, &c.
&c., running close round the walls; fiddlers and harpers
stuck up in one corner of the apartment; and in the center a set of quadrille dancers moving about with that
happy absence of animal spirits, so characteristic of
English recreations, while some three or four small,
wasp-waisted exquisites, too delicate to endure the
fatigues of the quadrille, look on with a supercilious
smile, lisping the while in soft undertones their opinions
of the fair exhibitors; such are the usual constituents of
a modern ballroom; while in the adjacent apartment —
should there chance to be one adapted to the purpose —
card-tables are laid out for the use of the elderly folks,
at which you will be pretty sure to see a squat dowager
or two, together with divers lean, prim spinsters, with a
slight patch of red at the end of their peaked noses,
watching each other's play as viciously as two cats
watch each other's movements on the tiles at midnight.
This last room is the very temple of dulness, where
speech is doled out in monosyllabic whispers, and where
at certain critical points — particularly if the game be
whist — faces lengthen visibly, and jaws drop to an
extent provocative of dislocation.

When poor Francis Welsted of "Passion and
Principle" arrives at London after leaving his beloved Fanny with the knowledge that she is to wed
another, he enters the Bell and Crown, a low-class

London inn. In the dining-room a group of rugged
and boisterous farmers are eating:

> Contrasted with these hale and hearty specimens of
> English yeomanry, stood the smoke-dried waiters,
> whose pale and yellow cheeks gave horrible evidence of
> the confinement which they suffered in the atmosphere
> they were doomed to breathe; for, in addition to the
> ordinary smells of London, a stable-yard, a coach office,
> the country farmers and the London lawyers; coffee,
> rum, hollands and water, tea, toast, brandy and to-
> bacco, all conspired at one and the same moment, with
> the never-failing odour of gas, . . . to give fragrance to
> the residence of poor Francis Welsted. . . . And ac-
> cordingly the waiter . . . spread over the table (ren-
> dered clammy by sundry circular deposits of ale and
> porter, the accidental spillings of last night's carouse) a
> cloth, not larger than an ordinarily sized napkin, darned
> in sundry places, and bearing strong evidence upon its
> face that eggs and mustard had been eaten upon it for
> several previous mornings. He then proceeded to ex-
> hibit a pewter tea-pot, with a Davenanted spout, a
> small jug, containing three or four tablespoonsful of a
> light-blue liquid, professing to be milk, which, with
> some half-dozen lumps of dingy sugar, recumbent in a
> basin, and attended thereon by a pair of brown ja-
> panned tongs, shared the board with a bit of salt butter,
> and a French roll, three inches long by two inches in
> circumference.

Brimmer Brassey, the sharp-practising lawyer
of "All in the Wrong," had an attack of gout
while at a client's house, and was thereupon put to
bed:

> It had been found necessary to confide to the foot-
> man, to whose care he had been consigned, the key of
> his "carpet bag," which contained so small a supply of

shirts, stockings, &c. as to betray the economical character of his wardrobe; while a file, as he would have said, of collars and fronts, with holes in them for his emerald studs, gave evidence of the superficiality of that delicate dandyism which dazzled the eye with its snowy whiteness. One tooth-brush twisted up in a piece of whitey-brown paper; a razor by itself — razor, tied with a piece of red tape to a round pewter shaving-box (enclosing a bit of soap) with the top of its handle peeping from the bottom of a leathern case, like the feet of a long-legged Lilliputian sticking out of his coffin; a remarkably dirty flannel underwaistcoat, edged with light blue silk and silver; one pair of black silk socks, brown in the bottoms; an ill-corked bottle, half full of "Russia oil"; a very suspicious-looking wiry hair-brush, and one shaving ditto, were amongst the most striking items of the omnium gatherum.

When Gervase Skinner called upon the provincial actress, Mrs. Amelrosa Fuggleston, he was ushered into a room in Mrs. Riley's boardinghouse:

The room presented a novel appearance to the country squire — indeed so novel as to startle him: opposite the door, turned up within itself, stood a half-tester bed, the furniture of which was chequered: under its shadowy canopy on the floor, which was sanded, rested two or three bandboxes, a washing-basin and ewer of pure white crockery, together with tea-things, and other things of similar ware, conducive generally to comfort and convenience. Before the fire, suspended by some twisted worsted, dangled four or five bones of a neck of mutton, in a forward state of culinary preparation. On the hob of the grate stood a black saucepan containing potatoes, covered with a saucer; and on a small single-clawed table, scantily covered with a huckaback towel, appeared two plates with knives and forks; a tea-cup contained the vinegar, and an old rouge-pot was filled with the salt; the mustard . . . filled a *ci-devant* pomatum pot; while the half loaf rested plateless on the table, on one side of which was placed a rush-bottomed chair, and on the other a three-legged stool.

The walls, pure in colour as the crockery, were not quite unadorned — here and there a brightly-coloured print attracted the eye: the late Mr. Incledon, as Captain Macheath, in a scarlet coat, hung as a pendant to a portly lady with a huge plume of feathers in her hat, sitting in a great chair with St. Paul's in the back ground. . . . The chimney-piece was adorned with two green parroquets, with bright yellow beaks, in earthenware; a plaster figure of Shakespeare without a head, and a small effigy of Liston in Paul Pry; two phial bottles and a tin tea-cannister comprised the decorations of this part of the apartment, across which hung, upon an extended line, divers and sundry articles of wet wearing apparel which had been recently removed from a tub which reposed itself securely upon a four-legged stand near one of the windows. A white cat, a black coalscuttle, and a brass "footman," completed the "properties" of the saloon, which had the happiness to call the amiable Isabella Riley, mistress.

Unfortunately, a few excerpts from Theodore Hook's descriptions of London life can do no more than indicate, perhaps, the photographic distinctness and minuteness of the detail. The most remarkable quality of the descriptions, however, is their cumulative effect, and this can be appreciated only by one familiar with all of Hook's stories. The range, the inclusiveness, the completeness of the scenic background then appears almost startling. The external trappings of an entire civilization (minus its lowest tenth) are before the reader's eyes. And there seems, then, only one fit phrase by which to characterize Hook's achievement — that applied by Walter Bagehot to Charles Dickens: "He describes London like a special correspondent for posterity."

The ethical background of Hook's stories exhibits a curious duality, caused by the conflict of his personal experience with the tradition of the novel — particularly of the romance. On the one hand, Hook was a man of the world and knew well how certain matters went on in the world — among his aristocratic acquaintances, for instance. On the other hand, he was a novelist and found himself facing a tradition established after 1770 by the romance writer. One may say without much exaggeration that the romancer recognized only one inexcusable crime, laxity in sexual relations, and that the penalty for such laxity is death. The villain is a villain because of his lasciviousness; the murders he commits are, in comparison, almost minor matters. The hero and heroine are always above even the suspicion of a libidinous idea. With the long predominance of romance, its moral code became almost obligatory for the novelist, and Hook adopted it for his major characters. Thus when George Grindle of "Fathers and Sons" lives with a young woman without marrying her, he has transgressed the romancer's laws and he must die. He must die even though he is not otherwise villainous, and although he finally acknowledges the woman as his wife. When Helen Batley of "All in the Wrong" marries Francis Mortimer, the result must be tragic because he had eloped in his youth with the wife of another man. And when Caroline Crosby of "Cousin William" continues to receive visits from her cousin after her marriage to another, her fate is certain. Her adultery causes the death of her only son, and she herself goes insane. Thus the letter of the code is upheld. But the author intimates again and again that none of these situations could be called exactly uncommon in the England of his day, and that the issue was not always tragic. The "John Bull," together with most of the other newspapers of the time, reported fully the testimony in all interesting *crim. con.* cases, and Hook probably knew a hundred more which were not aired in the courts.

For his minor characters Hook went straight to reality. As a result they act with surprising freedom. They have more audacity in action, it seems safe to say, than have the characters of any other English novelist of the entire first half of the century. There are almost a dozen immoral women among them. And two or three of Hook's scenes are reminiscent of Smollett — one in "Merton" in

which a visit is paid to the house of "ladies" at
two o'clock in the morning; another in "Gilbert
Gurney" involving Daly's adventure in a double-
bedded room at an inn. It is true that Hook's
touch is heavy when he attempts to inject the airy
Gallic spice into his off-color incidents. He cannot
depict the seductively erotic, and his attempts at
subtle *double entendre* are hopelessly *de mauvais
goût*. Yet the world in which his minor characters
move is refreshingly free from the romancer's code
and the Richardsonian sentiment. The virtue of
maids and servants is not pronounced, and when
any of the minors is immoral he is not killed off by
the author for his errors. Hook does not even lecture such characters upon their frailties. His attitude is that of the man of the world who accepts
human nature as it is and who hates the reformer,
the Methodist, the purity crusader. "Hang the
Society for the Suppression of Vice!" exclaims
Harry Dartford in "Doubts and Fears"; "I hate
cant and pretension wherever I find them, and
cannot choose but sneer at the virtue which fines
a poor woman for selling apples on a Sunday, and
winks at the commission of all sorts of mercantile
cheating every other day in the week."

Do these novels support their author's reputation as a humorist? If the elements of the humor
in them are collectively considered, the answer is
an affirmative. In the first place, Hook's descrip-

tions of London life are amusing by their faithful
reproduction of minute detail and circumstance.
Another comic element is added by the addiction
of the minor character to his "humour." Jim
Salmon of "Jack Brag" invariably addresses his
fifty-year-old wife as "Titsy," and repeats his un-
failing "D' ye twig?" In "The Marquess," Elizabeth Oldham's mother never speaks but to wander
hopelessly from one subject to another; and Mr.
Dumbledore of "Peregrine Bunce" utters a pun
with every exhalation of breath. A third element
is the relation of practical jokes and farcical incidents — the staple of "Gilbert Gurney," "Jack
Brag," and "Peregrine Bunce." Of these, "Gurney" is by a great deal the best, and Hook should
emphatically have done more things like it. That
the public was eager for this type of picaresque,
plotless story is shown by the great vogue in England of Paul de Kock's novels,[1] by the popularity
of Pierce Egan's "Life in London" (1821–24) —

---

[1] There is a curious parallel between Hook and de Kock.
The latter stands between the picaresque tales of Pigault Le-
brun and the realism of Balzac in somewhat the manner in
which Hook stands between Smollett and Dickens. *Mon voisin
Raymond* (1822) and *Gilbert Gurney* are similar in tone and
material. Both novelists use the motive of ridicule of the
bourgeois. That Hook had read de Kock's novels seems unquestionable. But he owed the Frenchman no debt. There
is, as Professor Saintsbury writes in his *History of the French
Novel* (1919), ii, 56, only a Plutarchian parallel between the
two. Hook is undoubtedly, I think, the better novelist.

and it is proved beyond question by the "Pickwick Papers" of 1836.

Finally — a matter not yet dwelt upon — Hook makes considerable use of humorous satire. He loves to lay bare fraud and pretension; he delightedly attacks the hypocrite, the mountebank, the person who attempts or professes to be what he is not. Among his many religious hypocrites there is the daughter of Amos Ford of "The Friend of the Family":

> He had a daughter, Rachel Ford, who was a pattern to her sex: she was as demure as the hand-maidens of the most unsophisticated days; she was full of religion — her mind constantly fixed on things above; her countenance (though plain) was serious and contemplative — her manner cold — her conversation chaste, almost to prudishness; she dealt out maxims even upon the pinning of a cap, and would quote scriptural authority for the tying up a geranium.

In "Jack Brag" Hook pays respects to the female education of the day:

> And after a sort of half-and-half education at a suburban boarding-school, where she learned astronomy, the mathematics, netting, knitting, knotting, the use of the globes, dancing, geometry, drawing, embroidery, rug-working, purse-making, flower-painting, botany, singing, geology, plain needle-work, natural history, stencilling, Italian, French, Spanish, German, the harp, guitar, piano-forte, tambourine, and triangle, together with many other sciences and accomplishments, "too numerous for the brief space of an advertisement," she . . .

Dr. Munx, also of "Jack Brag," explains his new system of medication:

Our system, in fact, is composed of a combination of what to the vulgar appear most ridiculous contradictions: for instance, a great deal of poison kills a man, — *ergo*, a little poison will do him good; — therefore, we take care to give him sufficient poison to produce a disorder which we know we can cure, in order to prevent his having some other disorder which we equally well know we cannot.

One of Hook's numerous political hypocrites is Sir Oliver Freeman of "Danvers":

He moreover spent much of his time in endeavoring to improve the condition of poor prisoners, and introduced the tread-mill into the County Gaol; he subscribed for the Irish rebels, and convicted poor women at Quarter-Sessions for the horrible crime of mendicity; was President of a Branch Bible Society, and seduced his wife's house-maids; was a staunch advocate for Parliamentary Reform, and sat ten years for a rotten borough; made speeches against titles, being one of the greatest lay-impropriators in the kingdom; talked of the glorious sovereignty of the people, and never missed a levee or a drawing-room in his life. Thus qualified, Sir Oliver Freeman stood forward a Son of Freedom, who on this special occasion had declared he would spend fifty thousand pounds to maintain the independence of his native country.

CHAPTER VIII.

HOOK'S IMPORTANCE AS A NOVELIST.

IT has been seen that Theodore Hook, at the beginning of his career as a novelist, passed through a period during which he emphasized society and fashion. From the beginning of the century there had been novels which occupied themselves with the same subjects. These fall into certain fairly distinct groups. The earliest comprises such works as Mrs. Parsons's "The Miser and His Family," of 1800 ("a severe satire of the fashionable world, so as to deter young people," writes the "Monthly" reviewer), and Hannah More's "Cœlebs in Search of a Wife" (1808). The intention in these novels is to make invidious comparisons between a life in high society and one devoted to plain living and sound religious principles. A second group may be illustrated by T. S. Surr's tremendously popular and frequently imitated "A Winter in London; or, Sketches of Fashion" (1806), and by Lady Caroline Lamb's "Glenarvon" (1816). These two novels are pure romances, into which the theme of fashion has been quite incidentally introduced. A third group began, shortly before 1820, to vulgarize the society theme, and to depict the wild pranks and practical jokes of the young London "sports." The high point of this sort of thing was Pierce Egan's "Life in London," which appeared in shilling instalments from 1821 to 1824.

Theodore Hook possessed an immeasurable advantage over nearly all other writers about fashion. He had been admitted, in his youth, to fashionable society of the most aristocratic sort. Thus he was able, in his "Sayings and Doings," to give an account of fashionable life far broader in scope and far closer to reality than such an account had ever been before. The reader is made familiar with all the interests of the aristocracy: the after-dinner gossip, the quarrels, the affairs of honor, the debts, the balls, the week-end visits, the large house-parties, the political affiliations, the haggling over valuable appointments, the *sub rosa* manoeuvrings at election times, the marriage settlements. To give spice to these descriptions there was the author's pose of ridicule of the middle class. In this Fanny Burney had already set the precedent by her raillery against the vulgar Branghtons of "Evelina." In short, with the first series of "Sayings and Doings" in 1824, the theme of society entered a new and final stage. With Hook the genuine "fashionable novel" took the form in which it was to exist until it fell into disfavor about 1835.

In spite of the dominance of romance during the first twenty-five years of the century, there existed various types of realism. In the first place there were the domestic novels of Maria Edgeworth, Jane Austen, and Susan E. Ferrier. Again, there were large numbers of "dialect" novels dealing sympathetically with the Scotch or Irish peasantry. The type began with Maria Edgeworth's "Castle Rackrent" (1800), and included, before 1830, the works of such writers as Lady Morgan, Mrs. Elizabeth Hamilton, John Galt, Alexander Balfour, Allan Cunningham, "Christopher North," Lockhart, Gerald Griffin, and John Banim. Thirdly, there were novels of the sea and of military life — such as Michael Scott's "Tom Cringle's Log," G. R. Gleig's "Subaltern," and, beginning in 1829, the numerous sea stories of Captain Marryat.

It is evident, however, that the realism of these three types is of a limited, circumscribed sort. They are of the side waters, the shallows of realism. Each of the three deals exclusively with some small portion or aspect of British life — the tea-table, peasant life, the battlefield, the quarter-deck. Now, a true realism must not be thus restricted. It must boldly enter the many-sided world of reality; it must draw a broad picture of contemporary life. A search for novels written between 1800 and 1825 which deal realistically with current English life yields very unsatisfactory results. There were a few weak and sporadic attempts that could make no headway against triumphant romance. They usually insist in their titles that they are "founded on fact" or "drawn from real life," and by that very insistence show that realism was rare and sadly on the defensive.[1] The situation does not change even at the end of the quarter-century. Thomas Love Peacock was interested in humorous satire, not in descriptions of current life. Scott's "St. Ronan's Well" (1824) was not considered a success. Indeed, perhaps the

---

[1] 1800. Tales of Truth.
1802. The World as It Goes.
1804. A Picture from Life.
1809. The Cottage of Merlin Vale; a History Founded on Facts.
1810. Characteristic Incidents drawn from Real Life; or, The History of the Rockinhams. By Mrs. Pilkington.
1811. Brighton in an Uproar: a Novel Founded on Facts.
1812. *Crim. con.;* a Novel Founded on Facts.
Friends Unmasked; or, Scenes in Real Life Founded on Facts.
1813. Tales of Real Life. By Mrs. Opie.
1815. Life, Smooth and Rough, as it Runs.
1818. Sophia; or, The Dangerous Indiscretion: a Tale Founded upon Fact.
The Cumberland Cottager; a Story Founded upon Fact.
1819. No Fiction; a Narrative Founded on Recent and Interesting Facts.
1820. Tales Founded Upon Facts. By M. A. Grant.
1823. Hauberk Hall: A Series of Facts.

only satisfactory broadly realistic novel of the period is Lockhart's "Reginald Dalton," of 1823.

Thus the appearance, early in 1824, of Theodore Hook's first series of "Sayings and Doings" was an event of first-rate importance to realism. Here at length, after a half-century of romance, is the beginning of a series of novels which consciously and boldly direct themselves toward realism. For Hook, between 1824 and 1841, endeavored in every one of his stories to set forth what he saw in the life about him. Moreover, he began his efforts at a very important time in the career of the novel. The popularity of Walter Scott was causing the novel to rise to the importance, relative to other types of literature, that it still maintains. David Masson, in the middle of the century, records

the curious fact that the annual yield of British novels had been quadrupled by the time of Scott's death [1832] as compared with what it had been when he was in the middle of his Waverley series [about 1824] — having risen from 26 a-year, or a new novel every fortnight, to about 100 a-year, or nearly two new novels every week; and, moreover, that this proportion . . . has continued pretty steady since Scott's death.[1]

Hook, then, strove continuously toward realism. But he had also two personal contributions to make to it — his minor characters, with "hu-

---

[1] *British Novelists* (Macmillan, 1859), p. 218.

mours," and his descriptions of London life. He was not an innovator, it has been seen, with his minor characters, for the example of Smollett lay before him. Yet he must be given credit even here for logically developing Smollett's practice to demonstrate the full advantages of the "humours" method. Hook's second contribution, however, marks him as a genuine innovator. He was the first to introduce into the novel descriptions of the externals of English life. This is not to say that the reader receives no idea of English life from "Tom Jones" or "Roderick Random." It is generally agreed that Ann Radcliffe first brought descriptions of natural scenery into the novel — which does not mean that novels previous to hers lacked all mention of natural scenery. The assertion regarding Hook means that he was the first novelist to present contemporary life with all its local color — to regard the externals of English life as documents to be minutely examined and descriptively reproduced.

Hook's importance as a novelist thus lies in the fact that he altered the nature of the fashionable novel, and that he was a pioneer of nineteenth-century realism; furthermore, that the most characteristic qualities of his realism are his minor characters with "humours," and his descriptions of London life. When it is observed that the fashionable novel, in the form given to it by Hook, was very much in favor during the decade 1825 to 1835, it is logical to suppose that Hook's influence did much to create that favor. When it is noted that between 1835 and 1840 the success of realism became assured, it is logical to conclude that Hook's efforts did not a little to cause realism to be in the air and to direct public taste and the efforts of novelists in that direction.

To trace Hook's influence more specifically is to examine the fashionable novels and the realistic novels which were published after he had established himself as a novelist, in order to discover examples, in those works, of his manner of using the fashionable theme or of his characteristic minor characters and descriptions. Such an investigation must be conducted with the utmost caution. It is easy to convict a writer of borrowing an artificial figure of romance, such as Mrs. Radcliffe's villainous monk. But it is very difficult to pronounce that one realist borrowed a character from another realist when people who might serve as models for both writers were daily walking the streets of London.

After 1825, the fashionable novel had a decade of popularity. Three noteworthy examples of it were Robert Plumer Ward's "Tremaine; or, The Man of Refinement" (1825), his "De Vere; or, The Man of Independence" (1827), and Thomas Henry Lister's "Granby" (1827). It is difficult to

explain the vogue of "Tremaine," for much of it is
heavy theological argument and there are few
"silver fork" descriptions. It added, however,
another element to the fashionable theme as employed by Hook — the situation of a young man,
rich and of high birth, who tries everything (society, politics, gambling, dissipation) in a search
for some soul-satisfying occupation. In "De Vere"
the political theme is emphasized almost to the
exclusion of other fashionable interests. The
work thus created a new type of novel. It is the
first English political novel.[1] Lister's "Granby"
has a plot much like that of Hook's "Merton" of
the first series of "Sayings and Doings" — which
was enjoying its full popularity when Lister began
to write. Lister's most characteristic ability is
that of conducting sprightly drawing-room conversations. He also holds up to scorn a vulgar
middle-class family, and he describes a ball at
which there are many plebeians and *parvenus*.

Thomas Hamilton's "The Youth and Manhood
of Cyril Thornton" (1827) has none of the characteristics of a fashionable novel. It is a piece of
realism after the pattern of Lockhart's "Reginald
Dalton" (1823). It is almost the only, and it is
certainly the best, realistic novel of the twenties

---

[1] For the type, see Dr. Morris Edmund Speare's *The Polit-
ical Novel* (Oxford University Press). I do not agree with Dr.
Speare when he qualifies the achievement of Ward and calls
Disraeli the true creator of the type.

of the century. Hamilton knew of Theodore Hook (Cyril once says: "None but Theodore Hook can fully understand my discomfiture when . . ."); yet the novel contains no traces of Hook's typical descriptions or characters.

The year 1828 was perhaps the high-water mark of the fashionable novel.

Do you know the modern recipe for a finished picture of fashionable life? Let a gentlemanly man, with a gentlemanly style, take of foolscap paper a few quires, stuff them well with high-sounding titles — dukes and duchesses, lords and ladies, *ad libitum*. Then open the Peerage at random, pick a supposititious author out of one page of it, and fix the imaginary characters upon some of the rest; mix it all up with a *quantum suff.* of puff, and the book is in a second edition before ninety-nine readers out of a hundred have found out that the one is as little likely to have written, as the others to have done, what is attributed to them.

But real lords did sometimes write fashionable novels, for the author of the words just quoted is one. He is Constantine Henry Phipps, Lord Normanby, posing in his "Yes and No: a Tale of the Day" — like Hook in "Sayings and Doings" — as the genuine man of *ton* decrying the false pictures of aristocratic society drawn by authors not in the least familiar with it. Lord Normanby evidently knew the society he described in his novel — and if he did, Hook's scenes are also genuine, for the details the two writers present are similar in almost all respects.

The popularity of the novel of fashion continued into the eighteen-thirties. Horace Smith, Lady Charlotte Bury, the Countess of Blessington, were among those who produced numbers of them. These writers were intimately acquainted with aristocratic society. Lady Charlotte had been one of Caroline's maids of honor, and the Countess's salon was visited by practically every person of note in England. But the elegant sentiments and refined dialogue of the novels they wrote have not sufficed — since other merits were almost totally absent — to keep these works alive. And, toward 1835, the vogue of the fashionable novel ceased. During the following ten years it found only a few belated practitioners, like the indefatigable Mrs. Gore, and it furnished excellent material for one of Thackeray's parodies — "Lords and Liveries" — in "Punch" in 1847.

In "Romance and Reality" (1831), the first novel of Letitia Elizabeth Landon, there is the following disdainful description of a plebeian dinner:

At the top was a cod's shoulders and head, whose intellectual faculties were rather over much developed; and at the bottom was soup called mulligatawny — some indefinite mixture of curry-powder and duck's feet, the first spoonful of which called from its master a look of thunder and lightning up the table. To this succeeded a couple of the most cadaverous fowls, a huge haunch of mutton, raw and red enough even for an Abyssinian, flanked by rissoles and oyster patties, which had evidently, like Tom Tough, seen "a deal of ser-

vice": these were followed by some sort of nameless
pudding — and so much for the luxury of a family dinner, which is enough to make one beg next time to be
treated as a stranger.

These lines do indeed give evidence of that desperate endeavor to say something "fetching" which
injures much of L. E. L.'s prose writing. They
are, however, in the vein of Theodore Hook's descriptions. One suspects, thus, that Miss Landon
had read Hook's stories, particularly "Maxwell,"
which had appeared just when she was about to
write her novel. The suspicion is confirmed later
in the work:

Edward Lorraine. — "How full of wit, point, and
what is best expressed by a phrase of their own, such
exquisite *tournure*, some of the short French stories are!
Hook is, I think, the only English author who possesses
their analysis of action — that bird's-eye view of motive, and the neat keen style whose every second sentence is an epigram; he is Rochefoucault illustrated; and
he unites, too, with his vein of satire, the more creative
powers, the deeper tones of feeling, that mark our English writers."

Mr. Morland. — "I give him credit for one very
original merit. Do you remember Charles Somerford's
letter in Maxwell? — it is the only love-letter I ever
read without thinking it absurd. It is equally passion-
ate and natural."

Theodore Hook's name appears neither in the
novels of Edward Bulwer nor in the Life of him
begun by his son and completed by his grandson.
Hook and Bulwer knew each other, of course. The

latter was editor of the "New Monthly Magazine" in 1832, four years before Hook assumed that office. Both had the same publishers — Colburn and Bentley. Both belonged to the Athenæum Club. Yet Bulwer was a vehement Whig, while Hook belonged to the Carlton Club, the inner circle of Torydom. Hook, also, was a friend of Maginn, the editor of "Fraser's Magazine," which, through the agency of the young Thackeray, vigorously attacked Bulwer's novels.

Four of the novels Bulwer wrote before 1840 are of interest here: "Pelham" (1828), "Godolphin" (1833), "Ernest Maltravers" (1837), and "Alice" (1838). The first two were written in the decade 1825–1835, and are, properly enough, fashionable novels. "Of all my numerous novels," writes Bulwer in 1840, "'Pelham' and 'Godolphin' are the only ones which take their absolute groundwork in what is called 'The Fashionable World.'"

When "Pelham, or The Adventures of a Gentleman" appeared, Hook was already the author of two series of "Sayings and Doings" and was just publishing the third. That Bulwer had read and profited by Hook's stories seems scarcely questionable, although it cannot be proved in any direct way. All the elements which Hook had introduced into the fashionable novel are present in "Pelham." Like Hook, Bulwer adopts a pose of extreme fastidiousness. As in Hook's stories, the fashionable world is completely presented. There are intrigues, duels, heavy gaming, roistering night life, political machinations, as well as "silver fork" detail. There is an electioneering scene, such as Hook had introduced into "Danvers." Polite conversation is emphasized in the description of the elegant coxcombry of Pelham. Plebeian villagers and a middle-class ball are brought in for purposes of humor and satire. Bulwer does not have Hook's interest in detailed descriptions of places. But he devotes considerable pains to his minor characters. A number of them are minutely described, and a few are modelled after real people — Russelton, for instance, being Beau Brummell. Several, moreover, are presented by "humours" in Hook's manner. Such are certainly Lord Vincent, the inveterate punster, Christopher Clutterbuck, the henpecked scholar, and Lord Guloseton, the epicure.

In 1833, when "Godolphin" appeared, the decade of the fashionable novel had almost run its course. "It is not my intention," writes the author, "to reiterate the wearisome echo of novelists who descant on fashion and call it life." "Godolphin" is not altogether, then, a fashionable novel. But neither does it pass beyond into the broad current of realism, as Hook's "Maxwell" of 1830 had done in part. For "Godolphin" is really a philosophical novel. That obscure and tragic pall

which Bulwer threw over many of his novels is
here already apparent. The reader is introduced
to Truth, Reason, Memory, Genius, and other
capitallized abstract nouns. He meets also German metaphysics, Byronic heroes engaged in endless self-tormenting strife, fervent outpourings of
natural and unspoiled hearts, nympholepts, moths
desiring stars. The way is already being cleared
for "Zanoni" (1842) and the "Strange Story."

This same preoccupation with metaphysics and
Rousseauistic sociology is evident in "Ernest
Maltravers" and its sequel, "Alice." Little attention is paid to the events of the everyday world,
where the action is supposed to take place. Instead, the interest is in Alice Darvil, a "natural"
character, with all the unspoiled, naïve (and therefore truly moral) impulses of a child of nature, and
in her relations with Maltravers, a philosopher
searching for his soul's happiness. Some readers
there are who do not think that these interests
injure Bulwer's novels, but who are willing to
accept him as a deep and original thinker. Considered from the point of view of realism, however, the injury they cause is grave.

And there is a further reason why Bulwer's
name cannot be pronounced significant for the up-
building of nineteenth-century realism. Theodore
Hook strove for realism in every one of his novels.
But Bulwer frankly drifted with the tide. He

frittered away his energies by attempting all of the current types of fiction. His first novel, "Falkland" (1827), is a romance. His next, "Pelham" (1828), is a fashionable novel. In 1829, with "Devereux," Bulwer turned to the historical romance. "Paul Clifford" (1830) is a *Tendenzstück* directed against the existing penal laws; "Eugene Aram" (1832) is the study of a criminal after the manner of Godwin's "Caleb Williams." With "Godolphin" (1833), Bulwer returned to the fashionable novel. But he is again in the field of the historical novel with "The Last Days of Pompeii" (1834) and "Rienzi" (1835). Then he goes back to a realistic theme in "Ernest Maltravers" (1837) and "Alice" (1838), but injures it by his German rationalism. Thus Bulwer tried all types but continued in none. He was not particularly concerned with realism — in fact, he did not attempt unmixed realism until "The Caxtons," of 1849.

In 1825, Benjamin Disraeli returned from his German tour, and Theodore Hook emerged from his confinement for the Mauritius defalcation. The two probably met in London in that year. For, in "Vivian Grey," of 1826, Hook is brought upon the scene in this way:

"I was rather disappointed [writes Cynthia Courtown to Vivian] at the first sight of Stanislaus Hoax. I had expected, I do not know why, something juvenile and squibbish, when lo! I was introduced to a corpulent individual, with his coat buttoned up to his chin, looking dull, gentlemanlike, and apoplectic. However, on acquaintance, he came out quite rich, sings delightfully, and improvises like a prophet, ten thousand times more entertaining than Pistrucci. We are sworn friends; and I know all the secret history of 'John Bull.'"

But it was probably not until Disraeli, about 1834, entered politics and society that he became acquainted with Croker and the Marquis of Hertford, or saw much of Theodore Hook.[1] It is well known that Disraeli brought all three of these characters into his "Coningsby" of 1844. Hertford appears as Lord Monmouth, Croker as his toady, Rigby, and Hook (three years after his death) as Lucian Gay:

Nature had intended Lucian Gay for a scholar and a wit; necessity had made him a scribbler and a buffoon. He had distinguished himself at the University; but he had no patrimony, nor those powers of perseverance

---

[1] *Life of Benjamin Disraeli*, William Flavelle Monypenny, (New York, 1912), ii, 33: [Disraeli, in a letter of July 4, 1838, describes a ball at the Salisburys' the night before] "Exmouth came up to Theodore Hook, full of indignation at the 31 Baronets in the night's Gazette. 'Thirty-one Baronets! Here's a pretty game of the Whigs!' says he. 'They'll make a bloody hand of it, at any rate,' said Theodore. The same wit and worthy was abusing the foreigners, and particularly Prince Poniatowsky, who, *on dit*, is anxious to turn the rich and pretty Mrs. Craven into a Princess. 'I suppose he can't show his face in his own land, the Radical scamp,' said T. H. Whereupon he was informed the Prince was no Rad, and had refused the crown of Poland. '*Peut-etre*,' replied Theodore. 'He may have refused a crown, but he looks very much now as if he would accept half a crown.'"

which success in any learned profession requires. He
was good-looking, had great animal spirits, and a keen
sense of enjoyment, and could not drudge. Moreover
he had a fine voice, and sang his own songs with considerable taste; accomplishments which made his fortune in society and completed his ruin. In due time he
extricated himself from the bench and merged into
journalism, by means of which he chanced to become
acquainted with Mr. Rigby. That worthy individual
was not slow in detecting the treasure he had lighted on;
a wit, a ready and happy writer, a joyous and tractable
being, with the education, and still the feelings and manners, of a gentleman. Frequent were the Sunday dinners
which found Gay a guest at Mr. Rigby's villa; numerous
the airy pasquinades which he left behind, and which
made the fortune of his patron. Flattered by the
familiar acquaintance of a man of station, and sanguine
that he had found the link which would sooner or later
restore him to the polished world that he had forfeited,
Gay laboured in his vocation with enthusiasm and
success.

Rigby wished Gay to remain entirely his own
property:

It, however, necessarily followed that the guests who
were charmed by Gay, wished Gay also to be their
guest. Rigby was very jealous of this, but it was inevitable; still by constant manoeuvre, by intimations of
some exercise, some day or other, of substantial patronage in his behalf, by a thousand little arts by which he
carved out work for Gay which often prevented him
accepting invitations to great houses in the country, by
judicious loans of small sums on Lucian's notes of hand
and other analogous devices, Rigby contrived to keep
the wit in a fair state of bondage and dependence.

But Lord Monmouth, Rigby's patron, desired to
be amused:

He wanted a jester: a man about him who would make him, not laugh, for that was impossible, but smile more frequently, tell good stories, say good things, and sing now and then, especially French songs.

Rigby, therefore, delivered up Gay to Monmouth:

It was a rule with Rigby that no one, if possible, should do anything for Lord Monmouth but himself; and as a jester must be found, he was determined that his Lordship should have the best in the market, and that he should have the credit of furnishing the article. As a reward, therefore, for many past services, and a fresh claim to his future exertions, Rigby one day broke to Gay that the hour had at length arrived when the highest object of reasonable ambition on his part, and the fulfilment of one of Rigby's long-cherished and dearest hopes, were alike to be realized. Gay was to be presented to Lord Monmouth and dine at Monmouth House.

The acquaintance was a successful one; very agreeable to both parties. Gay became an habitual guest of Lord Monmouth when his patron was in England; and in his absence received frequent and substantial marks of his kind recollection, for Lord Monmouth was generous to those who amused him.

The circumstance in Hook's life which makes this entire situation impossible is that he had met Croker and Hertford long before "his ruin" was accomplished — long before he left for the Mauritius. But, surely, it does not need to be argued here that the interpretation placed by Disraeli on the relations of these three men is purely fictional. What is of greater note is that he was not able to make a literary success of Gay. It is not enough

to introduce a character and assure the reader that
he is a wit. The real test, which Disraeli shirks, is
to show him in action.

Disraeli did not attain his full maturity as a
novelist until his trilogy, "Coningsby" (1844),
"Sybil" (1845), and "Tancred" (1847). The
years before 1840, then, comprise his early experiments with prose fiction. His first two novels,
"Vivian Grey" (1826) and "The Young Duke"
(1831), are fashionable novels. The romantic action of "Contarini Fleming" (1832) takes place
entirely on the Continent. "The Wondrous Tale
of Alroy" (1833) is a story of mediaeval Asia
Minor. "Henrietta Temple" (1836) is a realistic
novel. "Venetia" (1837) has an historical background. The young Disraeli evidently possessed
some of Bulwer's willingness to attempt all types
of fiction.

There is scarcely any basis for comparison between Disraeli's two fashionable novels and
Hook's "Sayings and Doings." Hook was familiar
with the fashionable scenes he describes; the
young Disraeli created them from his imagination.
In "Vivian Grey" the theme of high society is
restricted to the first part of the work, the scene of
which is laid in England. The remaining part,
which describes a tour in Germany, enters frankly
the realm of farce and grotesque fairy tales. The
author realized later the juvenility of the novel,

and, after trying vainly to suppress it, reissued it in 1853 with a prefaced apology for its boyish affectation — "the results of imagination, acting upon knowledge, not acquired by experience." Nor is the account of the dissipated career of the Duke of St. James, in "The Young Duke," much closer to reality. It is the worst of Disraeli's novels.

It is [writes his biographer, William Monypenny] a picture at once flashy and conventional of a society of which Disraeli had little direct knowledge when he wrote. "The Young Duke!" exclaimed his father, according to a family tradition, when he first heard of the book. "What does Ben know of dukes?"

The love story "Henrietta Temple" is the best of the early novels of Disraeli. The dinner-table scene with which the novel ends shows the author at length at the height of his powers, and is in striking contrast with the puerilities of some of the scenes in his earlier works. The fashionable phase has worn off, both because, in 1836, the decade of that type of fiction had definitely passed, and because Disraeli, with his green coat and massive gold chains, was entering aristocratic society and was on the eve of membership of Parliament. Details based on observation now succeed a pose founded largely on imagination. Several of the characters are portraits of well-known men and women — a practice which so grew upon the author that "Coningsby," eight years later, is a *roman à clef*. "Henrietta Temple" is a genuine realistic novel. Yet it was scarcely a pioneer in that respect. By 1836 a number of realists had appeared.

In the "Prologue" to the first number of "Bentley's Miscellany," in January, 1837, there is written: "Another [magazine] may shake our sides with the drolleries of Gilbert Gurney and his fellows, poured forth from the inexhaustible reservoir of the wit of our fellow contributor Theodore Hook." If young Charles Dickens, the editor, wrote this "Prologue" (and the fact seems unquestionable), it is the only one of his writings, seemingly, wherein he has mentioned Theodore Hook. Moreover, Theodore's name does not occur in John Forster's "Life of Charles Dickens." Hook and Dickens undoubtedly knew each other, but circumstances apparently forbade any close acquaintance. Hook was the elder by twenty-four years. He was of the original generation of the Garrick and the Athenæum; Dickens and Thackeray were of the second. Again, the social standing of the two men was not equal. Theodore Hook was a familiar figure at the houses of the great families of England. The young Dickens had no such *entrée* to society. Their only "mutual friend" was Ingoldsby Barham, and the three of them were all concerned in some degree with the found-

ing of "Bentley's Miscellany." [1]   Bentley had
probably thought of Ingoldsby for the editorship.
Certainly he had considered Hook, for it will be
remembered that Colburn, in 1836, suddenly became afraid that he would lose the leading contributor to his "New Monthly." But the man
finally selected was Dickens, practically unknown
except for the astounding success of the opening
numbers of "Pickwick."

The facts of Dickens's early career have been
often rehearsed. He began with "Sketches by
Boz," which appeared all through 1835 in the
"Monthly Magazine" and the "Evening Chronicle." There was a second series in 1836. His next
work was the "Pickwick Papers," which began to
appear in 1836. "Oliver Twist; or, The Parish
Boy's Progress" was contributed in instalments
to "Bentley's Miscellany," beginning in January,
1837. "The Life and Adventures of Nicholas
Nickleby" came out in monthly shilling numbers
during 1838 and 1839. In 1840 there began to
appear in the same manner that amorphous production known as "Master Humphrey's Clock,"
which contained the two full novels, "The Old
Curiosity Shop" (1840) and "Barnaby Rudge"

---

[1] Barham is the author of the excellent *bon mot* made on the
occasion. The name first decided on was *The Wit's Miscellany*.
Then the name *Bentley's Miscellany* was proposed. "Why,"
said Ingoldsby, "why go to the opposite extreme?"

(1841). Late in 1841 Dickens decided to visit the United States, and this first American trip may be said to mark the completion of the early period of his literary career.

"Among the writers of the present time," writes the "New Monthly" in 1836, in reviewing "Pickwick," "Theodore Hook alone has trodden the walk into which he has entered, and alone excels him in rich humour and playful yet pointed satire." A critic in the "Westminster Review" of July, 1837, when reviewing "Sketches by Boz" and "Pickwick," writes: "We are not surprised that Mr. Dickens has been frequently classed with a writer who has exhibited a good deal of comic power in depicting the same class of persons and circumstances. We mean Mr. Theodore Hook." In the same magazine a year later (volume xxviii, page 169), this same critic begins a review of Hook's "Jack Brag" with these words: "Though it may not be the position to which his talents entitle him, we are obliged to examine the merits of Mr. Hook immediately after those of his rival, Mr. Dickens. . . . Next to 'Boz,' he is most in the public eye."

Why was Dickens recognized as one who followed in the path which Hook alone had trod before him? In the first place, Dickens was preeminently a realist dealing with the life of his own day. In 1835 Hook was already the author of the three series of "Sayings and Doings," and of the novels "Maxwell," "The Parson's Daughter," "Love and Pride," and "Gilbert Gurney." In these he had striven consistently toward the realistic portrayal of contemporary life — and there was no other writer of his day comparable to him in this respect. To describe the broad current of English life meant, in 1835, to follow in the steps of Hook.

But the parallel between the two writers extends further than the fact that both were realists. Characteristic of Hook's novels are his minor characters with "humours" and his descriptive reproductions of the externals of English life. Dickens's novels possess these same two characteristics.

The minutely detailed descriptions (to consider them first) were, it has been seen, Hook's original contribution to the novel. His stories, and his alone, possessed them when Dickens began to write. The striking similarities in method and kind between Hook's descriptions and Dickens's are thus significant. Hook most frequently creates his pictures by piling up details — as in the following from "Passion and Principle":

Mrs. Rodney began rummaging in a pocket, apparently as large as a *sac de nuit*, and after a considerable rattling of sundry objects hidden from mortal eye, produced a handful of its contents, consisting of seventeen differently-sized keys, a piece of wax candle, a thimble, three old letters, a hard-hearted pincushion, a pair of sheathed scissors, a large toothpick-case, a dingy red-morocco purse, containing silver and half-pence, a small packet of white-brown paper, a pair of tweezers, and a flattened thimble; ranging all of which before her, on the table-cloth, she proceeded to select from amongst them the required key of the store-closet.

Dickens's use of the same method may be illustrated by a passage from "The Old Curiosity Shop":

There was not much to look at. A rickety table, with spare bundles of papers, yellow and ragged from long carriage in the pocket, ostentatiously displayed upon its top; a couple of stools set face to face on opposite sides of this crazy piece of furniture; a treacherous old chair by the fire-place, whose withered arms had hugged full many a client and helped to squeeze him dry; a second-hand wig box, used as a depository for blank writs and declarations and other small forms of law, once the sole contents of the head which belonged to the wig which belonged to the box, as they were now of the box itself; two or three common books of practice; a jar of ink, a pounce box, a stunted hearth-broom, a carpet trodden to shreds but still clinging with the tightness of desperation to its tacks — these, with the yellow wainscot of the walls, the smoke-discoloured ceiling, the dust and cobwebs, were among the most prominent decorations of the office of Mr. Sampson Brass.

Sometimes Hook will describe a person who perfectly illustrates a type, or a place in its characteristic and unchanging aspects. An example may be taken from "Danvers":

Society means with her an assembly of hundreds; her acquaintances are numerous, her friends scant: religion, with her, means the possession of a well-curtained, well-cushioned, well-carpeted pew in a fashionable chapel; her notions of charity are comprised in an annual donation or two to a lying-in hospital, or a female penitentiary: but without a crowd she dies; and then, to exist, she risks her life night after night by the disreputable exposure of her aged person, bedizened with the ornaments which graced her figure in its youth, and after feverishly enduring the loudly-whispered satire, and the ill-concealed laughter of the next generation, who stand round about her, she sinks into her crimson velvet coffin, without creating a sensation, except perhaps in the breast of her heir who . . . is relieved from the painful necessity of paying her Ladyship a jointure.

When describing a person or (as in the following instance from "Nicholas Nickleby") a place, Dickens frequently follows the same plan:

It is a great resort of foreigners. The dark-complexioned men who wear large rings, and heavy watchguards, and bushy whiskers, and who congregate under the Opera Colonnade, and about the box-office in the season, between four and five in the afternoon, when they give away the orders, — all live in Golden Square, or within a street of it. Two or three violins and a wind instrument from the Opera band reside within its precincts. Its boarding houses are musical, and the notes of pianos and harps float in the evening time round the head of the mournful statue, the guardian genius of a little wilderness of shrubs, in the center of the square. On a summer's night, windows are thrown open, and groups of swarthy mustachioed men are seen by the passer-by, lounging at the casements, and smoking fearfully. Sounds of gruff voices practising vocal music invade the evening's silence; and the fumes of choice tobacco scent the air.

As for minor characters—Hook's custom of presenting them by "humours" is, as is well known, that followed by Dickens. In "Pickwick" the fat boy is always asleep except when he is eating, and Jingle always speaks in jerks. Dick Swiveller of "The Old Curiosity Shop" continually quotes from popular songs. Mantalini of "Nickleby" utters his "demmit" with every speech. Dickens's novels overflow with these characters.[1] For the idea of them Dickens had before him, it is conceded, the example of Smollett, for the young David Copperfield (the young Dickens) grew up with those immortals "Roderick Random, Peregrine Pickle, Humphrey Clinker, Tom Jones, the Vicar of Wakefield, Don Quixote, Gil Blas, and Robinson Crusoe." But when he came to face the literary world of his own day, Dickens could not have failed to read the very popular novels of

---

[1] They were attacked by George Henry Lewes in the *Fortnightly Review* of February, 1872 (whose words are quoted by Forster near the conclusion of his biography of Dickens), in this fashion: "Their falsity was unnoticed in the blaze of their illumination. In vain critical reflection showed these figures to be merely masks; not characters, but personified characteristics; caricatures and distortions of human nature. The vividness of their presentation triumphed over reflection; their creator managed to communicate to the public his own unhesitating belief." The answer to such a criticism is, as I have asserted elsewhere, that the unreality of each character, considered by himself, may be granted; but that, nevertheless, the presence of large numbers of them acting together in a realistic setting creates a decided conviction of vivid reality, and so justifies the method.

Theodore Hook, where he would find, not a few, but scores of "humorous" characters, and a power of using them so as to bring out the advantages of the idea.

The general similarity of type between Hook's minor characters and those of Dickens extends frequently to similarities between individuals. The minor characters of Dickens are generally of a somewhat lower class of society than those Hook creates. Hook holds to the upper middle class and frequently enters the highest class. Dickens is more at home in the lower middle classes, with frequent excursions into the submerged tenth of society. When he tries the aristocracy — in the persons, for instance, of Sir Mulberry Hawk and Lord Verisopht of "Nickleby" — the result is not felicitous. But there are many places in which the two novelists meet on common ground, for they both describe the same civilization. Both depict rascally lawyers: Hook has his Screwman in "Gervase Skinner" (1828); Dickens his Dodson and Fogg in "Pickwick" (1836–37). "Gilbert Gurney" (1834–35) presents an eccentric foreigner, Count Stickinmeyer; "Pickwick" possesses Count Smorltork. Kekewich of "Gervase Skinner," the manager of the Taunton theatre, has charge of the affairs of a provincial theatrical troupe; in "Nickleby" (1838–39) Vincent Crummles manages the same sort of troupe. The

fact that Dickens and Hook regularly use significant or humorously descriptive names for their
minor characters strikes the eye of the reader,
but it scarcely proves a debt, for both the farce
stage and the novel had long known characters
thus named.

A somewhat more significant likeness is that
existing between Jingle of "Pickwick" and two of
Hook's characters — the strolling player of "The
Friend of the Family," and Kekewich of "Gervase Skinner." The player, for example, speaks
habitually in the following manner:

"First night of performance started at Guildford in
Surrey — long room, White Hart — Serjeant Onslow in
the church-yard; gothic house with pretty maids opposite the inn — telegraphed them all the morning —
roasted loin of pork and apple-sauce for dinner —
opened — seventeen people full grown, and two little
girls under age. Did n't pay for candles. Tried at Peters-
field — wore a hat like the mayor; the likeness was *felt*,
but not appreciated — *semper eadem*, worse and worse;
— cut the connexion, and once more embarked, as you
see."

This is exactly the "humour" of Jingle. That
Dickens borrowed the idea directly from the farce
stage (where it was not unknown, although not
common) is possible but not likely.

Lady Katherine Oldham of "The Marquess"
(1833) is an old woman who is borne incoherently
from one subject to another by the very rush and
flow of her speech. For instance:

"Mr. Richardson," continued Lady Katherine, "is full of talent, and so handsome, Lady Hester; — it is not always that personal attractions are supported by mental acquirements. I remember Lady Bustle, whose husband, poor dear old man, died of three slices of venison at a corporation dinner in his own borough — it is wonderful how some people eat, to be sure; for my part, as I was saying one day to Elizabeth, I cannot understand the difference of disposition and constitution in the same species. By the way, poor old Lady Bustle lost the use of her limbs by going to a fête in a foggy night; — supped in a tent — and sat on the damp grass; — poor thing, never was able to move afterwards, and is now pulled about in one of those chairs — which in my time were called Merlin's chairs — and a very curious exhibition that man Merlin had: there was a large Turk swallowed stones; close by the concert rooms in Hanover Square, where the bazar is to be. By the way, have you made anything for the poor Poles? Poor dear things, I am so distressed about them, you can't think."

Mrs. Nickleby, belonging to a lower class of society, has the same "humour" that characterized Lady Katherine. To illustrate:

"She always was clever," said poor Mrs. Nickleby, brightening up, "always, from a baby. I recollect when she was only two years and a half old, that a gentleman who used to visit very much at our house — Mr. Watkins, you know, Kate, my dear, that your poor papa went bail for, who afterwards ran away to the United States, and sent us a pair of snow shoes, with such an affectionate letter that it made your poor dear father cry for a week. You remember the letter? In which he said that he was very sorry he could n't repay the fifty pounds just then, because his capital was all out at interest, and he was very busy making his fortune, but that he did n't forget you were his god-daughter and that he should take it very unkind if we did n't buy you a silver coral and put it down to his old account? Dear me, yes, my dear, how stupid you are! and spoke so affectionately of the old port wine that he used to drink a bottle and a half of every time he came . . . that Mr. Watkins — he was n't any relation, Miss Knag will understand, to the Watkins who kept the Old Boar in the village; by the bye, I don't remember whether it was the Old Boar or the George the Third."

The similarity is striking, but there are complicating circumstances. Miss Bates, of Jane Austen's "Emma," spoke in the same way long before the creation of Lady Katherine. And also: "The character of Mrs. Nickleby," writes Mr. Arthur L. Hayward in his "Dickens Encyclopaedia," "was largely founded on that of Dickens's mother." The situation shows the difficulty and the danger of tracing "influences" between realists.

"Jack Brag," which was published on March 15, 1835, contains a character, Dr. Munx, who has an unusual system of medication:

"Our success I tell you does not depend upon the application of a remedy homoeopathically, so much as upon the minuteness of the dose; the effects of which are the greater as it approaches the finite bounds of dilution."

"I perceive," said Buckthorne, "that the poor-law commissioners have regulated their proceedings upon precisely the same system. According to their dictum, the less a man eats and drinks the fatter and stronger he gets. Minute medicaments in the shape of half-ounces of Dutch cheese and half-pints of water, 'approaching as near as possible the finite bounds of dilution,' are most judiciously substituted for the vulgar beef and beer which the allopathic asses of other days administered to the old and weak and infirm. . . ."

"The whole thing resolves itself into this one principle," said Munx, — "minuteness of application." [He then enters with considerable detail into the principles of dilution.]

In October of the same year Dickens contributed to "Bentley's Miscellany" his "Report of the First Meeting of the Mudfog Association" — a satire on learned societies. The following is an extract from the minutes:

Professor Muff related a very extraordinary and convincing proof of the wonderful efficacy of the system of infinitesmal doses, which the section were doubtless aware was based on the theory that the very minutest amount of any given drug, properly dispersed through the human frame, would be productive of precisely the same result as a very large dose administered in the usual manner. Thus, the fortieth part of a grain of calomel was supposed to be equal to a five-grain calomel pill, and so on in proportion throughout the whole range of medicine. . . .

A member begged to be informed whether it would be possible to administer — say, the twentieth part of a grain of bread and cheese to all grown-up paupers, and the fortieth part to children, with the same satisfying effect as their present allowance.

It may be granted that the satire in both cases was directed against some actually existing group in the medical profession. Nevertheless, the debt of Dickens to Hook appears here to be clear, specific, and conclusive.

When one compares the novels of Hook and Dickens with respect to the incidents in which the characters take part, one is conscious of a number of general similarities. In "Pickwick" there is a duel, an elopement, a fancy-dress reception, and a trial — all humorously portrayed; Hook has these in "Gilbert Gurney." There is a comic Parliamentary election in "Pickwick" and there is one in "Danvers." "Nicholas Nickleby," contains Crummles's dramatic company; "Gervase Skinner," Kekewich's troupe. Dotheboys Hall is a boys' school in "Nickleby"; Tickle's Academy is a boys' school in "Passion and Principle."

There are two cases in which the resemblances are more arresting. When Francis Welsted of "Passion and Principle" arrives at Tickle's Academy as the new instructor, he finds that Tickle has two vulgar daughters. Nicholas Nickleby, after his arrival at Dotheboys Hall, is thrown with Squeers's daughter Fanny and her friend, Tilda Price. Again, the unfortunate Merton, in the story bearing his name, is taken before the magistrate, Sir Martin Sowerby, who, although fortified by a gruff and aggressive manner, is really hopelessly subject to the influence of his daughter. Mr. Pickwick is likewise taken before Mr. Nupkins, who is savage and arbitrary in his official demeanor, but who quails before his wife and daughter. In both cases the proceedings are a travesty of justice.

In the following instance the similarities become pronounced. Young Edward Maxwell, attempting to discover the identity of a fair unknown, learns to his chagrin that he is pursuing Martha Scrimshaw, an old and hideous housemaid. Nicholas Nickleby, thinking that he is about to succeed in meeting and learning the identity of the young woman who visits the office of the Cheeryble brothers, encounters instead one Cecilia Bobster, who is decidedly not the object of his search. The accounts of both authors are alike in each stage of the incident. The hero wishes to learn only the name of the beautiful unknown and her place of residence. He finds himself fortunate beyond his dreams when he hears that she has consented to meet him. But he is also disappointed at finding his goddess so willing. He learns her name — Scrimshaw, Bobster; he thinks at first it is the name of her servant. He becomes more and more puzzled as he receives further details — where she lives, who her associates are, what she has said or written. But he sets forth, nevertheless, to keep the appointment. Then there is the meeting — a farcical scene.

A debt of Dickens to Hook appears in the following case unquestionable. Gervase Skinner has become involved with the mercenary Mrs. Fuggleston. He tells her that he is to marry another.

"Oh!" exclaimed the agitated wife, and uttering a piercing shriek, fell senseless into Skinner's arms; at which precise moment, the party coming up to proceed upon their agreeable walk, old Gray pushed open the street-door, according to local custom, and exhibited to the astonished eyes of Mr. Benson, and Miss Gray, the interesting spectacle of Amelrosa in another fit, supported by the suitor for the hand of the young and artless Emma.

The servants of the house hearing the noise, rushed to the scene of action, and the whole party was in an instant grouped like the characters at the end of a German play.

Pickwick's famous scene with Mrs. Bardell terminates in the same manner:

But entreaty and remonstrance were alike unavailing: for Mrs. Bardell had fainted in Mr. Pickwick's arms; and before he could gain time to deposit her on a chair, Master Bardell entered the room, ushering in Mr. Tupman, Mr. Winkle, and Mr. Snodgrass.

Mr. Pickwick was struck motionless and speechless. He stood with his lovely burden in his arms, gazing vacantly on the countenances of his friends, without the slightest attempt at recognition or explanation. They, in their turn, stared at him; and Master Bardell, in his turn, stared at everybody.

Hook's latest novels, "Fathers and Sons" (1841) and "Peregrine Bunce" (written in 1841), contain incidents reminding one of Dickens's. Jacob Batley, in the former novel, is a heartless miser having much in common with Ralph Nickleby. Peregrine's uncle Oliver wanders accidentally into the hotel room of a strange female very much as does Pickwick. But in these cases, of course, the debt is reversed — Hook is following Dickens.

"I think," writes Forster of Dickens, "it was not until the third book, 'Nickleby,' that he began to have his place as a writer conceded to him, and that he ceased to be regarded as a mere phenomenon or marvel of fortune." The period 1835 to 1839 may well be regarded as Dickens's period of apprenticeship. During these years Hook's reputation as the portrayer of the living English scene had risen to its height. Into the field which Hook commanded, Dickens entered. He adopted with completeness the idea which distinctively characterizes Hook's tales — that of characters with "humours." And he set down minute descriptions of everyday life of a kind which had appeared previously in Hook's pages and nowhere else. In "Oliver Twist," Dickens enters a level of society below the range of Hook. But in "Pickwick" and "Nicholas Nickleby" (as well as in a humorous satire like the "Mudfog Papers") the two meet on common ground. It is to be granted that when realists describe the same society their works will contain a certain number of general similarities. But the relations of many characters and incidents of Dickens's two novels with many of those in Hook's works extend to definite and particular ideas. It is certainly true that a writer of Dickens's ability would not copy verbatim from another. But that he had read the stories of the older novelist with an attention which caused him, perhaps half-unconsciously in most cases, to borrow specific characters and situations therefrom — that conclusion follows from the evidence which has here been surveyed.

Dickens followed in Hook's footsteps. But why is he so obviously superior as a novelist? Two circumstances account for a considerable portion of that superiority. In the first place, Hook in several of his novels surrendered unconditionally to farce. Dickens tried to keep farce in a subordinate position. It did, indeed, escape his control sometimes — as in the whole business, at the beginning of "Nickleby," of the "United Metropolitan Improved Hot Muffin and Crumpet Baking and Punctual Delivery Company." But he knew the danger. He zealously tried, writes Forster, "to keep the leading characters in his more important stories under some strictness of discipline. To confine exaggeration within legitimate limits was an art he laboriously studied; and, in whatever proportion of failure or success, during the vicissitudes of both that attended his later years, he continued to endeavor to practise it."

In the second place, Hook's major characters stand in unfortunate contrast with his "humorous" minors. The former, although lifeless, are necessary to carry on the action of the story; while the latter, although intensely real, have no place in the story. Dickens regularly abandons the story to the minor characters. He avoids using an organic plot such as Hook employed. "Pickwick" has no plot at all. "Oliver Twist" and "Nicholas Nickleby" follow the picaresque pattern, in which only the *terminus ad quem* is prescribed. Thus the major characters (who are not presented by "humours") need be very few in number — Nicholas, his sister, and the heroine in "Nickleby"; Rose Maylie, Harry Maylie, and a few of their associates in "Oliver Twist"; none at all in "Pickwick." Dickens, therefore, greatly reduced the blemishes which here injure Hook's work. He did not reform them altogether. Something of Hook's dilemma is evident in "Barnaby Rudge," where the plot makes definite demands of the major characters, and the minors, in consequence, have little connection with the story. Moreover, even the two or three solitary major characters in "Nickleby" and "Oliver Twist" are not unimpeachable. "His novels," writes Adolphus W. Ward,[1] "do not altogether avoid the common danger of uninteresting heroes and insipid heroines; but only a very few of his heroes are conventionally declamatory like Nicholas Nickleby,

---

[1] *Dickens* (English Men of Letters), p. 213.

and few of his heroines simper sentimentally like
Rose Maylie."

In 1829, when William Makepeace Thackeray
was a Cambridge undergraduate, he contributed
several articles to the student papers, the "Snob"
and the "Gownsman," signed "Dorothea Julia
Ramsbottom." These, as Mr. Lewis Melville
notes in his biography of Thackeray, were "inept
parodies of Theodore Hook's Mrs. Ramsbottom,
which are interesting only because in them may,
perhaps, be detected the germ from which, seven
years later, sprang the later correspondence of the
erudite Mr. Yellowplush."

In April, 1834, Thackeray wrote for "Fraser's
Magazine" a long review entitled "A Dozen of
Novels." Among the works thus reviewed were
Hook's "Parson's Daughter" and "The Widow
and the Marquess." Now, since Theodore was a
friend of editor William Maginn and was considered a Fraserian, he was to be shown as much
favor as might be. Young Thackeray took the
cue:

Are we about to puff Hook? God forbid! Why
should we puff Hook? There are some things so wholly
superfluous that they may be well left unattempted.

Be the other man who he may, Theodore Hook is
simply the wittiest man in this country, or in any other
we happen to know of. What fun, what drollery, what
flashes of wit, what coruscations of humour, flow — or

whatever else is the proper word — from Hook when he is in the proper key! Then his singing, his capital chants, his improvisings beyond example — who can compare with them? Even Lord Byron, jealous as he was of every other person's fame, acknowledged that Hook alone had conquered the English sputtering guttural. "As for the Italians," said his Lordship, "there is no great thanks to them if they improvise; their terminations are all so similar and so vocal, that the difficulty is, not to find, but to avoid, a rhyme. With us it is quite the reverse. I never knew but one that could accomplish the feat, and he was Theodore Hook. Theodore Hook is certainly an *improvvisatore.*"

"I do not know," said Hook, when this was told to him — (he was then persecuted by the sneaking government of the day — the government which he had mainly contributed to keep in office — for the Mauritius affair, in which he had been, from the beginning, most unjustly and most tyrannically treated) — "I do not know that I am an *improvvisatore* but I'm sure I am an unlucky Tory."

The critic does not rate Hook's two novels very highly. In "The Parson's Daughter" there "is a rather uninteresting hero, in love with a wholly uninteresting heroine"; yet "many of the minor characters are well executed." There is great ability in Hook, but he is hampered by his time-worn plots and uninteresting principals. Would that he would set forth the story of his many experiences and observations —

Would that he would some time or another seriously sit down to write what he knows! A novel from Hook, with Sheridan, for instance, as a hero — by name, if he liked — for the author of the *School for Scandal* is now as much a historical person as Rochester — and with Hook's own compotators and companions for characters, and the adventures of Hook himself and friends for incidents, would be a work that would bring us back to the days of *Tom Jones* and *Humphrey Clinker*.

Between 1838 and 1840 Thackeray contributed to the "New Monthly Magazine" his "Mary Ancel," and two pieces which appeared in instalments — "Major Gahagan's Historical Reminiscences" and "The Bedford Row Conspiracy." During those years Theodore Hook was editor of the magazine.

"Pendennis" was put out in monthly shilling numbers from 1848 to 1850. It is this novel which presents the entire literary world in which Thackeray had moved about the year 1832. As is well known, a number of the characters are modelled after real people. Pendennis is young Thackeray, Harry Foker is Andrew Arcedeckne, Shandon is Maginn, Bungay and Bacon are Colburn and Bentley respectively, the Marquis of Steyne is Hertford, Wenham is Croker, and Wagg is Theodore Hook.

But it will appear from the following extracts that Mr. Wagg is not the Theodore Hook whom Thackeray had praised in "Fraser's" in 1834:

"Yes, I've heard that joke about Venus's turtle and the London tavern before — you begin to fail, my poor

Wagg. If you don't mind I shall be obliged to have a new jester," Lord Steyne said, laying down his glass.

Mr. Wagg made his obeisance, with florid bows and extra courtesy, accompanied with an occasional knowing leer at his companion.

Wagg thrust his tongue in his cheek, thought the tea utterly contemptible and leered and winked at Pynsent to that effect.

If there was one thing laughable in Mr. Wagg's eyes, it was poverty. He had the soul of a butler who had been brought from his pantry to make fun in the drawing-room. His jokes were plenty, and his good-nature thoroughly genuine, but he did not seem to understand that a gentleman could wear an old coat, or that a lady could be respectable unless she had her carriage, or employed a French milliner.

. . . Mr. Wagg to hang on to a Baronet's arm, as he was always pleased to do on the arm of the greatest man in the company.

Wagg's white waistcoat spread out . . . with profuse brilliancy; his burly, red face shone resplendent over it, lighted up with the thoughts of good jokes and a good dinner. He liked to make his *entrée* into a drawing-room with a laugh, and, when he went away at night, to leave a joke exploding behind him. No personal calamities or distresses (of which that humourist had his share in common with the unjocular part of mankind) could altogether keep his humour down. Whatever his griefs might be, the thought of a dinner rallied his great soul; and when he saw a lord, he saluted him with a pun.[1]

---

[1] Steyne, Wenham, and Wagg are also in *Vanity Fair*. At a dinner Wagg is egged on by the ladies to try a passage of wits with the acute Becky Sharp. She defeats him ignominiously. Thereupon: "Wagg's great patron, who gave him dinners and lent him a little money sometimes, and whose election, newspaper, and other jobs Wagg did, gave the luckless fellow such a savage glance with the eyes as almost made him sink under the table and burst into tears."

Hook's literary labors are referred to in these
ways:

Accordingly she [Mrs. Bungay] hated Mr. Wagg
with female ardour; and would have deposed him from
his command over Mr. Bungay's periodical, but that
his name was great in the trade, and his reputation in
the land considerable.

Wenham and Wagg both knew him [Shandon] and
his circumstances. He had worked with the latter and
was immeasureably his superior in wit, genius, and ac-
quirement; but Wagg's star was brilliant in the world,
and poor Shandon was unknown there. He could not
speak before the noisy talk of the coarser and more successful man; but drank his wine in silence, and as much
of it as the people would give him.

"My brother, Major Pendennis, has often mentioned
your name to us," the widow said, "and we have been
— amused by some of your droll books, sir," Helen
continued, who could never be brought to like Mr.
Wagg's books, and detested their tone most thoroughly.

Even Wagg, whose books did not appear to him to be
masterpieces of the human intellect, he yet secretly
revered as a successful writer. He mentioned that he
had met Wagg in the country, and Doolan told him how
that famous novelist received three hundther pounds a
volume for every one of his novels. Pen began to cal-
culate instantly whether he might not make five thousand a year.

One cannot deny Thackeray's right to create
Mr. Wagg as a character in "Pendennis." Unfortunately the creation has worked some injury
to the memory of the man he is supposed to represent. A biographer of the real Theodore Hook
must, therefore, call attention to the evident fact
that Mr. Wagg is a character in a work of fiction.

There can be no certainty of any influence of Hook's novels upon Thackeray. In the "Man of Many Friends" Hook has a French chef who exhibits many of the qualities of Mirobolant of "Pendennis." Mrs. Fuggleston of "Gervase Skinner" is the same sort of provincial actress as is the famous Fotheringay. But by 1848 there were many novelists depicting all parts of contemporary London life. French chefs and provincial actresses had become common property. And Hook himself had been superseded in his own field by a greater man, Charles Dickens.

But the position of Hook as a novelist is not a mean one. His name takes on most literary significance in relation to the history of the English novel. Writing in an age of romance, he led the novel back to realism. To realism he made contributions of his own. That he was completely superseded by Dickens is not a disgraceful fate. It shows that he dug the channel for the current which overwhelmed him.

During the period 1825 to 1840, Theodore Hook was, one may contend, the best and most popular novelist. Scott at one end of this period, and Dickens at the other, must of course be omitted. The best work of Disraeli and Bulwer belongs to the next decade. This leaves, as a possible rival, only Captain Marryat. The popularity of "Peter Simple," "Jacob Faithful," and "Mr. Midshipman Easy" was undoubtedly great. But is Marryat as good a novelist as Hook? The present writer thinks not. When Marryat left his own field of novels of the sea to write "Japhet in Search of a Father," he clearly showed his inferiority. That "Japhet" is the equal of "Gilbert Gurney" cannot for a moment be conceded.

Among the novelists of the first half of the nineteenth century, Hook, in point of pure merit, takes a respectable position among novelists of the second class. His novels have not survived, it is true. The reasons are clear. The reader is repelled by the commonplace plot and the unreal major characters. As for the excellent descriptions and the vivid minor characters — there is no need to go to Hook for these things. They are present in greater numbers in the novels of Dickens. But that Hook's novels must remain entirely dead does not at all follow. They should be known to every serious student of the English novel. "Maxwell" and "Gilbert Gurney," in particular, well repay reading. From them can be derived the most favorable opinion of the novelist Theodore Edward Hook.

APPENDIX.

APPENDIX.

SYNOPSES OF HOOK'S NOVELS.

DANVERS.

(Sayings and Doings, 1st series.)

At twenty-eight, the fortunate young Burton has an amiable wife and two daughters, and a legal appointment which brings him two thousand a year. But the supercilious attitude of the Duke and Duchess of Alverstoke, who own the neighboring estate, Milford Park, causes the Burtons to become dissatisfied with their own peaceful lot, and leads them to attempt some form of emulation. They get word suddenly that Mrs. Burton's uncle intends to pay them an extended visit. He is old and immensely rich, but is a "mannerist and an egotist — self-opinionated, obstinate, positive, and eternally differing with everybody around him." His menagerie, collected during his travels, arrives before he does; and the various animals cause wild turmoil in the quiet house. The uncle himself appears, and soon causes the Burtons every sort of trouble by his self-centred impertinence. Worse still, he is attracted by the vulgar daughter of a low-class neighbor and marries her. Despite this, it is discovered, after the eccentric old man's death, that, with the exception of a small annuity settled upon the wife, his magnificent fortune has been left to Burton, provided that he will adopt the family surname — Danvers.

Now in the breast of the *parvenu* arise enormous ambitions. Sycophants of all kinds toady to him. He buys Milford Park from the Duke, sets up a princely estab-

lishment in London, goes to every social gathering to
which he can gain access, disburses huge sums in order
to be returned to Parliament. In short, he squanders a
half-million in less than two years; he is swindled by inferiors, and deferred to by titled acquaintances only
because of his money. His wife becomes painfully
aware that she is not fitted for aristocratic London
society; and the children are neglected. The final crash
is not long delayed. Considerably wiser now than
before, Danvers saves enough from the ruin to live
decently in a retired manner in his own class of society.

THE FRIEND OF THE FAMILY.

(*Sayings and Doings*, 1st series.)

The proud Lord Belmont is abroad filling a diplo-
matic post, and he has leased his estate, Burrowdale
Park, to another family. However, his son, Edward
Bramley, just out of Oxford, spends his vacations at the
village parsonage because he has fallen in love with
Rose Dalling, daughter of the worthy parson. Amos
Ford, Methodist and attorney, has charge of Belmont's
property. Knowing that his own daughter, the pale,
thin, religious Rachel, has no chance of becoming Edward's wife, he determines to cause trouble between
father and son because of the affair of Rose Dalling.
After Edward declares himself to Rose, and is accepted
pending the arrival of Belmont's approval, Ford writes
Belmont an unjust account of the proposed match.
Influenced by this, and having already practically
pledged the youth to the daughter of a titled family,
Belmont forbids his son to marry Rose, and even refuses to see him when he comes to England to see Ford.
Changing his initial plans, Ford represents that Edward
has seduced Rose. Thereupon, Belmont orders the
marriage to take place, but intimates that he will disinherit Edward. The youth attempts to find his father,

but is arrested by Ford upon a writ for debt — an invalid and dishonest charge. However, Belmont accidentally encounters the Dallings, finds out the truth, and approves the marriage. Ford flees the country because he is afraid that the many irregularities existing in his accounts will be discovered. His pious daughter elopes with a strolling player.

MERTON.

(*Sayings and Doings*, 1st series.)

Young Henry Merton is madly in love with Fanny Meadows. Her mother, however, prefers the young dandy, Felton. So Fanny and Merton elope to Gretna Green. But Fanny is followed and taken away by her mother just as the marriage is about to be concluded. Felton challenges Merton to a duel, but Merton's old friend, Fitzpatrick, fights Felton first and kills him. By a series of unlucky accidents, Merton continually fails to meet Fanny, either on the road from Gretna or in London. He therefore returns home, and finds his father certain that the marriage can be arranged. But the father dies suddenly. No will can be found, and apparently the estate is not large, but there is evidence of secreted funds. Soon after this, Merton falls ill at the house of Lord Castleton, and is nursed by the lord's protegée, Kate Etherington. This unprincipled woman tells Merton that Fanny is married to another, and the report finds support. Lord Castleton promises Merton a colonial appointment, and Merton marries the designing Kate.

Immediately after his marriage Merton finds out that Fanny is not married, and he leaves his wife to see her. Kate renews her relations with a former lover, Sir Henry Lavington. Merton's house burns down a few days after the insurance policy has lapsed. Kate elopes with Lavington. Merton proceeds against him by law, but is unsuccessful because it is proved that Merton left Kate a few days after marriage to see Fanny. Lord Castleton withdraws Kate's settlement and takes away Merton's colonial appointment. Merton tries to find Castleton. He gets to a crowded inn, and is placed in a room with a man who proves to be Lavington himself. The next morning Lavington has disappeared, and there are signs of blood. Merton is arrested and convicted. He escapes, but is recaptured and just about to be hanged when Lavington arrives, explaining his disappearance by the fact that he wished to slip away secretly to France to throw his creditors off the trail.

Penniless now because a lawyer he has trusted has run away, Merton is put into the insolvent debtors' prison. But he suddenly hears that he is the heir of the deceased Lord Mildenhall. This proves later to be an error, but the real heir, who is Merton's half-brother, provides liberally for him. Merton and Fanny now plan their marriage with her mother's consent. Kate has been reported dead. But Merton suddenly meets her again — she is now a woman of the streets. He nurses her back to health, and she rewards him by running away again. Merton is given a divorce. Fanny is ill and is taken to Madeira for her health. Hearing that she has returned, Merton rushes to her — to be told that she has died.

MARTHA, THE GYPSY.

(Sayings and Doings, 1st series.)

See pp. 245–246.

THE SUTHERLANDS.

(Sayings and Doings, 2nd series.)

The Sutherland family consists of a widow and three children: Jane, plain and unattractive; the heir, George, careless and susceptible to female charms; and James, penurious and calculating. George visits Leamington, and falls in love with the dashing Emily Busbridge, whom he meets at a ball. He marries her, and brings her home to his family. She soon proves to be exceedingly vulgar, and in morals no better than she should be. George's mother, grieved and shocked, leaves the house and takes her daughter to Bath. Emily thereupon invites her friends, who take control of the house, win George's money at cards, and demoralize his servants. George finds that Emily's father is about to be transported for theft, and that Emily has been in charge of various other gentlemen, none of whom has married her.

Meanwhile, James has determined to acquire a rich wife. He discovers that Grace Lazenby, the only daughter of a rich and high-placed Indian merchant, is at Mrs. Trainer's school close by. To be sure, Grace is unattractive, cold, and silent. He arranges with Mrs. Trainer to pay her £1500, if by her aid he succeeds in marrying Grace. Much to James's surprise, Lazenby approves of the match and invites James to his London residence. When he arrives there, Lazenby is very kind. However, several other visitors, including a Colonel Fitzmaurice, are not. There is also a brilliant and accomplished girl, Emma Fisherton, Lazenby's niece, whom the Colonel is wooing. Certain of success, James cancels Mrs. Trainer's note for the £1500. To his dismay he discovers later that Grace is Lazenby's *natural* daughter with only a life interest in £300 a year, and that the sparkling Emma is to be the heiress. The Lazenby household has thus forced itself to be kind to James because he is to take this daughter off their hands. It is too late to recede, and James lacks the initiative to do so. He therefore marries the unfeeling Grace. He takes her to Bath, to his mother and sister. There George also appears, with the news that Emily has eloped with one of his grooms. Both the brothers have thus been thoroughly "done."

THE MAN OF MANY FRIENDS.

(*Sayings and Doings*, 2nd series.)

Young George Arden, orphan heir to an immense estate, is in London, and is rapidly being turned into a worthless profligate by a set of unprincipled hangers-on. One of them wins a large sum of money from George at cards; another elopes with a worthless woman to whom George had become engaged. He is now in the hands of three swindlers — Arthur Dyson, a shrewd cheat; Bertie Noel, a libertine; and Wilson, a thieving butler.

Word of the young man's situation comes to old Colonel Arden, George's uncle, a "man of the world; shrewd, odd, and penetrating; rigidly honourable, high principled, and apparently to George, a little severe." The Colonel determines to make a vigorous effort to rescue his nephew, and to fulfil his plan of marrying George to his cousin, Louisa, the daughter of the Colonel's sister. George has not seen Louisa for many years. The Colonel, himself very wealthy, descends upon London, and sets up an establishment rivalling his nephew's. He wins away Wilson, the butler, from George. Noel and Dyson, too, fly to the Colonel, for they see new opportunities for plunder. Louisa is introduced as the daughter of a retired clergyman. George now has the mortification of seeing his "friends" abandon him and prey on his uncle just as they have preyed on him. His eyes are opened. Dyson begins his usual dishonest practices at cards; Noel tries to seduce Louisa. George has fallen deeply in love with her, and is filled with concern for his uncle, and regret for his own worthless life. Thus the change of heart that the Colonel has longed for is brought about. Louisa and George are united, and the professed friends are exposed and ejected.

DOUBTS AND FEARS.

(*Sayings and Doings*, 2nd series.)

Mathew Grojan owns the Imperial Hotel, at a fashionable watering-place. To this hotel comes Lady Almeria Milford, much agitated by a report that her son is about to propose for Miss Rosemore, the daughter of a widow whose antecedents are unknown. Sir Harry Dartford is also at the hotel. He, although a dangler by temperament, and a married man living apart from his wife, is of excellent birth and rank and is sound at heart. Although he has never seen the Rosemores, he promises Lady Almeria, who knows and likes him, that he will disillusion her son, Milford, and extricate him from the clutches of the fortune-hunters. Sir Harry thereupon writes a letter to Mrs. Rosemore, and, to his surprise, he is invited to visit them. He goes further — he asks the daughter, Maria, to appoint a meeting. Again he is successful. Milford hears of this, and is almost ready to give up the girl he loves. But that night when Sir Harry goes to the rendezvous, he discovers that Maria is his daughter, and that "Mrs. Rosemore" is his wife. A reconciliation takes place, and there is now no objection to the marriage of Milford and Maria.

PASSION AND PRINCIPLE.

(*Sayings and Doings*, 2nd series.)

Mr. Rodney, the master of a boys' academy, has a domestic, matter-of-fact wife, and a beautiful daughter, Fanny. Young Francis Welsted is also domesticated in the house. He had been a student in the school before the death of his father. After that event, the almost-penniless lad had been cared for by Rodney, sent through Oxford, and retained at the academy as an instructor. He and Fanny, thrown much together, began to love each other. This natural and fitting circumstance should have been greeted with rejoicing by Rodney. But the impractical old schoolmaster has other views for his daughter. She has been asked in marriage by the veteran, Major-General Sir Frederick Brashleigh, an elderly, imperious tyrant who has risen to his present rank by acting the part of *mari complaisant* to the governor-general of India who had been attracted by Brashleigh's first wife. Hearing of this proposed union, Welsted leaves the academy and goes sorrowing to London, leaving Fanny heartbroken. The General does not know of Welsted, for then, to do him credit, he would have drawn back from the match, particularly since his further acquaintance with Fanny's family does not increase his ardor. So this ill-advised match — detested by Fanny and half regretted by the bridegroom — takes place. From it Rodney reaps only sorrow, for the General takes Fanny to India immediately.

In London, Welsted, after much discouragement, becomes an instructor at Tickle's Academy. He also falls in accidentally with the young Viscount Feversham, son of the Earl of Farnborough. That family owes him a debt of gratitude, because, many years before, at Rodney's school, Welsted had saved the Viscount's life. He is therefore made tutor to the Viscount, and is thus able to spend three additional years at Oxford, preparing to take orders. At the end of that time he is ordained, and accepts a benefice in Ceylon — being anxious to leave England because one of Farnborough's daughters has fallen in love with him. Arriving at the Cape on his trip out, he meets the miserable, unhappy Fanny with the General. The three sail together from the Cape. The ship founders in a storm. Brashleigh is lost; Welsted rescues Fanny — but, at the very moment of succor, himself perishes.

COUSIN WILLIAM; OR, THE FATAL ATTACHMENT.

(*Sayings and Doings*, 3rd series.)

Caroline Crosby has a father who is an imaginary invalid, and a step-mother who does not like her. Caroline is in love with her wild and dissipated cousin, Captain William Morley, despite the fact that he is to make a marriage of money with the unattractive Jane Seward. In desperation Caroline accepts the proposal of Sir Mark Terrington, a passive, well-meaning, elderly gentleman. As the date of William's marriage approaches, he unfeelingly ridicules the unattractive Jane to his friends in a moment of intoxication. Word of this reaches her father, and when William and his father arrive at Seward's mansion, they are turned away. William thereupon rushes back to Caroline and succeeds in persuading her to elope with him. The design is thwarted by his arrest for debt, and his action in the Seward affair offends Caroline and her father — the latter had not been averse to the marriage of the cousins. Therefore Caroline, although loving William, marries Sir Mark.

Twenty-one years later, in 1825, William Morley, after an heroic career in the army, is domesticated in the family of Caroline and the now invalid Sir Mark. She has an excellent son, William Terrington, who is engaged to marry a young flirt, Flora Ormsby. It is evident to everyone except Sir Mark and Caroline's son, that William and Caroline are carrying on an intrigue. One night young Terrington discovers the guilty ones. He immediately challenges William, but before the meeting can take place the young man kills himself, unable to endure the thought of his mother's disgrace. William flees to the Continent. Caroline goes mad.

GERVASE SKINNER.

(*Sayings and Doings*, 3rd series.)

Gervase Skinner is a rich landowner, every act of whose career illustrates the saying of "penny wise and pound foolish." At his house in Somersetshire he likes to entertain provincial actors in order to get free seats for their performances. He is introduced to the blooming and food-loving actress, Amelrosa Fuggleston, and to her husband. She is really the vulgar child, out of wedlock, of some titled young scion, but she wins Gervase's deep admiration. She quarrels with the local theatrical manager, and leaves with her husband for London at Gervase's expense.

The beautiful young Emma Gray has, since her childhood, been betrothed to Gervase through the dying wish of her father. Gervase now travels to London to arrange his affairs before going to meet his fiancée to make plans for the wedding. In a dozen incidents during this journey, Skinner's desire to save a few shillings causes him the loss of many pounds, besides great vexation. He falls in with the Fugglestons, who force him to give up a large sum of money by employing the ancient "badger game." Meanwhile, Emma Gray has fallen in love with an impecunious young artist, and she succeeds in getting her father to call off the match with Skinner. The penny-saver subsequently elopes with Mrs. Fuggleston, but she leaves him when she finds that sudden misfortunes (all caused by attempts to save trifles) have apparently ruined him. Emma and her young husband now show their friendship for Skinner by furnishing him money until his disordered affairs can be straightened. Skinner afterwards gives up his miserly ways.

MAXWELL.

The London residence of the distinguished surgeon, Maxwell, contains the following members: Edward Maxwell, the son; Kate Maxwell, the daughter; and Godfrey Moss, a gruff-spoken but good-hearted elderly idler. They are talking about the sad case of a respectable merchant, Hanningham, who that day has been hanged for murder. Maxwell himself suddenly enters. He has been experimenting in anatomy on bodies provided by resurrection men, and he shows by his perturbation that he has just met with an experience which has unnerved him, and which he wishes to keep secret. Kate knows it also, but she is pledged to secrecy.

Edward Maxwell is supposed to be engaged to his cousin, Jane Epsworth, but he shows no resentment when she elopes with another. Kate has been in love with Charles Somerford, the almost penniless orphan of a physician who had been Maxwell's friend. But Maxwell objected to the match because Charles's mother was apparently an illegitimate child. He had, therefore, purchased an army commission for Somerford and thus had him sent to India. Word now arrives that Somerford is at the Cape, hopelessly ill. So Kate accepts the offer of marriage of Apperton, a stockbroker. Edward Maxwell saves the life of a beautiful young woman, and finds that she is in some way connected with his father. But the physician forbids his son to inquire further after her identity. Kate and Apperton are married. At Brighton, on her honeymoon, she sees Somerford, who has returned to England after recovering from his illness. They love each other, but it is now too late. Apperton proves not only to be, himself, an illegitimate son, but also to be a rascal who loses or makes away with his father-in-law's money. He represents the ruin as complete, and advises Maxwell to flee to escape arrest.

The Maxwells flee to Madeira, where they are met by young Hanningham, the son of the merchant who was hanged. Here Edward enters business as Hanningham's partner. After some time, Maxwell, young Hanningham, and Kate go back to England for a visit. They stop first at an island in the Azores, where they meet an old man and his beautiful daughter. When the party arrives in London, it is found that Apperton has absconded, but that Maxwell's affairs are not as hopeless as he was led to believe. Young Hanningham discovers the real perpetrator of the crime for which his father had been hanged. At Madeira, Edward finds Apperton on a ship which touches at Funchal. Apperton dies. Edward also discovers that his fair unknown is known to the Hanninghams. He takes a boat for England. While these events are in motion, Charles Somerford discovers that his mother had been legally married, and that his grandfather, the Earl of Lessingham, still lives. The kind old Earl acknowledges Charles on his death-bed, and Somerford finds himself a lord. Matters now draw to a conclusion. The old man at the island in the Azores is Hanningham the elder, himself. His still living body had been brought to Maxwell's house. The surgeon had revived him and aided him to escape. The mysterious beauty is his daughter. As proof is now forthcoming of his innocence, he is pardoned by the King. Edward and the daughter, Maria Hanningham, are united. Somerford, now Earl of Lessingham, marries his old love, Kate.

THE PARSON'S DAUGHTER.

Lady Frances Sheringham is a widow of aristocratic birth but of narrow means. She establishes herself, together with her son, Captain George Sheringham, a navy officer on half-pay, in modest Dale Cottage at Binsford. Here they meet an old-time country squire, Harbottle — excessively rich, drunken, vulgar, and opinionated — and his beautiful wife, Fanny. Young

Charles Harvey is visiting the Harbottles. He is enamored of Fanny, and, while she is not indifferent to him, she begs him, for the sake of her honor, to leave. The squire soon hears of this. Lovell, the rector of the parish, has a charming daughter, Emma. George falls in love with her, much to his mother's disgust. An accident sweeps away all the members of a family who stand between George and a title; consequently he becomes Lord Weybridge, with an enormous revenue. He nevertheless pledges himself to Emma before leaving for London to take possession of his fortune. But George and Emma are separated by many adverse circumstances.

Harvey is found dead one morning at the bottom of a pit into which he had ridden during the night. Fanny, with Lovell's approval, leaves her husband, Harbottle, and is taken by Emma to the house of a relative a long distance away. Emma does not know the secret of this separation; she soon returns in the company of a young French count. Hearing of this, George becomes very jealous. So he allows himself to be persuaded by his mother into a pledge of marriage to Lady Catherine Hargrave, daughter of the Duchess of Malvern. After he is pledged, a report of Harbottle's illness calls him to Binsford. There the dying squire confesses that it was he who directed Harvey to take the path across the fields which would surely lead him to the ditch. For this reason Fanny had left him. George also discovers that the French count is a nine-year-old boy. It is now too late, however, for George's mother writes Emma a letter announcing her son's engagement to Lady Catherine. So the heart-broken Emma gives him up, and he unwillingly returns to keep his promise to the daughter of the Duchess. But George learns suddenly that one of the unlucky family, whose extinction has given him his title, has survived. Thus George has now not only to relinquish his estates but also to make good many expenditures which his mother has made. When his plight is known, the Duchess breaks off the marriage. The rich widow, Fanny Harbottle, soon dies, leaving all her money to Emma. Immediately the parson's daughter forgives her errant lover, pays his debts, and marries him. Two years later the title comes back to George.

THE WIDOW AND THE MARQUESS; OR, LOVE AND PRIDE.

1. *The Widow.*

Charles Saville, a law student with a very moderate income, is in love with Harriet Franklin. The love is returned, but Mrs. Franklin, although she likes Charles, cannot consent to her portionless daughter's marriage to a poor man. She therefore chooses for Harriet an old and very rich invalid gentleman named Smith, and removes her daughter from Charles's society. But the youth secretly follows her, and finally gets her to consent to elope with him when she arrives at Cowes in the Isle of Wight. But at Portsmouth the unlucky Charles boards what proves to be not a Cowes steamer, but a Channel packet, and it conveys him to Bordeaux. Thus the lovers are separated, and Harriet has to marry Smith.

The Smiths reside in Italy until the husband's death, soon after, makes Harriet a rich widow. She now understands how it was that Charles failed to keep his promise, and she is eager to hear further from him. He hears that she is a widow and that she will soon return to England. He pays a visit to his old friend, Alvingham. There he meets one Major Brown, who announces that he is soon to marry. It develops also that he knows Harriet intimately. Charles is about to conclude in despair that Harriet is false when the Major and his wife arrive, bringing with them the blooming Harriet — the secret being that Brown is Harriet's half-brother. So Charles and Harriet are united.

2. *The Marquess.*

The Marquess of Snowden personifies pride of family and position. He has a son, Lord Malvern, now abroad under the care of an estimable young tutor, Charles Burford. He has also a daughter, Lady Hester Plinlimmon, whom he bullies. He announces to her that she is to marry the good-natured but spineless Lord Elmsdale. Unknown to her father, Hester has fallen in love with the tutor, Burford. The Marquess intends, after his daughter is married, to wed Elizabeth Oldham, a young woman for whom the Marquess's son has had a decided affection. The Marquess's daily life is marked by many blows to his excessive pride — particularly on the day when the King visits Lionsden Castle and everything goes amiss. Nor do Elizabeth and Hester like each other, for the former has become a brainless flirt. The day of the marriage between Hester and Elmsdale approaches. Hester hates the thought of it.

Lord Malvern, in France, discovers that Burford loves his sister Hester; he hears also that his father is to wed the woman whom he (Malvern) admires. Both the travelers are, therefore, unwilling to attend the wedding. Instead, Malvern accompanies his tutor to visit the latter's mother and sister, Maria, at Paris. After a time, Burford's mother decides to leave for England in order to remove her daughter from Malvern's society; the two are obviously falling in love, and Mrs. Burford thinks that the match could never take place because of Malvern's rank. But Malvern follows the party.

In England, meanwhile, Hester faints during the ceremony, and it has to be postponed. Elmsdale, suspecting the truth, gives up his claim. The Marquess denounces his daughter in strong terms, but Malvern suddenly arrives and takes his sister away to an aunt's house. There she and Burford meet and avow their love, while Malvern declares his intention of espousing Maria. The misfortunes of the proud Marquess rapidly accumulate. He has set his heart on becoming governor-general of India. He deserts the Whigs and becomes a Tory in order to accomplish his purpose, but suddenly, for the first time in decades, the Whigs come into power. Moreover, his affianced Elizabeth elopes with a worthless lieutenant. Broken in spirit, he becomes reconciled with his children.

GILBERT GURNEY.

Gilbert Gurney describes his early life. He finds no interest in the study of law, and so decides to write a farce for the Haymarket. It is hissed off. Disappointed, he starts back to see his mother. He meets a coarse wit and practical joker, Daly, who is always concocting not altogether innocent jokes. Gilbert's mother wishes him to join his brother Cuthbert, who has made a fortune in India. Back in London, Gilbert goes to various places with Daly, and is waked up one morning after a night's dissipation with the news that his mother is dead. She has left him a very moderate income. He plans, therefore, to make a wealthy marriage with Emma Haines (whom he had previously courted but whose mother had not been favorable). He sends Daly to discover where she is and to prepare the way for him. But Daly, after meeting Emma, marries her himself, thus betraying Gilbert's trust. However, after a comic duel, the two are reconciled. Gilbert next meets Mrs. Fletcher Green at a ball. He likes her very much, and, thinking her a widow, proposes to her — to discover that she already has a husband. During the next few months he has many amusing adventures. Then he again meets Daly. He finds that the charming Emma has lost all her money and is a nagging shrew who leads her husband a miserable life.

Soon Gilbert gets a letter from Cuthbert telling him to come to India, but first to have a talk with his old

business partner, Nubley, who is now in England. So
Gilbert goes to Hampshire to see Nubley. He there
becomes acquainted with the parson Wells and his
daughter, Harriet. Wells talks him into promising to
marry Harriet. But when he suggests taking her to
India, Wells refuses his permission and breaks the engagement. Gilbert begins his preparations for departure. But as he is about to board his ship he meets his
brother Cuthbert, who has returned. Cuthbert had
married a widow with three children at school in England, but she had died on the journey from India. He
promises to aid Gilbert, and the voyage is called off.
News arrives that Harriet has fled from her parents because she feels that her place is at Gilbert's side. He
finds her in Portsmouth seeking him. She is ill, but she
recovers and the two are married.

GURNEY MARRIED: A SEQUEL TO GILBERT GURNEY.

Cuthbert establishes Gilbert and his wife, Harriet, in
a pretty cottage near the residence of the Reverend
Wells. Cuthbert lives with them. The lazy tropical life
of India and the effects of a fever he contracted there
have rendered him nearly helpless. He rapidly makes
himself a nuisance by his affected inability to do more
than sit in a chair and order about the entire household.
Soon Cuthbert's step-children, the three young Fal-
wassers, — Kitty, a pert miss of fifteen; Jane, younger
and more docile; and Tom, an *enfant terrible*, — come to
visit. They are the children of the widow whom Cuthbert
had married in India. The girls have been at Mrs. Brandyball's school, and they invite their preceptress. Kitty
and Tom set the house in an uproar, and Mrs. Brandyball begins her plan to get the helpless Cuthbert into her
clutches. The opportunity comes when Tom gets the
smallpox. Cuthbert goes with the other two children to

Mrs. Brandyball's seminary. Tom dies, and Cuthbert is soon persuaded to show animosity against Gilbert. The Brandyball–Cuthbert marriage soon becomes a certainty. Even the remonstrances of old Nubley, who likes Gilbert very much, have no effect. But Cuthbert suddenly loses his money in the crash of an India house, and Mrs. Brandyball shows her real character by scorning him and reviling his step-children when she hears of it. So the penniless Cuthbert and the children return to Gilbert's cottage and a reconciliation takes place. Cuthbert recovers some of his money later, and Nubley designates Gilbert as his heir.

JACK BRAG.

Jack Brag is the son of a deceased London tallow-chandler. He refuses to help his mother keep up the business because he has an idea that he is destined for higher society. Actually he is a vulgar, blustering, impertinent, low-class "dandy," a hanger-on of good society — tolerated by Lord Tom Towzle because he is a good jockey. His career is a succession of attempts to worm himself into good company — attempts which invariably meet with failure. Thus he has the temerity to propose both to a rich widow and to her unmarried sister at the same time. He scorns the love of the modest Anne Brown, whose brother had married Brag's sister. This brother rises in the army through merit, and when his wife, Brag's sister, dies from drink, he marries the rich and lovely daughter of a general. Anne herself marries a physician, Dr. Mead. Seeking a rich wife, Brag answers a glowing matrimonial advertisement only to find that the woman is his own mother. His vulgarity and presumption soon disgust Lord Towzle, and he discards him.

Brag's mother marries her young apprentice, Jim Salmon, who immediately begins to spend her money upon women and wine. Travelling about the country imposing upon well-bred people, Jack meets with one ignominious exposure another after. He finally arrives at Cowes, where he takes possession of a yacht, promising to buy it. Here again his advances to a widow meet with a deserved rebuff. Now penniless, Jack seeks out his deserted mother. He is obliged to go to Spain in an army commissary department in order to recoup his fortunes. Salmon is killed in a fall, and Mrs. Brag gets back her property again. Jack, now wiser and humbler, makes plans to return to her and to the tallow business.

ALL IN THE WRONG; OR, BIRTHS, DEATHS, AND MARRIAGES.

The rich, miserly, and selfish Jacob Batley has a brother, John Batley, who is a sociable and pleasant, though not an affluent, man. John Batley's attractive daughter, Helen, accepts one of her suitors, Colonel Francis Mortimer, despite the fact that he had eloped in his youth with the wife of another man — which wife he had later married and lived with till her death. After Helen and Mortimer are married, they go to the Continent, where Mortimer gradually gathers about him the evil companions of his youth — particularly Colonel Magnus and the Countess St. Alme. He invites them to Sadgrove, his English country residence. There the Countess sows distrust between Helen and Mortimer by deceitful practices and by recalling to Mortimer the events of his former marriage. Thus husband and wife gradually become estranged. Helen's father, John Batley, now determines to marry. He is thwarted at his first attempt by a ludicrous error. But he soon meets Mrs. Teresa Catling, a widow whose executor is his brother, Jacob Batley. This widow he marries and lives happily with, although he discovers that Jacob has swindled him out of considerable money connected with the lady's jointure. At Sadgrove, the Countess St.

Alme finally leaves, but sends her son, the nineteen-year-old Francis Blocksford, there to stay for a long visit.

Two and a half years pass. At Sadgrove are Helen and Mortimer, — now almost totally estranged despite their two children, — Francis Blocksford, and Mary Mitcham, a beautiful and unfortunate gentlewoman who has been forced to enter Helen's service as a maid. Helen is called to London to see her dying father. With her goes Miss Mitcham. Blocksford suddenly disappears from Sadgrove. Mortimer assumes that Blocksford and Helen have eloped. He closes up the house, takes away the children, refuses to hear from Helen except through his legal advisers, and hurries to France to see the Countess. There he learns the truth: that Blocksford has married the beautiful Mary Mitcham, and that Helen is absolutely innocent. But the Countess nevertheless poisons his mind and keeps him from returning to his wife. He gives the children into the care of his sister, Mrs. Farnham, who brings them to England. Helen, disguised, enters her service as governess to her own children. She nurses them through the smallpox, but catches it herself, and expires just as the penitent Mortimer reaches her side.

FATHERS AND SONS.

Colonel Bruff and Sir George Grindle agree that they will marry Grindle's elder son, George, to Bruff's daughter, Jane. Young George, a "dandy" of the second water, has a half-brother, Frank, quiet and studious, with intellectual interests — the very opposite of George. Jane Bruff is at this time on a visit to her friends, the Amershams. She meets there one Miles Blackmore, whom, however, she does not love. Bruff sends notice that she is to come home to London. When she arrives he tells her that she is to marry George Grindle. Bruff has fallen into the hands of his scheming housekeeper and mistress, Smylar, who, at first, wishes to marry off Jane so that she can begin her attempt to get Bruff to agree to the same ceremony with her. But Smylar suddenly changes her plans and urges Jane not to consent to marry George — thinking that the refusal will so enrage the irascible Colonel that he will cast out his daughter and disinherit her. Jane despises the brainless and dandyfied George, but she likes Frank very much. Her father, however, roughly insists that she follow his orders, and preparations for her marriage to George are set in motion. They have to be postponed, however, because of the death of Frank's uncle, who leaves Frank a handsome fortune.

George decides that, before his marriage, he will do well to take his mistress, Ellen (by whom he has had a child), back to her mother in Paris and leave her there. Ellen's mother has always believed her daughter married to George. George does as he has intended, but in Paris they fall in with Miles Blackmore, whose curiosity is aroused. In England the Amershams meet Frank. They learn that there is a Mrs. Grindle in Paris, and they write to ask Blackmore about it. The wedding day of George and Jane approaches. Smylar urges Jane to flee or elope. But Jane will not. On the marriage morning Blackmore brings in Ellen just in time to stop the marriage. They have an attested document stating that George, before witnesses in Scotland, has referred to Ellen as his wife. According to Scotch laws, George and Ellen are therefore legally married. There is now no obstacle separating Frank and Jane, and Smylar is exposed and removed from the household.

PEREGRINE BUNCE; OR, SETTLED AT LAST.

Peregrine Bunce's rich uncle will provide liberally for Peregrine if Peregrine helps provide for himself by making a rich marriage. And so this scheming, mercenary "bounder" — a complacent, penny-squeezing Cœlebs in search of a rich wife — begins his peregrinations. He tries his fortunes with the Minton girls. He woos the religious Margaret, but she elopes with another. Her father in anger announces that he will give her dower to her gay sister, Dorothea. This announcement is heard by the eavesdropping Bunce, but Dorothea accidentally sees him in hiding. Hence when Bunce transfers his affections to her, she shows him the door.

At Brighton he woos the rich widow Mimminy and wins her consent. But a Miss Atkins, who is employed as governess to the widow's daughter, proves to be a former mistress of Bunce's, and her appearance breaks off the match.

The rich merchant, Mr. Nobbatop, has a beautiful and estimable adopted daughter, Maria Grayson. She is not averse to Bunce's advances, but the mercenary lover suddenly hears that Nobbatop's firm has failed. He therefore abandons the family, only to hear later, to his infinite mortification, that Maria Grayson has an independent fortune not affected by Nobbatop's bankruptcy.

At Leamington, Bunce meets the hoydenish Betsy Misty. Just as he thinks he is ingratiating himself, Betsy informs him that she knows the history of his affair with the Mintons. Bunce's uncle, disgusted by his nephew's actions, now casts him off. (An account of how Bunce is taken in by, and marries, a penniless adventuress posing as a rich widow, is added by another writer.)

BIBLIOGRAPHY.

BIBLIOGRAPHY OF THE WRITINGS
OF THEODORE HOOK.

1805

THE SOLDIER'S RETURN; OR WHAT CAN BEAUTY DO? *A Comic Opera in Two Acts.* As Performed at the Theatre Royal, Drury-lane. The Overture and music entirely new, composed by Mr. Hook. London, 1805. Also, Philadelphia, 1807.

1806

THE INVISIBLE GIRL. Theodore Edward Hook. London, 1806. Also, London, no date, but probably 1826. Also, Cumberland's British Theatre, vol. 40 (1829). The songs in the piece were published separately in 1806.

CATCH HIM WHO CAN. *A Musical Farce.* Theodore Edward Hook. Music by Mr. Hook, Senr. London, 1806. Also, Cumberland's British Theatre, vol. 40 (1829).

TEKELI; OR, THE SIEGE OF MONTGATZ. *A melodrame in Three Acts.* By Theodore Edward Hook. The music by Mr. Hook, Senr. London, 1806. Also, London, Davidson, no date; Cumberland's British Theatre, vol. 220; New York, 1807, 1808, and 1815; Philadelphia, 1823.

1807

THE FORTRESS. *A Melodrama.* From the French. Theodore Edward Hook. Music by Mr. Hook, Sen. London, 1807.

1808

THE SIEGE OF ST. QUINTIN; OR, SPANISH HEROISM. (Not printed.)

MUSIC MAD. *A Dramatic Sketch.* Theodore Edward Hook Esq. London, 1808. Also, Boston, 1812.

THE MAN OF SORROW. By Alfred Allendale. London, 1808. Reprinted as "Ned Musgrave; or, The Most Unfortunate Man in the World." London, 1842. This second edition, also, London, 1854; New York, 1854; Philadelphia, no date.

1809

SAFE AND SOUND. *An Opera in three acts.* Theodore Edward Hook. London, 1809. Also, New York, 1810.

ASS-ASS-INATION; OR, THE ORACLE. Printed in *Bentley's Miscellany,* vol. 22 (1847) as: "Ass-ass-ination. An historical tragedy in Two Acts. Edited by Theodore Edward Hook Esq."

KILLING NO MURDER. *A farce in two Acts.* Four editions, London, 1809. Fifth edition, London, 1810. Also, New York, 1809, and vol. 31 of Cumberland's British Theatre. The Buskin plot was printed separately as "A Day at an Inn."

1810

THE WILL AND THE WIDOW; OR, PUNS IN PLENTY. (Not printed.)

1811

BLACK AND WHITE; OR, DON'T BE SAVAGE. (Not printed.) Remodelled in 1819 as "Pigeons and Crows" (not printed).

TRIAL BY JURY. *A Comic Piece.* In Two Acts. Theodore Edward Hook. London, 1811. Also, New York, 1811.

DARKNESS VISIBLE. *A Farce in Two Acts.* Theodore Edward Hook. Two editions, London, 1811. Also, London, 1817.

1819

FACTS ILLUSTRATIVE OF THE TREATMENT OF NAPOLEON BONAPARTE IN SAINT HELENA. London, William Stockdale, 1819. Also printed in Clement K. Shorter's *Napoleon in His Own Defense* (Cassell & Co., 1910).

1820

TENTAMEN; OR, AN ESSAY TOWARDS THE HISTORY OF WHITTINGTON, LORD MAYOR OF LONDON. London, William Wright, 1820. Also in *Choice Humorous Works of Theodore Hook* (1889).

THE NEW CHRISTMAS BUDGET. *Old Tom of Oxford.* London, W. Wright, 1820. (Not certainly by Hook.)

THE RADICAL HARMONIST; OR, A COLLECTION OF SONGS AND TOASTS GIVEN AT THE LATE CROWN AND ANCHOR DINNER. *Collected by Old Tom of Oxford.* London, W. Wright, 1820.

Perhaps a few more anonymous Tory pamphlets.

EXCHANGE NO ROBBERY; OR, THE DIAMOND RING. London, 1820. Also, Cumberland's British Theatre, vol. 37 (1829).

THE ARCADIAN. Printed by Miller. A monthly magazine. Two numbers only.

Editor of *John Bull*, a weekly newspaper, from first number on December 17, 1820, to his death in August, 1841. Practically all of the poems, and many of the facetiae and book reviews are in Barham's *Life and Remains of Theodore Edward Hook*. Many are also in the *Choice Humorous Works* (1889). In both are "The Ramsbottom Letters," which appeared first in *John Bull*. These letters were also printed by Bentley (1872) and by J. C. Hotten (1873). Practically all the original material in the newspaper until 1824 may be safely ascribed to Hook. After that time his interest waned, and it is impossible to recognize his articles.

1821

PETER AND PAUL; OR, LOVE IN THE VINEYARDS. (Not printed.)

1824

SAYINGS AND DOINGS: A SERIES OF SKETCHES FROM LIFE. London, Colburn and Bentley, 1824. Four editions in 1824–25. Also, vol. 13 in Colburn's Modern Standard Novelists. Routledge, 1872.

1825

SAYINGS AND DOINGS; OR, SKETCHES FROM LIFE. Second Series. London, Colburn and Bentley, 1825. Also, vol. 14 in Colburn's Modern Standard Novelists. Philadelphia, 1825. Routledge, 1872.

1826

THE REMINISCENCES OF MICHAEL KELLY, OF THE KING'S THEATRE, AND THEATRE ROYAL, DRURY LANE, including a period of nearly half a century; with original anecdotes of many distinguished persons, political, literary, and musical. Two vols. London, Colburn and Bentley, 1826.

1828

SAYINGS AND DOINGS; OR, SKETCHES FROM LIFE. Third Series. London, Colburn and Bentley, 1828. Also vol. 15 in Colburn's Modern Standard Novelists. Routledge, 1872, in two vols. "Cousin William" published in New York, 1835 and 1837.

CAUTIONARY VERSES TO YOUTH OF BOTH SEXES. In Ainsworth's "The Christmas Box," of 1828. Reprinted in *Choice Humorous Works*.

1829

THE SPLENDID ANNUAL. Contributed to the first number of *Sharpe's London Magazine*, edited by Allan Cunningham. Reprinted in *Choice Humorous Works*.

1830

MAXWELL. *By the author of Sayings and Doings.* London, Colburn and Bentley, 1830. Also, no. 35 in Bentley's Standard Novels, 1849 and 1854. Also, London, 1878.

Between 1830 and 1834 Hook probably wrote several articles for periodicals — perhaps *Fraser's* or *Blackwood's*.

1832

A review of Prince Puckler-Muskau's account of his travels in England. In the *Quarterly Review* for January, 1832 (vol. 46, pp. 518–544).

THE LIFE OF GENERAL, THE RIGHT HONOURABLE SIR DAVID BAIRD, BART. Two vols. London, Bentley, 1832.

1833

THE PARSON'S DAUGHTER. London, Bentley, 1833. Also, no. 46 in Bentley's Standard Novels, 1835. Also, Railway Library, 1867; Routledge, 1872; Philadelphia, 1833.

LOVE AND PRIDE. London, Whittaker and Co., 1833. Also, no. 87 in Bentley's Standard Novels, with title, *The Widow and the Marquess; or, Love and Pride*, Also, Railway Library, 1868; Philadelphia, 1834.

1834

GILBERT GURNEY. In the *New Monthly Magazine* in 1834 and 1835. Later, with added chapters, in book form, London, Whittaker and Co., 1836. Also, Paris,

1836; Philadelphia, Waldie's Select Circulating Library, 1835–36; vol. 86 in Bentley's Standard Novels, 1841.

Boots. Short story contributed to "Angelo's Picnic; or, Table Talk." London, 1834.

Magpie Castle, *by the Author of Sayings and Doings.* In *New Monthly*, 1834 (I).

Ditton. In *New Monthly*, 1834 (II).

1835

Precept and Practice. No. I, Fanny Vane. No. II, Life after Death. *By the Author of Sayings and Doings.* In *New Monthly*, 1835 (II).

Precept and Practice. No. III, Captain Gray. *New Monthly*, 1835 (III).

About the middle of 1835 Hook began to write the Monthly Commentary in the *New Monthly*.

1837

Jack Brag. London, Bentley, 1837. Also, Paris, 1837; vol. 75 in Bentley's Standard Novels, 1839; Parlour Library, vol. 276; Routledge, 1872; English Library of Standard Works, 1884.

The Gurney Papers. By instalments in the *New Monthly* in 1837 and 1838. Published as *Gurney Married: A Sequel to Gilbert Gurney*, London, Colburn, 1839. Also, Baudry's European Library, 1839; Philadelphia, 1839; Standard Novel Library, 1863; London, David Bryce, no date.

Fashionable Fictions. *By the Author of Sayings and Doings.* Practical Jokes. *By the Author of Sayings and Doings.* In *New Monthly*, 1837 (II).

Pascal Bruno. Edited by Theodore Hook Esq. London, Colburn, 1837.

1838

RUSSIAN POLICE AND ENGLISH PRISONS. By the editor. WINE AND WATER. By the Editor. In *New Monthly*, 1838 (II).

1839

BIRTHS, DEATHS, AND MARRIAGES. *By the Author of Sayings and Doings.* London, Bentley, 1839. Also in Bentley's Standard Novels, vol. 38 (1842), with title, *All in the Wrong; or, Births, Deaths, and Marriages.* Also, Standard Novel Library, 1863.

WIDDLEZIG. THE ATONEMENT. CIVIL WAR. ODD PEOPLE. A FRAGMENT OF MODERN HISTORY. A STIR IN THE HOUSEHOLD. PUBLIC AMUSEMENTS. PUBLIC BUILDINGS. THE PLANTER'S BIRTHDAY. EMILY; OR, THE UNEXPECTED MEETING. FOREIGN MORALITY. All in the *New Monthly*, and all signed, "By Theodore Hook Esq."

1840

FATHERS AND SONS. By instalments in the *New Monthly* in 1840 and 1841. Also in book form, with preface containing sketch of author's life, London, Colburn, 1842. Also, vol. 207 in Parlour Library, 1847; Routledge, 1872; Philadelphia, 1842.

PRECEPT AND PRACTICE. London, Colburn, 1840. Also, London, 1857; Standard Novel Library, 1863. This is a collection of Hook's *New Monthly* contributions as follows: *Captain Gray, Life After Death, The Widow's Dog, The Man and His Master, The Little Man, Fanny Vane, The Atonement, Widdlezig, A Fragment of Modern History, A Stir in the Household, Civil War, Fashionable Fictions, My Last Tour, Russian Police and English Prisons, Odd People, Magpie Castle, A Trip Over London, Practical Jokes, Ditton, The Planter's Birthday.*

Cousin Geoffrey, *by Harriet Maria Gordon Smythies.* To which is added a tale, Claude Stocq. Edited by Theodore Hook. London, Bentley, 1840. Also, Routledge, 1873.

Peter Priggins, the College Scout. *By the Rev. James J. Hewlett.* Edited by Theodore Hook. London, 1840.

1841

The French Stage and the French People, *as illustrated in the Memoirs of M. Fleury.* Edited by Theodore Hook. London, Colburn, 1841. In two vols. There was a second edition in 1842, with the title, "Adventures of an Actor, comprising a Picture of the French Stage during a period of Fifty Years. Edited by Theodore Hook Esq." London, Colburn, 1842. In two vols.

The Parish Clerk. *By the author of Peter Priggins.* Edited by Theodore Hook. London, 1841.

1842

Peregrine Bunce; or, Settled at Last. London, Bentley, 1842. Also, Railway Library, 1857; Routledge, 1873. Hook was engaged on this novel at the time of his death in August, 1841. It was finished by another hand.

The following translations of Hook's novels were made:

Theodore Hook's ausgewählte Romane. *Aus dem Englischen von E. A. Moriarty und J. Seybt.* Leipzig, 1842, 1843. (*Jack Brag, Gilbert Gurney, All in the Wrong, The Parson's Daughter.*)

Ma Vie de Garçon: Réminiscences d'un vieux gentleman. Par E. D. Forgues. Paris, 1861. (Abridged from *Gilbert Gurney.*)

Merton, Scènes de la Vie Anglaise. *Roman Nouveau par Théodore Hook.* Par M. Erasme de Saint Clair. Paris, 1828. Four vols. (*Merton,* and also *Danvers.*)

INDEX.

INDEX.

Ainsworth, W. H., 157, 161, 163, 368.

All in the Wrong, 230, 249 n., 266–267, 273, 274, 284–285, 288, 359–360, 371.

Angelo, Henry, 23, 29, 91, 162, 175, 177, 370.

Arcadian, The, 125, 197, 367.

Ass-ass-ination, 77, 366.

Athenæum Club, 171, 196, 206, 304, 313.

Bannister, John, 23–24, 34, 41–42.

Barham, Richard Harris ("Ingoldsby"), 9, 10, 28 n., 65, 70, 76, 136, 144, 163, 164, 198, 201, 205, 231, 313, 314.

Barham, Richard Harris Dalton, 9, 10, 28 n., 65 n., 198.

Bayley, Thomas Haines, 144, 156, 194 n., 204–205.

Baylis, T. Ashton, 186–188, 217.

Beazley, Samuel, 32, 68, 78, 94, 119, 153, 178, 194 n., 195, 201.

Bennett, Henry Gray, 104, 107, 111, 120, 130, 131, 136, 138, 140, 142, 143.

Bentley, Richard, 6, 9, 10, 150, 154, 155, 156, 159, 208, 224, 226, 227, 229, 230, 231, 233, 234, 304, 314, 333.

Bentley's Miscellany, 6, 77, 154, 156, 157, 162, 313, 314, 324.

Berkeley, The Hon. Grantley F., 132, 179, 202.

Berners Street Hoax, 71–74.

Blackwood's Magazine, 143, 163, 224, 225–226, 279, 369.

Blanchard, Laman, 157, 207.

Blessington, Countess of, 156, 188, 194 n., 215, 302.

Broderip, William John, 4–5, 161, 187, 205, 233.

Brougham, Henry Lord, 88, 120, 131, 133, 138, 139, 140, 272.

Bulwer, Sir Edward, 54, 153, 303–307, 336.

Bunn, Alfred, 56–58.

Byron, Lord, 27–28, 38–39, 41, 91, 120, 121, 148, 187, 209, 332.

Campbell, Thomas, 81, 82, 85, 152–153, 156, 194 n., 195, 206.

Cannon, Edward, 89, 176, 198–199, 201.

Caroline, Queen, 117, 118, 122, 128–132, 140, 143.

Catch Him Who Can, 35, 42–43, 49, 365.

Clermont, 247–248, 252, 254, 256, 258.

Coates, Robert, 74–75.

Colburn, Henry, 5, 6, 7, 149, 152, 153–156, 157, 159, 208, 224, 225, 226, 227, 228, 229, 230, 231, 233, 234, 304, 314, 333.

Coleridge, Samuel Taylor, 189, 190, 191, 193, 195.

Colman the younger, George, 31, 33, 50, 57, 85, 92 n., 112, 162, 205.

Coningsby, 116, 213, 308–310, 311, 312.

Cousin William, 226, 249 n., 253, 258, 274, 275, 288, 349.

Covent Garden Theatre, 18, 31, 40, 51, 52, 56, 98, 113.

Croker, John Wilson, 106–107, 116, 133–135, 142–143, 158–159, 194 n., 208, 209, 210–213, 308, 333.

Cunningham, Allan, 162, 207, 228, 295, 369.

Danvers, 224, 236, 250, 272, 274, 276–277, 292, 305, 317–318, 325, 341–342.

Darkness Visible, 47–48, 50, 367.

Diamond Cut Diamond, 23.

Dickens, Charles, 13, 156, 162, 163 n., 287, 313–331, 336, 337.

Disraeli, Benjamin, 116, 164, 194 n., 211, 213, 217, 307–313, 336.

D'Orsay, Count Alfred, 188, 213.

Double Disguise, The, 22, 33.

Doubts and Fears, 225, 238, 250–251, 289, 347.

Drury Lane Theatre, 18, 31, 34, 35, 36, 37, 40, 41, 44, 51, 52, 56, 65.

Dubois, Edward, 85, 144, 153, 195–196, 197, 201.

Egan, Pierce, 17, 60, 240, 290, 294.

Elliston, Robert W., 36, 47, 125.

European Magazine, 144.

Exchange No Robbery, 112–113, 367.

Man of Many Friends, The, 225, 238, 277, 281, 336, 346.

Man of Sorrow, The, 75, 148 n., 224, 366.

Marryat, Captain Frederick, 156, 171, 194 n., 295, 336–337.

Martha, the Gypsy, 224, 245–246, 344.

Mathews, Charles, 31, 36, 42, 43, 44, 46, 47, 53, 55, 67–68, 76, 85, 96, 98, 160, 167, 196, 201.

Mathews, Mrs., 42, 43, 44, 67 n., 68, 76, 77, 160–161, 196.

Maxwell, 226, 227, 234, 246 n., 249 n., 253, 258, 268 n., 270–271, 280, 282, 303, 305, 326, 337, 351–352, 369.

Merton, 224, 236–237, 249 n., 250, 278, 300, 343–344.

Mitford, Mary Russell, 18, 29.

Monthly Mirror, The, 37, 38, 40, 48, 49, 85, 86, 195, 197.

Moore, Thomas, 93, 120, 143, 148, 176, 186, 194 n., 209, 218.

Murray, John, 8, 180, 203–204, 206.

Music Mad, 39, 43–44, 49, 366.

New Monthly Magazine, 5, 6, 7, 152–158, 159, 164, 195, 202, 204, 215, 228, 229, 230, 233, 234, 245, 304, 315, 333, 370, 371.

Nicholas Nickleby, 314, 318, 319, 320, 322–323, 325, 326, 328, 329, 330.

Noctes Ambrosianae, 143, 163, 226–227.

"Old Tom of Oxford," 123–124, 126, 367.

O'Meara, Barry, 114, 115–116.

Parke, W. T., 20–21, 78.

Parson's Daughter, The, 227, 244, 249 n., 255, 260–261, 274, 331, 332, 352–354, 369.

Passion and Principle, 225, 249 n., 253, 255, 261, 273, 275, 276, 282, 283–284, 316–317, 325, 347–348.

Pelham, 304–305, 307.

Pendennis, 333–335, 336.

Pen Owen, 25.

Percy Mallory, 25.

Peregrine Bunce, 231, 233, 239, 241, 242, 251, 267, 268, 283, 290, 327, 361–362, 372.

Peter and Paul, 113, 368.

Phipps, Constantine Henry, 300.

Pickwick Papers, The, 163 n., 314, 315, 319, 320, 321, 325, 327, 328, 330.

Pigeons and Crows, 77, 112, 366.

Pixerécourt, Guilbert de, 35, 36, 37.

Planché, J. R., 54, 156, 174–175, 203–204.

Poole, John, 155, 156, 207.

Precept and Practice, 154, 157, 230, 370, 371.

Price, Stephen, 199, 201.

Quarterly Review, 8, 149, 162, 163, 369.

Raikes, Thomas, 89, 213.

Ramsbottom Letters, 10, 148, 166, 331, 367–368.

Redding, Cyrus, 84, 149–150, 153, 207.

Reminiscences of Michael Kelly, 149–150, 368.

Reynolds, Frederick, 33, 63.

Reynolds, Frederick Mansell, 182, 189.

Richardson, The Rev. J., 218, 220.

Roche, Regina Maria, 247, 252–253, 254, 256.

Rogers, Samuel, 178, 186, 208, 209, 218.

Rolls, John, 76–77.

Safe and Sound, 35, 43, 49, 366.

Sayings and Doings (three series), 61, 208, 224–226, 227, 232, 235–238, 271, 276, 278, 279, 280, 294, 297, 300, 304, 311, 341–350, 368.

Scott, Sir Walter, 13, 41, 133, 149, 161, 170, 195, 197, 201, 208, 212, 245, 263, 296, 297, 336.

Shackell, William, 126, 137, 139, 141, 144–145, 169, 232.

Sheridan, Richard Brinsley, 19, 31, 32, 33, 38, 55, 79, 87, 88, 89, 205, 332–333.

Sheridan, Thomas, 87, 93, 103 n., 185, 215.

Siege of St. Quintin, 37–38, 366.

Smith, Horatio, 59–60, 69, 80–81, 85, 156, 194–195, 201, 302.

Smith, James, 34, 59, 85, 156, 178, 194–195, 201.

Smith, Sydney, 179, 191, 209.

Smollett, Tobias, 227, 240, 262–263, 264, 265–266, 288, 298, 319.
Soldier's Return, The, 33–34, 262, 365.
Southey, Robert, 164–165.
Sutherlands, The, 225, 238, 344–345.
Sutton, Charles Manners, 213.

Talfourd, Thomas Noon, 153, 207.
Tekeli, 36, 37, 38, 39, 365.
Tentamen, 122–123, 124, 135 n., 367.
Terry, Daniel, 41, 68, 83, 112, 113, 125, 126, 135, 196–197, 201, 208, 232.
Thackeray, W. M., 14 n., 157, 163, 217, 302, 304, 313, 331–336.
Trial by Jury, 47, 50, 366.
Twiss, Horace, 87, 165, 178, 183, 215.

Vauxhall Gardens, 17–18, 59, 166, 220.
Vivian Grey, 307–308, 311–312.

Ward, Robert Plummer, 299, 300.
Wellington, Duke of, 133, 136, 151, 152, 212, 213, 214, 215, 217, 272.
Widow and the Marquess, The, 227–228, 237, 239, 249 n., 250, 253, 255, 272, 275, 281, 282, 290, 321–322, 331, 354–356, 369.
Wilson, John ("Christopher North"), 143, 163, 295.